How I Revolutionize the Beauty Industry from Soul Train to Wall Street

I hope my memoir provides insight into the meaningful experiences that have shaped my mission to better America. Thank you for taking the time to read my story.

Warm regards,

George Johnson

AFRO
SHEEN

AFRO

How I Revolutionized an Industry with the
Golden Rule, from *Soul Train* to Wall Street

SHEEN

George E. Johnson

with Hilary Beard

LITTLE, BROWN AND COMPANY

New York Boston London

Copyright © 2025 by George E. Johnson

Little, Brown and Company
Hachette Book Group
1290 Avenue of the Americas, New York, NY 10104
littlebrown.com

First Edition: February 2025

Little, Brown and Company is a division of Hachette Book Group, Inc. The Little, Brown name and logo are trademarks of Hachette Book Group, Inc.

The publisher is not responsible for websites (or their content) that are not owned by the publisher.

The Hachette Speakers Bureau provides a wide range of authors for speaking events. To find out more, go to hachettespeakersbureau.com or email HachetteSpeakers@hbgusa.com.

Little, Brown and Company books may be purchased in bulk for business, educational, or promotional use. For information, please contact your local bookseller or the Hachette Book Group Special Markets Department at special.markets@hbgusa.com.

Book interior design by Marie Mundaca

ISBN 9780316577342
Library of Congress Control Number: 2024950056

Printing 2, 2025

LSC-C

Printed in the United States of America

To my mother, Priscilla Dean Johnson Howard,
and my father, Charles David Johnson.

To my wife, Madeline Murphy Rabb, who rescued me from a
lonely depression and brought light and happiness back into
my life. Without her unwavering support from the beginning to
the end, I could not have completed this book.

To S. B. Fuller, Dr. Herbert A. Martini,
and Dr. William J. Faulkner.

I hope the stories I share on these pages inspire fellow entrepreneurs and strivers with ambitious goals and dreams, just as many great people inspired me.

—George E. Johnson

Contents

CONTENTS

AFRO
SHEEN

Prologue

I STEPPED OUT of the jitney at Sixty-Third and South Parkway, and braved the snow and winter wind for three blocks, on my way to one of the consumer loan companies sprinkling Chicago's South Side. There was no doubt about it, this was gonna be a big day. All I needed was $250 (about $2,600 today) to start my own business.

It was February 1954, and I was a production compounder for the Fuller Products Company, one of the largest Black-owned businesses in the United States. Run by the master salesman and millionaire S. B. Fuller, this consumer products firm was one of the most significant employers in the community. During my off-hours working with a chemist there, I had co-created a revolutionary hair-straightening formula I knew would turn the Black men's haircare market upside down. Everyone knew that the Whiter you looked — whether it was because you had light skin, a narrow nose, thin lips, or straight hair—the more likely mainstream employers were to accept you, treat you humanely, or hire you. Many Black men wanted straighter hair, like the pompadour and finger-waved hairstyles some successful Black entertainers were wearing, from Cab Calloway to Chubby Checker, Little Richard, Duke Ellington, and Nat King Cole.

I needed a seed loan to match the funds my business partner had put up. Fortunately, I'd patronized this loan company several times and had a track record of repayment. Just $250 would provide me and my family a ticket out of poverty.

For ten minutes I waited in the large open room, listening to my neighbors, all of whom were Black, present their case to one of several White loan officers. I heard a housekeeper plead for money to buy a stove. A laborer who needed a loan to fix his truck. Before long, a middle-aged man wearing a gray suit stood up and motioned that he was ready for me.

"My name is George Johnson," I stated confidently as I settled into the chair across the desk from him. "I've got something that's going to allow me to build a great big business!"

I then described my professional expertise, my eight years of employment with Mr. Fuller, and my innovation.

"What kind of loan are you asking for?" the man inquired, raising an eyebrow.

"All I need is two hundred and fifty bucks," I told him. "Just give me the two fifty and I'm on my way!"

I spoke enthusiastically. However, something about the twinkle in the man's gray eyes and his barely there smile unsettled my stomach. He shuffled papers, then chuckled and cleared his throat.

"I'm gonna do you a favor," he began in a patronizing tone, leaning forward and running his fingers through his ash-brown hair. "If I loan you that money and your boss finds out that you are in the same business that he's in, he's gonna fire you. You're not gonna be able to pay the money back. So I'm not gonna loan you the money."

Then he sat back, crossed his arms, and grinned.

My stomach turned a somersault, but I didn't want the man to see my feathers droop. I stood up and put my cap on my head.

"Good day," I said, looking him straight in the eye. As I strode out, I didn't bother to close the front door. I kept walking until I was several storefronts up the street and out of his sight. At that point, I stopped and stood limp as a dishrag, as I considered my nonexistent alternatives. I was already working three jobs, and neither my mother nor John, my older brother, had money to lend me. The El train rumbling overhead jolted me back to the moment. I walked to South Parkway and flagged a jitney.

"Where you heading?"

"Sixty-Ninth Place and Indiana," I answered.

But somewhere along the ride, a warm thought wafted into my mind as softly as a leaf floats from a tree on an autumn afternoon.

This is just one branch of the loan company. There is a central branch where they clear people's credit. Just wait a few days and go to a different office.

Several days later I did just that. This time, I shared no stories of Black men with innovative chemical formulas, products, or business plans.

I made up a tale, instead.

"I'm taking my wife to California," I said, my smile as

bright as the Los Angeles sky. "I need two hundred and fifty dollars for a vacation loan."

I knew this request wouldn't rattle his belief that he was superior to me. Nor would it challenge his stereotypes of Black men as subservient or unintelligent.

Thirty minutes later, I walked out with a check in my hand.

1

This Is Black Power

IT WAS NOVEMBER 1966, and the first time Dr. Martin Luther King Jr. visited my company's offices. We had met four years prior, when he delivered keynote remarks at the banquet for hairdressers that Johnson Products Company held to increase awareness of Ultra Sheen, our new line of haircare products.

The entire team, including myself, were overjoyed to have Dr. King on the premises weeks after we moved into our brand-new thirty-thousand-square-foot headquarters. It was built from the ground up in less than two years.

Our modern two-story brick structure stood at 8522 South Lafayette Avenue, a highly trafficked location alongside the Dan Ryan Expressway. And boy did it capture attention. Right in the heart of the South Side of Chicago, each day, thousands of commuters could see our signs, "Johnson Products Company" and "Ultra Sheen," mounted on the pedestal out front. I wanted to inspire and educate people by the sheer physical presence of the building.

We opened in town when many businesses were moving to the suburbs and laying off workers. I wanted to motivate the community and show what was possible. Multimillionaire Black businessman S. B. Fuller would say that when Black folks see White people do things, they don't necessarily think they can do them themselves. But when Black people do things, other Black people believe they can accomplish them, too. The lesson stayed with me.

It was my hope, as Black people learned our building was owned by other Black people, that their pride and sense of possibility would increase. Our headquarters challenged White folks, as well. Many were forced to reconsider negative stereotypes and low expectations toward Black people and expand their view of what we could accomplish.

Our building was seen as a wonder. The front plaza featured an eleven-foot abstract sculpture by Richard Hunt, a Black sculptor. I commissioned it to complement several six-foot-tall redbrick pyramids evoking ancient Egypt. There were two entrances—the main entryway, which took you to the lobby, and the employee entrance, which led to the cafeteria and manufacturing plant.

Within our first month or two of opening, our headquarters was a source of such racial and civic pride that all sorts of visiting dignitaries made JPC a priority stop. There was the diplomat Ralph Bunche, the first Black Nobel laureate, who received the 1950 Nobel Peace Prize for his work as a United Nations mediator. Cassius Clay visited our plant as well. The first time he used his birth name; by the second time he'd changed his name to Muhammad Ali. William Tubman, the president of Liberia, came by, too.

Soon JPC began holding tours. I wanted local neighbors both to see the inside and what our company was accomplishing.

Most buildings in the area were older. JPC's decor was contemporary, with a split-level staircase, brown exposed brick walls, bright paintings, and African sculptures. Francine Hurst, a bubbly, welcoming receptionist who I'll never forget, had a desk in the lobby, surrounded by a large open area that contained a brown sofa and four stainless steel and brown leather Barcelona chairs, designed by the German American architect Ludwig Mies van der Rohe. A beautiful brown, burgundy, and pumpkin-colored area rug atop the tan carpet pulled the space together.

My office was sleek, in a gray-and-brown color palette, the walls exposed brick, furnished with stylish and contemporary Herman Miller furniture. Beautiful art adorned the walls. From my private garage, I could walk up a set of stairs right into my office.

JPC's boardroom was contained by glass walls. We had an art department that designed the packaging for our products, as well as sometimes helping with advertisements. My older brother John, an extraordinary manager, led our sales efforts. Out in the plant, our brother Robert ran the shipping department. Manufacturing took most of the space. It was nice to finally have a plant equipped the way I needed it, after years in smaller buildings where I'd had no contribution to the design. Everything here was customized for our own products, to get excellent manufacturing results.

During a time when too many Black people struggled to obtain decent employment, Johnson Products offered a dignified and professional environment to everyone. On any given day, you could walk the halls and come across a Black woman in a white chemist's smock, a Southeast Asian manager, or a young salesman sporting a suit and an Afro. Our workforce was 90 percent African American, the remainder a variety of ethnicities, divided mostly between Whites, Asian Indians, and Mexicans.

JPC saw all of our employees as assets to our company. We wanted them to work hard, care about the quality of their output, be concerned about the company, and stay with us for as long as possible. We believed in loyalty, not turnover. When each shift began, we played spiritual music to uplift and inspire them.

We took care of JPC's employees by giving them the most we could. There's a popular saying, "Live and *let* live." I embraced a different philosophy: "Live and *help* live."

JPC offered health insurance, as the big companies of the day did. We also offered six paid sick days each year, which was generous at that time. Even today about a quarter of America's workers have no sick days. We also implemented four-day holiday weekends. The standard even today is three days.

Each day, our chef prepared a delicious subsidized breakfast and lunch in the company cafeteria. The food was so good that people would often try to sneak their family and friends in. Even around 1970, hunger remained a problem in Chicago. We wanted as much of our employees' salary as possible to make it home to their families.

We also offered college tuition reimbursement. Most larger companies didn't begin to put that forward until after 1978, when the IRS made it tax-deductible for corporations. As someone who hadn't had the chance to go to college, I wanted to encourage as many of our employees as possible to obtain a higher education.

We provided paid maternity leave for women and a guaranteed job upon their return. The government didn't enact the Family and Medical Leave Act until 1993, almost thirty years after JPC provided the same benefits.

It was also an era in which few Black workers received health care benefits. In case our people had a headache, or a stomachache, or cramps from their period, or if they came down with the flu or got injured at work, JPC employed a full-time nurse and assistant nurse on-site.

And I can't forget JPC's experimental salon, where we tested our products for safety and improvements. Any employee could get their hair cut or styled there for free.

For a company our size, our salary was very competitive and our benefits were unique and extremely bighearted. In particular our profit-sharing program, in which every employee participated, rivaled Sears, Roebuck and Company's program. Our employees' fortunes rose as the company's did. JPC had good workers, and we wanted them to stay with us and invest themselves in the company while JPC reciprocated their efforts.

Just as important, JPC provided a loving work environment. We treated our workers like they were members of the family. Back then, there wasn't much conversation about a company's culture. At many companies, managers and leaders would walk around yelling. Some bosses berated their people. They didn't manage with skill but with fear. Too many Black people were targeted by abuse like this. I wanted our workers to know that we cared about them. Rather than leadership by intimidation, my management style was coaching people.

I chose not to pay myself an exorbitant salary. I didn't want to hoard our profits just for myself; I believed money should circulate.

This was an era when the national economy was dominated by industrial giants such as General Motors, Ford, and Chrysler; General Electric; U.S. Steel; and major oil companies. Chicago also was known for big meatpacking companies like Armour and Swift. The Montgomery Ward and the Sears department store chains were headquartered here, as well. Of course, JPC was a much smaller company. Still, our revenues exceeded $5 million annually—the equivalent of almost $49 million today—and we shared them.

In the 1960s, people took a tremendous amount of pride in having a neat appearance, both on the street and when they came to work. Our professional employees wore suits, dresses, and jackets. Our manufacturing workers dressed in a shirt and tie for their commute to work, then changed into JPC's sanitized green-and-blue uniforms to carry out their assignments. At JPC no one hassled or humiliated employees about their hair, which frequently happened in other environments, where Black people were expected to conform to a European standard of beauty. We wanted our people to feel comfortable no matter their identity, or what hairstyle they wore. At that moment, popular relaxed hairstyles included updos, bouffants, and pixies, and popular natural hairstyles included fades, cornrows, and Afros.

The same year I founded Johnson Products Company, Ralph Ellison won the National Book Award for *Invisible Man*; Willie Thrower of the Chicago Bears became the first Black quarterback in the National Football League; the Supreme Court ruled that state-sanctioned segregation of schools violated the US Constitution in *Brown v. Board of Education of Topeka, Kansas*; and a young NAACP lawyer named Thurgood Marshall successfully represented antilynching activist Mary Church Terrell in *District of Columbia v. John R. Thompson Co., Inc.*, before the US Supreme Court.

It was 1954, and I was JPC's single employee. A little more than a decade later, Johnson Products Company employed more than one hundred people of all racial backgrounds, offering both a loving environment and dignified jobs—from research to engineering, sales, and warehouse—and above average pay to qualified folk that mainstream employers normally excluded. Almost all mainstream workplaces refused to hire Black people for office jobs. They relegated the overwhelming majority of White women to the secretarial pool and Black women to menial labor or, at best, the factory floor. At JPC, women served on our leadership team.

I was satisfied with our new building, who worked there, and what we were doing to empower the community. And at this momentous time, Dr. King was here to visit. I wore my best gray suit, a light-blue button-down shirt, a blue-and-gray-striped tie, and my black Bally lace-ups. My hair was styled in the process, as always, using our men's hair straightener, Ultra Wave Hair Culture.

"It's an honor to have you here," I said, shaking his hand and placing my left hand on top of his.

"Now *this* is Black power!" exclaimed Dr. King, admiring our headquarters.

As we walked toward my office, I stopped to introduce Dorothy McConnell, my priceless administrative assistant. Next came my wife and business partner, Joan, who led the accounting department.

"We are excited to have you here," Joan said, her high-wattage smile illuminating the room. "We are grateful for everything you're doing for our people."

I led our visitors—Dr. King, the Reverend James Bevels, a leader with the Southern Christian Leadership Conference (SCLC), and another gentleman—into the swank glass-walled conference room between Joan's office and mine. Dr. King and his family had moved to Chicago a year earlier. A group of local leaders had asked him to bring his nonviolent approach to activism to help reduce hunger and end segregation in jobs, housing, and education here. Thousands of Chicagoans were marching with Dr. King to break the color line and integrate neighborhoods.

In the conference room the main table, made of zebrawood, was already set for lunch. Before we sat down, Edwin C. "Bill" Berry joined us. He headed Chicago's Urban League. Shortly thereafter JPC's chef, Al Davis, brought hot fried chicken, collard greens, macaroni and cheese, and corn bread to the room. As Al dished up the food, Dr. King thanked him for preparing it, and in that brief gesture I witnessed the reverend's grace, thoughtfulness, and unpretentiousness. Dr. King then said a blessing over both the food and JPC. We chatted as we ate, the conversation flowed.

Ironically, at that time, some of Dr. King's teachings were causing me fits in my business. When I founded Johnson Products, most Black people aspired to wear straighter hairstyles. But in the 1960s, Dr. King and other leaders were teaching "Black is beautiful" and encouraging Black folks to stop imitating White people's appearances. I particularly remember him communicating the importance of being yourself and appreciating the way God made you.

"What God gave you is good enough," he told Black women.

This was a novel idea to many of us and gave people who wore the badge of color a new understanding of our significance. Large numbers of women, in particular, believed this message. Suddenly our primary customers began to cut off their relaxers and wear their hair natural. After decades of desiring straighter hair, Black women began deserting hairdressers by the thousands and wearing their hair as it came out of their head. Nappy, kinky, curly, and wavy hair textures were in. Many women started wearing blowouts, naturals, Afro puffs, cornrows, and braids.

When Dr. King began speaking, I listened carefully. He brought me up to speed on the SCLC's mission to train people in the tradition of Christian nonviolence. Dr. King took his time, speaking methodically.

"Would you be willing to use your business as an instrument of social good?" Dr. King asked me.

Since its creation, I ran Johnson Products according to the Golden Rule, "Do unto others as you would have others do unto you." We were all about doing good. In addition to our generous salary and benefits, there were the Thanksgiving food baskets JPC gave the needy, the way we invited schools to bring their students to visit, and our new initiative with the nonprofit Junior Achievement, to teach entrepreneurship and financial literacy and prepare young people for the world of work. In our cafeteria and offices around our facility, JPC volunteers mentored kids who created their own companies. Our professionals taught them how to organize, produce, and sell their products. This was the least I could do, offering others what had been provided for me.

Through these small acts, we were building Chicago's Black middle class.

Most Black people were low-income or working-class—domestic workers, janitors, menial laborers, factory and assembly-line workers, mechanics, postal workers, auto workers, gas station attendants, and the like. Two of my uncles worked in Chicago's bloody slaughterhouses, where hogs were killed, cut up, and packaged for sale. In general, racial discrimination in the workplace was so bad that 40 percent of unskilled Black laborers earned less than their unskilled White peers had earned ten years earlier.

JPC changed that. We impacted our employees' lives and helped them to build up savings and possibly shake off the trauma of poverty. We provided hair products that allowed people to style their hair in a way that gave them the confidence to seek gainful employment and live as they aspired to live.

Dr. King explained that the SCLC particularly wanted voters newly empowered by the Voting Rights Act to understand that going to the polls and casting their ballot offered the best opportunity to improve their quality of life.

"Will you help me pull together a group of Black businessmen to come to our meeting?" he asked.

"It would be my pleasure," I told him.

Dr. King told me he also wanted to establish an initiative to improve Black people's job opportunities.

"Many mainstream retail businesses and industries deplete communities by selling to Black people but refusing to hire us or buy our goods," he explained. "Black Chicagoans shouldn't patronize businesses that deny us jobs, advancement, or basic courtesy."

I was well aware of the problem. Black business owners regularly shared strategies. One person who immediately came to mind was George Jones, the head of the Joe Lewis Milk Company, who was attempting to sell to White grocers.

The president of Parker House Sausage had been trying to secure distribution, as well. So was a man I knew with a frozen pizza business and another who ran an orange juice company. I could recite a long list of Black businesses being denied the chance to sell their products to mainstream firms that were doing business in our community. That's not to mention all the aspiring entrepreneurs who couldn't get off the ground.

"JPC is one of the largest Black-owned manufacturing firms and even we are struggling to get our biggest products sold in mainstream grocery stores," I added.

I reached out to people I knew. Word traveled and about thirty-five or forty businesspeople came to Dr. King's meeting. That day, Dr. King launched Operation Breadbasket from JPC's cafeteria. He also introduced a young minister, Reverend Jesse Jackson, to lead it.

I had first encountered Reverend Jackson a few months earlier. The tall, slender, handsome young man wearing a short Afro was speaking brilliantly about the Civil Rights Movement at the University of Chicago's campus chapel.

At the time, he was a seminary student and so poor he hardly owned a change of clothes. He and his young family lived in inadequate housing not far from the university. After witnessing his brilliance, I organized a group of six Black businessmen to meet with Reverend Jackson in my office. We talked for more than two hours. It was clear he had great potential and an amazing ability to analyze a situation and give an appropriate response in a snap. We decided to stand behind Reverend Jackson, chip in together, and get him a decent place to live, on Ridgeland Avenue in South Shore.

Using peaceful protests, boycotts, and strong negotiating tactics, Operation Breadbasket pressured a number of mainstream companies to start carrying Black-owned products.

For the first time, JPC obtained distribution in Jewel grocery stores.

I also spoke with the executive committee of Black-owned Independence Bank and proposed that they guarantee a loan to Dr. King. A few weeks later, he received a loan of $145,000, about $1.2 million today.

The day we handed him the check, Dr. King wept.

Nearly two years later, it was April 4, and I was sitting in the family room reading the newspaper with the TV running in the background, when a CBS News special report interrupted the normal programming.

"The Reverend Martin Luther King Jr. was shot to death by an assassin late today, as he stood on a balcony in Memphis, Tennessee," anchorman Dan Rather stated.

I doubled over and cried. Dan Rather introduced the news director at the Memphis television affiliate.

Joan overheard everything from the kitchen, came running, and began sobbing intensely. I did my best to comfort our children.

Our entire house was bawling.

As I grieved, I wondered if I'd been supportive enough, and I worried what would happen to the civil rights movement.

Black folks everywhere revered Dr. King. We didn't know what was going to happen next, but we sensed that whatever it was, it wasn't going to be good. People were grief-stricken, bewildered, angry. We worried that riots were about to take place.

I got myself together and drove to the office, where everyone was distraught. Chicago's Black police chief, Captain Fred Rice, called to invite me to attend the memorial that

Mayor Richard J. Daley planned at City Hall the next morning. I accepted. President Johnson delivered a television address, in an attempt to calm people down.

At some point that evening, Reverend Jackson called me. He looked at me as somewhat of a fatherly figure by this point.

"I just got back to Chicago," he said, then described how he'd been standing on the balcony next to Dr. King when he was shot. Speechless, I did my best to comfort him. But who had the right words for a horror like that?

"I've been invited to a memorial at City Hall," I told him. "Do you want to go with me?"

"Yes, George," he told me. "I definitely want to come."

The next morning, I drove to pick Reverend Jackson up at his home. Normally, he dressed neatly and was well kept, but he got in my car wearing the same bloodstained shirt and jacket he was wearing when Dr. King fell. Reverend Jackson's Afro looked unkempt, his spirit seemed broken, and he had an odd look in his eyes I'd never seen before—and I haven't seen since.

Certain city council members frowned when they saw me walk in with Reverend Jackson. The Chicago City Council was almost exclusively White and male. Many of its members and Mayor Daley had been actively supporting the very racial segregation Dr. King had been trying to break down. I was shown to my seat. There wasn't a place for Reverend Jackson. He walked to the front of the room and sat in the chair on the dais reserved for either the monsignor of Holy Angels Catholic Church or the cardinal of the Archdiocese of Chicago. I was amazed to see him occupy that place, just a seat or two from Mayor Daley. The entire chamber became agitated.

People began giving tributes to Dr. King. Before long, Reverend Jackson stood up and said something to the effect of, "I'm listening to all these crocodile tears, but yesterday Dr. King wouldn't have been welcome in this chamber." He made more remarks, then he turned and walked out.

After he left, quite a bit of grumbling took place about what he'd said. People reacted like he had insulted them. Several TV stations were televising the proceedings live, and caught both Reverend Jackson's comments and him walking out. I remained until the service was over. But since I had brought Reverend Jackson with me, many of White Chicago's leaders treated me as if I was a traitor. I experienced some cold shoulders for quite some time. But who could care given the fact that we'd lost a great man in the Reverend Martin Luther King Jr.?

I flew to Atlanta for Dr. King's funeral at Ebenezer Baptist Church. Afterward I joined the processional of thousands walking slowly behind Dr. King's casket, which pallbearers had placed in a wooden farm wagon and was pulled across Atlanta by two mules. All along the route to his *alma mater*, Morehouse College, where the final funeral service took place, enormous crowds of Black people lined the streets. They stood on balconies, sat on rooftops, and climbed into trees to see and pay their respects. I would never forget this incredible man. My ode to Dr. King's legacy would be my continued hard work on behalf of Black people.

2

The Secret to Success

WHEN I MET S. B. Fuller in 1944, he was already one of the nation's wealthiest Black men. Born in Louisiana in 1905, he grew up dirt-poor, the eldest child of sharecroppers. When he was nine, he left school to work the fields full time. The school system offered education to Black children only three months of the year, because they were expected to work in the fields the other nine, while White children went to school months longer.

In addition to sharecropping, Fuller's father bartered vegetables, eggs, and fish at the local market. This made their family unusually independent at a time when the South was racially segregated. When Fuller was fifteen, his family moved to Memphis, and he began selling mail-order products. Apparently, that was fine until he added women's dresses to his product line. Local White merchants complained to the sheriff. The sheriff told the teenager to quit doing business and get a job at the lumberyard.

During that era, Black people whom racist Whites perceived as "uppity" or "not knowing their place" at society's bottom ran the risk of experiencing violence. This included being lynched, killed publicly at the hands of a mob. In those days, the NAACP was running a national antilynching campaign because racial violence was so common nationwide.

Black business owners were frequent targets of racial hostility. The Greenwood District of Tulsa, Oklahoma, was home to ten thousand Black people and two hundred Black-owned businesses. The community was so prosperous that educator and leader Booker T. Washington began calling its downtown Black Wall Street.

Many White Tulsans resented Black people's success, and in 1921 ten thousand of them looted, vandalized, and torched Black Wall Street. They killed almost three hundred Black people, burned down two hundred businesses, and destroyed roughly twelve hundred homes. Attacks upon Black businesses took place around the nation. Black success proved the widely held belief in White supremacy to be a lie. Some people also feared Black people's economic independence in general, and many White businessmen depended on Black customers to feed their own families.

In 1928, S. B. Fuller walked and hitchhiked the 533 miles from Memphis to Chicago. When he arrived in the Windy City, he got a job delivering coal to buildings that burned it for fuel. He eventually became manager of the coal yard. He married, and his wife taught him to read by using the Bible, which was how many Black people became literate. At that point, he began studying books about selling. Ultimately,

Fuller became a salesman for the Commonwealth Burial Insurance Company, a Black-owned firm providing burial insurance to Black Chicagoans, who could not get it from mainstream insurance companies. At Commonwealth, he practiced the sales skills he was learning. He also read that only eighty-nine of the more than four thousand American millionaires at the time possessed a high school degree, and that the president of Lever Brothers made $485,000 a year (about $9.5 million today). The head of a soap company earned more than any other corporate leader. These facts raised his sense of what was possible.

In 1936 Fuller purchased a car and, after obtaining insurance, received a $25 rebate. Using the $25 as seed money, he bought soap at a reduced price from a company going out of business. After applying his own labels, printed "Fuller's Quality Soap," he sold one bar at a time, reinvesting his receipts in his business over and over. After transforming soap into money, he added more products and opened a retail store.

I learned of S. B. Fuller in 1944, after my brother John graduated from high school and became a sales agent for Fuller Products. During that era, on the South Side of Chicago, Black people operated more businesses than you could count. *Scott's Blue Book*, the city's directory of African American businesses, featured almost 340 pages of advertisements and stories about these enterprises. There were many entrepreneurs on the South Side, and a person rarely needed to leave the emotional safety of the community to shop in other neighborhoods or downtown.

Within blocks of our family's apartment, there were several Black-owned businesses — Sunbeam Cleaners, a barbershop, an ice cream shop, a live-chicken store, and Liberty

23

Life Insurance Company, the first Black-owned and operated insurance company outside of the South, and one of the
few to survive the Great Depression.

The Fuller Products headquarters was in a gray brick
building, one block from our home, next to the relief station,
where jobless people redeemed coupons for vegetables and
groceries. Although the Great Depression was over, many
people were still looking for work. In addition, thousands of
Black folks were fleeing the South, seeking better jobs,
greater freedom, and more opportunities in the North.
Southern migrants typically arrived in Chicago needing
jobs. Many employers either refused to employ them at all or
hired them only after hiring White people, including immigrants who didn't speak English. Black workers got the dirti-
est, most dangerous, and least desirable jobs. During World
War II some Black people would picket factories to protest
segregation, carrying signs reading "Hitler Must Own This
Plant; Negroes Can't Work Here," "If We Must Fight,
Why Can't We Work?" and "Bullets Know No Color Line,
Why Should Factories?" Many employers got away with what
they could, despite the 1941 executive order that President
Roosevelt signed prohibiting government contractors from
engaging in discrimination in the defense industry.

As the war dragged on and more White men were sent
off to the front, a labor shortage developed. Private companies hired more Black people for factory jobs, semiskilled
work they'd been barred from, and the area's airplane factories. While they got better jobs, they often received lower pay.
The doors to apprenticeship and trade schools remained
closed to Black people. Few were permitted in high-paying
skilled occupations, including as carpenters, plumbers, and
electricians. During the war, some Black men found jobs as

bus drivers and as operators of the elevated train. Many Black women were able to leave the domestic work they did for White families to obtain jobs in factories. Others found work as clerks and waitresses in mainstream stores and restaurants. But a campaign to increase opportunities in retail positions downtown failed. Lots of those jobs disappeared when White soldiers returned home after the war. Still, Black people's economic situation was improving overall, as compared to the desperate years of the Great Depression.

In a world that severely constricted Black people's possibilities, S. B. Fuller opened the windows of opportunity. By the time my brother John joined Fuller Products, the company's annual revenues likely totaled more than $300,000, a little short of $5 million today. It was a significant amount for any company, but it was a huge revenue for a Black-owned business. John became an independent sales agent for Fuller, lugging a black plastic case that must have weighed at least twenty pounds door-to-door, up and down the steps of South Side tenement buildings. John sold household products and cosmetics—face powders, hand creams, all kinds of skin products, hair products, lipsticks, deodorants, perfumed bath salts, and even vanilla extract. He did well "carrying that bag," as we called it. I was thrilled to see my brother prospering.

At the time, I was struggling at Wendell Phillips High School. I valued my education and had previously enjoyed my classes, excelling in English, math, and chemistry. My mother had raised us to do what we had to do in school. At St. Elizabeth's Catholic School, my cousin and I did well and were often taken into classes of older students to embarrass and perhaps inspire them. At Doolittle Elementary School, I had my first Black teacher. I could tell he cared about Black children, and he encouraged us to do well. Maudelle Brown Bousfield, the first African American principal of a Chicago public school, hired the first Black teachers who worked at Wendell Phillips. They were invested in our academics.

But our family was poor and times were hard.

Beginning when I was six years old, John and I worked to help our mother make ends meet. The job she held at Michael Reese Hospital kept a roof over our head and our stomachs from being empty, but there wasn't money left for anything else. John and I started out "junking," selling stuff we dug out of trash cans to the junk man in the alley. After that, when John got a job, he opened the way for me to follow him. When I was ten, we both got paper routes. Next, we worked in the noxious back room of a dry cleaner. He didn't work the jobs I held during high school—first, bussing tables at a famous nightclub, the College Inn at the Sherman Hotel downtown, then as a washroom attendant at the swanky Drake Hotel. Both these jobs ended late in the evening. I loved earning tips, having funds to give Mama, and still having money for myself. But I typically didn't return home until eleven p.m. or midnight. I started oversleeping my morning alarm. My grades suffered, and I felt ashamed as my prospects of earning my high school degree diminished.

John kept encouraging me to quit Wendell Phillips High School and start working for Fuller Products. Every morning, Mr. Fuller held a meeting at his office to recruit and motivate sales agents. The meetings were open to the public and lasted an hour or so. In the fall, my big brother finally persuaded me to attend. Impressed by how well John was doing financially, I figured why not and went with him. We passed the relief line, walked up a flight of stairs, and entered Fuller Products' headquarters and manufacturing facility. John and I stood in a large sales room surrounded by about seventy-five Black men and women of all ages, most neatly clothed in a shirt and tie or a dress. Many appeared to be Fuller Products sales agents, and several seemed to be curious about people like me.

"God did not intend for you to be poor," a tall, bespectacled, brown-skinned man proclaimed to the crowd standing before him, removing his jacket, as a minister might. "God has provided you with everything you need to overcome poverty! But you have to have a burning desire to escape it." I had listened to many sermons before, but I had never heard anything quite like this. S. B. Fuller was the most dynamic speaker I'd ever encountered, and his message that I didn't have to remain poor resonated with me and took root in my spirit.

By December I was disgusted with my academic situation and gave up on the idea of obtaining my high school diploma.

I'm going to try Fuller Products.

I knew that if John could do well there, I could, too. I dropped out of Wendell Phillips. I was enamored of my new boss. I still believed in the importance of education and felt I was leaving one type of classroom to enter another.

I'm going someplace that has promise.

I also quit the Drake Hotel.

Each morning I attended Mr. Fuller's sales meeting. "Anything a White man can do, so can you!" he told us, motivating and inspiring poor Black Chicagoans with messages extremely radical for that era.

To people who had fled the Cotton South to take charge of their own future, the idea that we could break out of poverty was groundbreaking. Few if any of us had ever seen such a successful Black man. But here he was standing before us six days a week.

I learned that Mr. Fuller read everything in sight, and his memory was photographic. Most of his messages were rooted both in his unapologetic love of Black people and his extensive knowledge of the Bible, whose ideas he understood, interpreted, and espoused quite clearly.

I came from a strong religious family. Both of my parents were very spiritual people. Mama had lots of faith and was always grateful to God. Even today, I can hear her crying out, "Thank you, Jesus. Thank you, Jesus!" Beginning early in childhood, we attended Olivet Baptist Church. My beliefs were further developed at St. Elizabeth's. I spent untold hours on my knees beneath the church's huge stained-glass rose window, memorizing the Catholic catechism, the principles of Christianity. I learned about faith and developed a sense of God's presence. The nuns taught us that God is looking over you; God is inside you; and God is taking note of your conduct.

Our mother left our father to move us children up north, and each month Daddy wrote from Mississippi to tell us how much he loved and missed us. Every envelope contained three new dollar bills. When I was ten, Mama sent us down south to spend a year with Daddy. The Bible and religion were his top priorities. He wanted us to love the Lord and obey God's will, and taught us to be polite and courteous, respectful toward others, and grateful for what the Lord provided. He took us to the Baptist church down the street and had us baptized. I will never forget getting dunked in that swollen creek. The water was cold as hell!

Because our upbringing emphasized spiritual development, the ideas that Mr. Fuller preached were not foreign to me. In fact, his sermons made the Bible more real and me more curious about its contents.

By far the most powerful lesson I learned from Mr. Fuller was the Golden Rule: "Do unto others as you would have others do unto you." Since I already knew the Ten Commandments and the Golden Rule from my home training and Catholic school education, I believed it was literally what I must do.

I saw Mr. Fuller practice trust first by demonstrating trust in his employees. His salesmen didn't have to put out money up front to get a black bag and to become an independent Fuller Products sales agent. He loaned people the heavy suitcase because he sensed they were honest, driven, worth the risk, and could help him grow his business.

I began selling Fuller Products door-to-door. I sold during the day and returned to the office the next morning to deposit the revenue. Whatever I sold on Monday, I turned in first thing Tuesday—Mr. Fuller didn't allow salesmen to keep the money in their pockets too long. Each day I sat down with him to review how much I'd earned the day before, then replaced the products I'd sold and headed out to sell again. On Saturdays he paid my commission for the entire week. Sundays were the only day he took off. Each time I handled Mr. Fuller's black bag, I benefited from his willingness to front me credit.

On a day-to-day basis, I witnessed Mr. Fuller teach ordinary working-poor and destitute Black Chicagoans how they could make money running their own independent business. Not only did he teach people how to start their own enterprise; he also financed us, shared the profits, and inspired us to increase our income. Fuller Products supplied the means to make a good living. "A man doesn't have to have a lot of degrees behind his name to earn ten thousand a year" ($230,000 today), he would repeat, invigorating his listeners with all sorts of great ideas, including but not limited to how selling his products could benefit us.

Mr. Fuller built his business one person at a time. The fact he started out with $25, and now had hundreds of successful Fullerites scouring the neighborhood for sales, was everyone's proof that his methods worked. Each Fuller Products salesperson told their family and friends both what he taught them and how well they were doing financially. Some Fuller salespeople were making $75 to $100 a week, the equivalent of about $68,000 to $88,000 a year today. This was an unheard-of income for almost any American, much less a Black one. With news like this, Mr. Fuller didn't need to advertise either his jobs or his products. Positive word of mouth spread across the South Side like wildfire. Tenement by tenement, house by house, block by block, people talked about how Mr. Fuller was helping people to become prosperous and financially independent.

Initially, I felt enthusiastic about my job. John and I strategized about where we could find our best prospects. While many Fuller agents were making good sales in poorer neighborhoods, we thought the better opportunities existed farther south. Since formal sales territories didn't exist, we walked to Forty-First Street, Forty-Third Street, and Forty-Seventh Street and worked our way toward the more affluent areas of the community. But while my big brother was a smart, loyal, and ambitious salesman, it didn't take long for me to develop a different attitude about selling. I had a hard time walking into somebody's shabby apartment—and because many of us were poor, many people's apartments were shabby—and seeing little children play on the floor in their underwear because the family couldn't afford play clothes, and then waving honeysuckle perfume or cologne under the person's nose and watching them suddenly want to buy it. Some people found the money, whether or not they should be spending it. *That lady should not have bought the cologne*, I thought more than once, a guilty feeling settling over me. I continued to sell, but I couldn't get those thoughts out of my mind.

Before long, John became enthralled with the idea of going to New York City. He asked Mr. Fuller if he could work out of the New York Fuller Products branch. John left Chicago for New York in early 1946. I missed my older brother, and he kept calling to tell me how well he was doing. After I argued with my high school sweetheart, Joan, and we broke up, I decided to go to the Big Apple. By the time I arrived, John and a couple of guys had gotten a three-bedroom apartment at 131 Convent Avenue in Harlem. I shared a bedroom with John; the two other guys shared a bedroom; and they rented the third bedroom to a woman.

The Big Apple was a tremendous place. The streets were more crowded than they were in Chicago. But in New York nobody spoke to you at all. When I said hello to a guy in our building, he didn't even grunt a reply. The rudeness startled me. And I had the same problems selling in New York as I had back in Chicago. In fact, it was worse because the people seemed more desperate. My emotions only permitted me to be just a so-so salesman. I made a little money, but I didn't have any savings. Then Joan began calling me, begging me to return. Now that I knew she wanted me back, I couldn't wait to go home.

Determined to get the money I needed to go back, I leveled down and sold as hard as I could. For two weeks I was the leading salesman in the branch, and I remained on top until I saved enough money to buy a train ticket home. On the ride back, I remember standing between two cars, smoking a cigarette. A man commented that he liked my jacket. I lied and told him that my father owned a big business, Fuller Products.

But not every Chicagoan struggled in New York. John was doing well. So was a young Chicago native, Rose Meta Morgan, who migrated to the Big Apple in 1938 and was making a name for herself as a hairstylist on the East Coast. During her teens, Ms. Morgan styled Black women's hair to help her family financially. She'd become good and even dressed singer Ethel Waters's hair when Ms. Waters performed at Chicago's Palace Theater. Ms. Waters encouraged Ms. Morgan to relocate to Harlem, where she later perfected the innovative approach to hairstyling that became her signature treatment. Until that point, most hairdressers used grease to straighten Black women's hair and curl it into tight coils. The technique left the hair heavy and with little movement. Ms. Morgan's approach involved blow-drying the hair and then curling it using oil, which left hair much looser and bouncier. Her method became all the rage.

In addition to her pioneering style, Ms. Morgan pampered Black women and treated them as human during a time when many White families saw their Black domestics as merely "the help." Her belief that Black women deserved to be indulged was unprecedented in the salon world. Stars like Sarah Vaughan, Ella Fitzgerald, Lena Horne, and Diahann Carroll flocked to her Rose Morgan House of Beauty and Rose Meta House of Beauty, which became sensations throughout the Northeast. In addition to styling hair, Ms. Morgan's cosmetologists applied her proprietary makeup and beauty products to Black women's faces. Her salons also offered massages, colonic irrigation treatments, and other services far ahead of their time. For years, Ms. Morgan served more than four hundred Black women a day. She claimed her salon business was the world's largest.

At some point Ms. Morgan came to Mr. Fuller's attention. They formed a partnership to sell her haircare and makeup products and opened a branch, Rose Meta Cosmetics, in Brooklyn. Mr. Fuller invited John to help launch this business, and my big brother went on to manage it.

When I returned to Chicago from my New York fiasco, mentally I was finished with sales. I continued to sell part-time to make ends meet, but carrying that heavy black bag now bothered my back. I knew I couldn't keep it up, and I asked Mr. Fuller if he would put me in a job in the lab. He agreed to give me this new opportunity for about $65 a week.

Now that I no longer had to do sales, rather than dress up each morning I threw on a pair of pants, a shirt, and an old pair of shoes. I made bacon and eggs or peanut butter and jelly sandwiches for breakfast. Then I walked the block to Mr. Fuller's offices, arriving by 8:30 a.m.

I headed up the steps and entered the small L-shaped facility, walking past a couple of offices and weaving through the people gathering in the open sales area for the 9:00 meeting, which typically lasted until 10:00 or 10:30.

"How'd you do yesterday?" I might hear someone ask as I passed through.

"Brother, I sold so much vanishing cream last night, you'd think women were turning into ghosts!" a fellow might reply, laughing.

"Don't listen to Willie—I saw him working at the gas station last night," another might retort.

"How do you know I wasn't selling vanishing cream there?"

The sales agents could be competitive.

Next I walked past the shipping room, then the production area, where the jars were filled and the bath salts made. Behind the production room was the small lab where I worked. I changed into my gray uniform and white smock there. My day often began with bringing raw materials up the fire escape. We used planks to cover the steps, and a pulley system to haul big, heavy black industrial drums up to the second floor. An entire drum of petrolatum might weigh four hundred pounds; mineral oil was lighter. Once we pulled the containers through the door, we stacked them at the end of the hall.

A fifty-year-old gentleman named Mr. Parsons taught me my job as a production compounder, most of which involved formulating small batches of Mr. Fuller's products, to prepare for manufacturing. I learned to make many products: cleansing cream, vanishing cream, cologne, deodorant, bath salts, hair pomades, cold cream, and more. The first ones I was assigned were vanishing creams. Vanishing creams are emulsion products. In high school chemistry, I learned that oil and water don't mix. At Fuller Products, I discovered that's true unless you incorporate an emulsifying agent, a product that breaks the ingredients down into small molecules that appear to be blended. The emulsifier holds the molecules closely side by side, and the naked eye cannot discern that they're separate.

When we finished formulating and mixing batches of each of the different products, we emptied these mixtures into large pots and dragged them over to where other workers filled the containers the products were sold in. A couple of these people, known as fillers, used a scooper to transfer the products from the large pots into a big hopper. True to their job title, the fillers stood along each side of the table and hand-filled the appropriate jars: small, round jars of face cream or tall jars of bath salts, whatever the product required.

One set of people filled the jars, another set wiped the jars clean, labeled them, and returned them, full, to the original boxes they came from. After that, the boxes went into the storeroom. My job also included moving the packages of finished product to the storage area.

As I walked around the facility, I often found myself in earshot of Mr. Fuller. To the extent I could, I listened in on his sales meetings. Sometimes I could hear every word of his sermons.

"God has put everything you need inside you. Use it and your mentality will grow. You will learn how to think and how to solve problems; it's within you. God has given us everything we need.

What had God given me?"

I wasn't always sure what Mr. Fuller meant. He clearly wasn't talking about material possessions—few of us had many material items. The more I listened to his inspirational messages, the more he seemed to be saying that God had given each of us some basic abilities, and they already existed within us.

"Latch on to those gifts and use them to create the life you want!"

What abilities do I have? What do I want?

I was seventeen when I started reading the Bible seriously. In the beginning, some of its stories seemed preposterous. How could a woman possibly come from a man's rib, or a snake speak to a woman? I wasn't convinced. And with World War II newsreels playing in movie theaters each week, I felt particularly frightened by the idea of armies killing people and the thought that God promoted war. But I kept reading and eventually found relief in Ecclesiastes, which started out as a mind-boggler— *Vanity of vanities, saith the Preacher, vanity of vanities; all is vanity*—but began to make a lot more sense over time. I also read the New Testament and developed the deeper biblical background that helped me to understand what the text was saying. *One generation passeth away, and another generation cometh: but the earth abideth for ever.*

We Fullerites were dedicated to our role model. We listened respectfully and were energized by his encouragement. It was beautiful and wonderful to see the type of people Mr. Fuller was able to get standing on their feet. Over the years I saw him help countless folks get off relief and earn a good enough income that they were able to take care of their kids, purchase a home, buy a car, and live a nice life. Some could afford to pay for their children's college. As his business expanded nationally, countless Black people around the country became affluent. Even teachers, who had among the highest-paying jobs Black people possessed, quit to come to work for him.

"If you really want to get out of poverty, you will find a way," he told us. "Racism stops a lot of people. Don't give in to it, overcome it."

Racism was rampant, but, rightly or wrongly, Mr. Fuller didn't think it had the power to hold you back. He wanted us to believe we could overcome it if we wanted to. He thought that if you really wanted to succeed, you would manage despite racism, as he had. We could use the power of our mind to project ourselves beyond our current situation, he told us, encouraging us to focus our thoughts on worthy and achievable goals, and envision accomplishing them.

"Mentally, you have to come up with something that

benefits others," he told us. "To succeed, you have to find a product or service that people will value."

"If you have the desire to be out of poverty and to do something for other people, God will help you," Mr. Fuller preached. "He will put you on your path, and you can follow it. Take what you have and make what you want. Combine a burning desire with the willingness to help someone. That's the secret to success, an eagerness to help other people. You help yourself by helping others."

He believed we were responsible for our own lives. If we wanted to get rich, we could get rich, but we'd have to work our butts off. He was the proof; he was the example. He also encouraged us to pray for wisdom, and if we were worthy, we'd get it.

Mr. Fuller tried to prepare us for the adversity we would encounter. Every now and then, I heard one sales agent advise another not to argue with Mr. Fuller, or to give him any backtalk.

"You can't win," they warned, "no, not with Mr. Fuller."

He attempted to shake up our beliefs—to build the courage of his people. "Last week, Ruby was our number-one saleslady again," he might say in his Monday-morning sales meeting. "I don't know what's going on with everyone else, but she has been in the lead for two straight weeks now. Seems like some of our former sales leaders are taking a little vacation. If you want to improve your condition, you cannot rest on your laurels."

People might become restless and squirm uncomfortably.

"Now, after Ruby, comes Hazel, then Tessie . . . ," he might continue. "Would you look at this? Women are in the top three spots."

When I first started at Fuller Products, most of the sales

agents were men, and men usually sold the most product. Over time, I noticed that women seemed to do a better job of recruiting and convincing people to come to the meetings. The sales room filled up with more and more women.

"Ruby been making all that money because she been selling to the women married to all those good livers at her church," some man might grumble. As the son of a courageous, hardworking, and resourceful single mother, I knew the competence of women.

From time to time, I also overheard Mr. Fuller counsel sales agents, one-on-one.

"Jimmie Lee, if you wanna make more money, all you gotta do is work harder and smarter," he might tell someone. "You could double your earnings and transform your life!" He really pumped people up.

The men's dressing room was located on the fourth floor. We went there to change before and after our shifts, and to smoke a cigarette, go to the bathroom, and lollygag around. The walls were high, but the top was open, and I could hear what people were saying from outside the dressing room. From time to time I got a kick out of scaring my fellow workers. I walked toward the dressing room, copying Mr. Fuller's stride and speaking in his vernacular. Guys got off their asses, scurried around the dressing room, and got back to work.

One day while I was a teenager, I found myself alone with Mr. Fuller.

"What do you want to do?" this great man asked me.

"I want to make a good living."

"Do you want to be rich?"

"Yes, I want to be rich."

"Then you have to take your fate into your own hands," he advised. "You have to be the master of your own fate."

I didn't know quite what my mentor was talking about, but I was definitely paying attention.

Months later he asked the same question in front of a larger audience. I'd brought Joan with me to the meeting so she could hear Mr. Fuller speak.

"Who in this room wants to be rich?" Mr. Fuller asked.

What fool would say, "I don't wanna be rich?" I rose to my feet. To my surprise, nobody else stood up.

Mr. Fuller took a long look, and I felt all the sales agents' eyes on me.

"JAWWWGH," he said, with his deep southern drawl. That's how he pronounced my name: "JAWGH."

"JAWWWGH, you don't wanna be rich," he said slowly, drawing out my name.

"I certainly do," I answered confidently, standing a bit taller to prove my point.

"JAWGH, you don't wanna be rich. You love your swine too much."

WHAAAT?

I was embarrassed and quickly sat down, struggling to make sense of what he'd said.

Is he talking about Joan? He must be!

I wasn't quite certain I understood what he meant; I assumed he was suggesting I was too involved with my girl-friend. Mr. Fuller was brilliant, very cagey, and known for putting people on the spot. Few Fullerites stood up to him because everyone knew you couldn't win.

One day in 1949 when I arrived at work, I discovered Mr. Fuller had taken another pioneering step. Having raised the money as covertly as possible, he'd purchased a well-known White-owned company, Boyer International Laboratories. Some said it was the first time in the history of the United States that a Black firm had bought a White-owned company. The fewer White people who knew that a Black man had bought it, the less the chance one would threaten, sabotage, or undermine him. Among Black folks, Fuller Products' purchase of Boyer became a thing of legends.

"Knock and the door shall be open to you," he told us. "Cast your bread upon the water and it will return tenfold, a hundredfold, a thousandfold."

Fuller Products relocated from the Cottage Grove facility to the much larger six-story, 91,000-square-foot Boyer International plant at 2700 South Wabash Avenue. The Boyer Building became the Fuller Building. Overnight, I found myself working in an oversize lab that was already outfitted with much better equipment. Growth required scaling up production to sizable machines and reworking our formulas to create larger batches.

Black folks were proud that Mr. Fuller was now the boss of many White people. When Boyer's all-White workforce learned they now worked for a Black man, the ones who had a bad attitude quit right away. Mr. Fuller did a great job retaining the principal people in charge of running the business. The majority of the supervisors stayed, and Mr. Fuller employed most of them until they retired.

Although White people continued to work for Mr. Fuller, it didn't mean they all liked it. Frequently the vice president of sales reminded Mr. Fuller that he needed a White man to be the contact between Boyer and its distributors. In response, Mr. Fuller reminded the vice president how much more money he had been making since Mr. Fuller purchased the company. Watching these inherited employees humiliate this outstanding man was painful to witness, but Mr. Fuller's hands were tied. He'd made a big investment in Boyer, and he had to tolerate what came with it.

Sometimes he would flip the script on others' racism. One day Mr. Fuller sent the White woman who managed Fuller Products' marketing department downtown to the Hilton Hotel to reserve a meeting space to host his annual convention. The Hilton was segregated at the time. By then, Fuller Products probably had several thousand sales agents around the country. There was a branch in New York City, Brooklyn, Philadelphia, Memphis, Boston, Savannah, Kansas City, and Los Angeles. Fuller Products branches were all over, especially in the Midwest. *Fortune* magazine reported that Mr. Fuller's business grossed $18 million ($205 million today). Hundreds of Black folks came to the Chicago Hilton to attend the convention. People showed up in droves, and there was no way the Hilton could have turned them away because of the volume. I can only imagine the proud reactions of the Black bellhops, porters, and staff, as Mr. Fuller desegregated such a major hotel.

What I learned working for Mr. Fuller was the equivalent of getting a college degree in business, religion, and psychology.

3

One Dollar in the Bank

IT WAS FEBRUARY 1953. My workday at Fuller Products had just ended, and I was riding the elevator from the fifth floor to the ground. The elevator stopped on three, and a neatly dressed chestnut-colored man wearing a gray suit and tie stepped on. The man's brow was furrowed, and he was rubbing his head like something bad had happened.

"What the *hell* is wrong with you?"

The words blurted out of my mouth before I knew I said them.

"I had an appointment with Mr. Fuller," the man answered. "I was hoping he'd help me, but he isn't interested."

"Help with what?" I asked, wondering what made this man agitated, downright dejected.

"I wanted him to make a product for me," he said as the

elevator descended. "I've been having problems with my product, and I need to improve it, so it won't be disastrous for my business."

"What line of business are you in?"

"I own the House of Nelson barbershop, over on Sixty-Fourth and Cottage Grove," he said, anxiously smoothing his hair, which was thick, about an inch long, conked, and styled in a Quo Vadis, an Italian Caesar.

"Yeah, I know the area," I said as we exited the elevator on the ground floor.

"I figured because this is a Black company, I could get Mr. Fuller to help me make a better product," the man continued. "But he said he's not interested in the barbering business, doesn't have any time to get involved."

I felt sorry for the guy. "Well, I don't know exactly what you're talking about, but I work in the lab—"

"You work in the lab for Mr. Fuller?" he asked, his eyes studying me intently.

"Yes, I work for Mr. Fuller," I said. "Maybe I could help."

"Yessir! The name's Nelson, Orville Nelson," he offered, reaching his right hand toward me.

I told him my name as he shook my hand vigorously. "Give me your card if you have one. When I have a chance, I'll try to come by and see what I can do."

"Yessir," he said, reaching into his suit jacket.

I headed downtown to Harrison's Restaurant, where I worked a second job to make ends meet. I washed cars on Saturdays and Sundays as well. By now, Joan and I had married. I was feeling the pressure of being a husband and father to our first child, Eric, who was a toddler, and our two-month-old named John, after my brother.

Late that night, as I undressed for bed, I put Nelson's card in my dresser.

One Saturday morning about two months later, I went to visit Orville Nelson. At about nine thirty, I took the streetcar over to 6430 South Cottage Grove. When I pushed the door of his storefront open, I was immediately shocked. All four barber chairs were occupied, and guys were lined up all along the wall, taking up every available space.

What's going on?

As I stepped farther inside, I noticed all the barbers moving quickly. It looked like they were racing each other.

Nelson was working on a man sitting in his chair. I approached him.

"Excuse me, I don't know if you remember me—," I began.

"Johnson! You're George Johnson from Fuller Products," Nelson exclaimed, briefly looking up from his client.

"Good to see you, Mr. Nelson." I stood in the middle of the floor near his chair. There was no other place to sit or stand.

"Look around. This is what I wanted Mr. Fuller to see." He motioned to the crowd with a comb in his hand. "All these cats are lined up to get their hair processed."

Ohh, that's what's going on.

Many Black men wore the popular style of straightened hair, sometimes with a finger wave or pompadour in the front. Fuller Products sold pressing cream, pressing oil, and hot combs to straighten the hair, but I'd never seen chemical straightening before.

I saw men carry empty jars to a one-gallon container filled with a three-layered substance. They stirred the stuff,

44

scooped it into their jar, stirred it again, and applied it to men's heads, pulling and stretching the hair.

"*Hurry up, man, hurry up!*" I heard a man yell. His barber quickly spun the client's chair around, lowered the man's head into the shampoo bowl, and began rinsing the concoction out.

Something about the frenetic pace unsettled and even frightened me.

"This is what I'm having trouble with," Nelson said, motioning toward the wide-mouth jug full of the white stuff, sitting on a shelf behind his chair. I could see the substance inside had separated, water on the bottom, solids in the middle, and oil floating on top.

Orville took a long brown stick and began to mix the ingredients together. As he stirred, the substance seemed to transform from heavy and stiff to smoother and more easily stirred. After the liquid became evenly consistent, he dipped a large black comb in it, using that comb to scoop the substance into the smaller jar he held in his hand.

Every few minutes a client shouted, "*Gotta go, gotta go!*" and the guy's barber spun his chair to the sink.

"So, how do you work with this stuff on men's hair?" I asked.

Nelson explained that he used his fingers to apply a thick layer of clear petrolatum onto his client's scalp to protect it. Then he spread the concoction, called conk, onto the hair, swiftly combing it from the roots to the ends.

"I've gotta get the hair straight enough but get the conk off before it burns his scalp," he told me as he swiftly combed, lifting the man's hair and stretching it straighter. I marveled at how quickly Orville moved.

"How ya doing, buddy?" Orville asked his client.

"My scalp's getting a little warm," the man replied with a grimace.

"Just a little bit longer," Nelson responded, continuing to comb.

As Orville's client squirmed uncomfortably, I glanced around the shop at the quick-handed barbers, the men in the chairs, the guys standing in line, and the fellows with their newly processed hairstyles.

My goodness, this is really unbelievable.

I barely had enough time to have that thought before Orville's client told him, *"That's enough, gotta go!"*

Orville spun the chair around to the shampoo sink and started rinsing the conk out.

"What's the active ingredient?" I asked, incredulously.

"It's a combination of potatoes, eggs, and sodium hydroxide," he replied, offering the chemical name for the substance many of us commonly knew as lye.

"Well, the solution seems simple," I told him as he gently toweled the man's head. "The product is crying to be emulsified."

As Orville began to style the man's hair, I explained what I knew about emulsification. I figured Orville's sodium hydroxide was so strong that it was also saponifying the petrolatum being applied to these men's scalp. In other words, the conk was chemically removing the protection from the man's skin and incorporating it into itself. That's why the barbers were having to work fast, to straighten the hair before nothing was left to protect the scalp.

"Come on, baby, hurry up!" a man moaned.

"I think I can do something about it," I said. "Can you give me a little bit to take back to the lab?"

"Here you go!" Orville spooned some product into a jar.

"And what's your competition?" I asked. "Is there anything out on the market that's any better?"

He gave me a list of three or four products.

"I don't have any money," I told him. "But I'll go buy them and take them into the lab to analyze them, if you give me some cash."

"Here you go, man." He reached into his pocket, pulled out a wad of bills, peeled off several, and gave them to me.

We shook hands, and I headed out of the shop.

Orville needed a stabilized product that straightened hair but didn't leave men with chemical burns or blisters on their scalp or thin their hair over time. Naively believing the chemistry easy, I hit a couple drugstores, purchased the list of products Orville had told me to buy, and took them back to Mr. Fuller's lab.

Shortly before he bought Boyer International Laboratories, Mr. Fuller had hired a German national, Dr. Herbert A. Martini, to become his head chemist. Dr. Martini had spent World War II in an internment camp in the United States. He said he had a difficult time finding work after the war ended and he was released. American companies didn't have a good taste for the Germans who'd been imprisoned, he told me.

Mr. Fuller decided to give him a shot. Right away, Dr. Martini took me under his wing as he performed his job, which included improving Mr. Fuller's existing products, creating new products, and cutting costs.

Dr. Martini called me "Yonsen," like I was Swedish, for fun.

I called him Doc.

When Doc Martini arrived, many of Mr. Fuller's products

needed improvement to make them more chemically stable. Doc identified which emulsifiers weren't working well enough and replaced them with better ones. He also helped reformulate the products as Fuller Products' sales volume went up and product batches that had once been, say, 250 pounds increased to 800 pounds, and then later to 1,200. One of Mr. Fuller's bestselling brands was a deodorant called Be Sweet. It had irritated some people's skin; Doc Martini changed the formula to address that.

In the process of working on all these projects, Doc taught me an awful lot about how you can emulsify oil and water to look like one smooth cream. Our job now was figuring out how to do it for Orville's substance.

At lunchtime, Doc and I went to work on this interesting challenge. First we tested the pH of Orville's product. For around the next nine months, coming in early and during our lunch hour, we tried every emulsifier we could find in the United States, attempting to identify one that could remain stable in a highly alkaline product. Doc Martini and I tested emulsifier after emulsifier, but none could endure a pH that high.

Doc Martini was like a wizard. Week after week, he and I made small batches and put them in the incubator to test them. Seven days in the incubator was like a month on the shelf. If the product started to separate, he knew we had not identified the right emulsifier.

I took some of the compounds to Orville in a small jar.

"This one's too weak," he might tell me. Then Doc and I would return to the lab to compound a different batch.

"Try this one," I would tell Orville a week or two later.

"It's still too slow," he'd say after trying it out.

"How's this?" I'd offer, taking yet a new formulation to him.

"It's better than the last one, but we're not there yet."

Doc and I headed back to the drawing board, over and over.

"Doc, your persistence and determination are amazing," I told him.

"Yonsen, you'll learn that it pays not to give up."

Doc's resolve reinforced some of Mr. Fuller's favorite lessons.

Learn how to think, how to solve problems, and your mentality will grow. God has given us everything we need, it's within us.

In this case, Doc Martini was the brains of our operation. He was intrigued by challenges. Month after month, chemical companies brought Doc different emulsifiers, and we tested various formulations for stability. We were careful not to neglect our work duties.

After a while, Doc had exhausted every emulsifying agent we could find in the United States. None of them worked. But I watched this amazing man both refuse to be defeated and practice the "burning desire" Mr. Fuller talked about. Instead of giving up, Doc reached out to some of his colleagues back in Germany, describing what we were attempting to accomplish and the alkalinity the emulsifier needed to tolerate. Several companies began sending him products. Finally a German firm, Hinkel Chemical, sent an emulsifier called acetyl alcohol that could tolerate a pH of 15.

"Ahh," Doc purred, after the formula with the new emulsifier held up for six weeks in the incubator. "Yonsen, it looks like we may have something here."

"I think we should go with it," I said. "Six weeks in the

incubator equals six months on the shelf, and this stuff isn't going to sit around that long in anyone's barbershop."

Finally, we created the perfect formulation. It straightened men's hair enough but not too much, quickly but not too quickly, and was chemically stable and didn't separate. "This one is perfect!" Orville told me. "Don't touch it— this is it!"

Between my determination to solve Orville's problem and Doc's curiosity, we had created something unique.

Many of the competitive formulations were 70 percent liquid and 30 percent solid. Ours was 60 percent liquid, 40 percent solid. Our product did a better job straightening men's hair without the discomfort or potential for burning skin or blistering the scalp. The difference was abundantly clear. There was nothing like the product we had created. All a guy would have to do was experience it to see.

"If it's perfect, then we ought to market it," I told Orville as he swept up his barbershop one evening.

"Well, let's market it." He stopped sweeping and looked at me squarely, his eyes dancing at the opportunity. "How much would that cost?"

I had already thought about it. I figured I could borrow $250 from a loan company I had done business with previously.

"It will take five hundred."

Orville opened the drawer in his barber stand, pulled out his checkbook, and wrote me a check for $250. The next day I braved the winter winds and snow and trudged to a neighborhood loan company, on a mission to borrow $250. I'd already done business with the firm and felt confident as I pitched the loan officer our opportunity. The man listened then sat back and crossed his arms.

"I'm not gonna loan you the money," he said, suddenly grinning.

I stormed out but I didn't give up. A few days I later went to a different branch and secured the $250 I needed for my share. Orville and I opened a checking account at the South Side Bank at Forty-Seventh and Cottage Grove and deposited $500.

Orville Nelson and I officially started our company on February 15, 1954, nine months after I started working on the straightener. We agreed I would make the product, and he'd sell it. He would sell on Wednesdays, when Chicago barbershops were closed—starting with shop owners he knew around town, but eventually going to Indianapolis, Detroit, Cleveland, St. Louis, and other cities nearby. We agreed he would leave town on Tuesday evenings. Wednesday would be his big selling day.

"We could name our company Johnson Nelson or Nelson Johnson," I told Orville as we stood in his barbershop one Saturday while he conked a man's hair.

"Don't worry about putting my name on it," he said, looking preoccupied.

"But either of those is a great name," I said, sounding out both names as I spoke them out loud.

"Just use your name, it's fine," he insisted.

"You sure?"

"Don't worry about that stuff, just sell me the product at your cost."

"You've got a deal!"

"And since my wife already orders my products, I'll just tell her to order our raw materials, too," he added.

Johnson Products Company became our name. I labeled our hair straightener Ultra Wave Hair Culture. Ultra because it signified the best; wave because that's what the men were after; and "hair culture" because that phrasing was common in the industry. Our product was unique, and I didn't want to call it a hair straightener.

Mr. Fuller's advice began to ring even more loudly in my ears.

God will help you. He will put opportunity on your path, and you can take it.

I needed a place to manufacture our product. By asking around, I learned about Leon Cooper, who owned the C&W beauty-supply store. Leon had a small manufacturing operation where he repackaged and sold C&W Products' haircare line for beauty shops. Leon purchased in bulk from a Black-owned company in Philadelphia. Someone told me that in the back of his shop, he had a burner big enough to heat a four-hundred-pound drum sunk into a concrete floor. Something like that could be perfect for me.

One day after work, I braved the cold and headed over to meet Leon.

"Good evening," I began, after unbuttoning my peacoat and removing my hat. "I'm a production compounder for Mr. Fuller, but I've developed my own product. I've been told you have a manufacturing facility."

"Sure, man, let's talk," he answered.

Leon listened carefully as I explained my product. He talked about his business and walked me in back and showed me his operation. He demonstrated how he melted his product and poured it into cans and jars, which he then labeled and packaged, and sold from his storefront. Leon and I struck a deal. We agreed that I would produce and package his products for him, and in exchange, I could use his operation for just $35 per month, about $425 today. I consented to do his work first, but after I finished, I could manufacture and package Ultra Wave Hair Culture.

"I'll operate in the evenings after work," I promised. "I'll keep the place clean and never be in your way."

Thirty-five dollars per month was not a lot, but Lord knows, I could hardly afford it. The agreement felt equitable to me, though, and it worked out for Leon. He liked to hunt and fish at his place up in Minnesota. Having my help took some of the load off him and gave him some time for recreation.

I could still hear Mr. Fuller's voice. *That's the secret to success—a willingness to help other people. You help yourself by helping other people.*

The arrangement permitted me to take what I had and to make what I wanted. To get it, I had to risk leaving my second job at Harrison's. When I quit, I lost the $65 (about $735 today) a week of income it provided.

Because I interacted with their products often, I was on good terms with all the Fuller Products raw-material and packaging suppliers. I began calling them. Max Holzman, the salesman who sold glass and jars, brought me six cases of sixteen-ounce jars and caps; the minimum purchase was normally five gross, five dozen cases. Mr. Fuller's mineral oil and petrolatum supplier got a fifty-pound pail and a five-gallon can from one of their customers to help me. I went to a used-equipment company I knew about and bought a hand vacuum filler to fill the jars. I also needed a mixing tank. I found a thirty-gallon drum and had a guy cut off the top with an acetylene torch and weld the sharp top edges smooth. I bought two-inch thick wooden clothes rods to mix the ingredients.

As I purchased each product, I wrote out a check, then

another, and another. After I bought all my supplies, it totaled $499. I had just one dollar left in our bank account, but I had everything I needed to make the first batch of Ultra Wave Hair Culture.

I left Fuller Products at four thirty, when my workday ended, took the streetcar over to Leon's place, arrived at about five, and began producing his product. I rolled a drum over to the top of the burner, pried off the top, ignited the burners, and kept an eye on the drum's contents as they melted. Then I manually filled and labeled both the five-pound cans Leon sold wholesale to beauticians and the eight-ounce jars he sold to the beauticians to resell to their customers. I usually finished Leon's work somewhere between eight thirty and nine.

After that, I started producing Ultra Wave Hair Culture, a two-step process that required heating the solid and liquid ingredients separately, then mixing them. I stirred the ingredients with the clothes rod until the components interacted chemically. The formula became thicker than mayonnaise and worked the hell out of my arm as I stirred.

These blended ingredients created Ultra Wave.

At that point, I dipped a large saucepan into the vat, filled it with Ultra Wave, and began pouring the product into the hand filler, one panful at a time. Next I positioned a jar underneath the filler and filled one jar at a time. I labeled the jars, then packed them into cases.

On the days when she could find a babysitter, Joan joined me at Leon's place. Sitters were hard to find. When I worked by myself, I might not head home until about eleven. Once our sales volume began to increase, I might not leave until midnight. I was wiped out. God gave me a lot of energy in those early days, but growing the business quickly was absolutely exhausting. Overly fatigued, a couple of times I left the formula to Ultra Wave lying out rather than taking it with me when I left the shop.

I took the first jars of Ultra Wave Hair Culture to Orville.

"Look what I've got for you," I told him.

"Oh, man!" he exclaimed. "Look at that. I guess we're in business now!"

I couldn't wait for him to start selling our product in Chicago on Wednesday. On Thursday, I returned to collect my share of the proceeds.

"How'd it go?" I asked excitedly, striding through the door.

"What do you mean?" he asked as he worked on a man's hair.

"How were sales?"

"Oh, that," he responded nonchalantly. "I didn't make it out."

"You didn't make it out?" I asked, surprised. "What happened?"

"I'm sorry, man, something important came up." His tone was matter-of-fact.

"What do you mean, something came up?" I asked, astounded.

"I had to take care of business around the shop. Next week, I'll go for sure."

"Well, make sure you do that. We really need to turn this product, Orville," I replied, looking in his supply closet. From the look of his inventory, I could see he and his barbers were doing a brisk business at the shop.

My mind was spinning when I left Orville's. My money was tight. I didn't have a week to waste waiting for him to hit the streets.

Anyway, if I could carry the heavy black bag for Mr. Fuller, I could certainly sell my own products. It was clear I would have to do that this week. Each day after work, I put on a suit, my peacoat, a hat, and my winter boots and headed out to barbershops, hoping to talk to these entrepreneurs.

"I'm the cofounder of Johnson Products Company," I said to each shop owner, bursting with pride as I reached out to shake his hand. "My partner Orville Nelson and I have created Ultra Wave, a new hair straightener for men that doesn't burn the scalp."

At that point, it wasn't uncommon for the man to stop and give me the side-eye.

"You work with Orville Nelson? I ought to kick you out of here . . ."

"*Huh?*"

"Maaan, the last time I saw that guy, he was running a scam," a barber told me. "Sold me some conk that blistered up my customer's scalp *and* made his hair fall out."

"Oh, wow, I'm sorry," I said. "Well, I've created a new formulation that straightens men's hair, but it doesn't burn the scalp. It's different and safer than anything you've ever seen before."

"Lemme see it then."

I opened a jar and handed it to him.

"Hmm. . . . It hasn't separated yet."

"No sir, and it won't!" I told him. "It is scientifically formulated to be stable. The product is the same from batch to batch, you don't have to stir it, and it will stay on your shelf for a good six months."

"Hmm! You say you made it yourself?"

"Yessir!" I replied. "I have a manufacturing operation at Leon Cooper's place."

"Leon Cooper? Oh, well then, how much does it cost?"

"Just one dollar a jar, same as what you're using right now, but it's a better and safer product!"

"Okay, give me one," he said, handing me a dollar.

"Thank you very much. You're going to be really happy, I promise you!"

"Well, I hope so," he said. "But you better watch out for that Orville Nelson character. I'm telling you, he's no good!"

"Okay, sir. Let me know what you think of our product." I handed him my card and left the shop.

As I departed, a part of me felt on top of the world. But what was all this crap about Orville?

Maybe they just had a personal run-in.

But then it happened again.

"You're in business with Orville? You better watch that guy!"

"What makes you say that?"

"Orville didn't tell you where he learned how to barber?"

"No . . ."

"Ask him about the time he spent in the Illinois State Penitentiary."

WHAT??!!

In shop after shop, I heard a similar story.

He's no good. He's always running a racket. He saves the good stuff for himself, then sells us the crap that sets our customers' scalp on fire. He scammed me and stole my clients.

One shop owner at a time, I learned more about Orville. Some guys told me that at one point, he conned them into coming to his barbershop under the promise he would teach them how to process and finger-wave their clients' hair. Apparently, to get his instruction, they had to purchase conk from him. He then sped through the lesson quickly, and no one could keep up with what he was doing. Truthfully, anyone could have straightened hair with the stuff that Orville was using, but he had to finesse the product to get outstanding results. The fact that it was exceptionally alkaline made it dangerous. Because he didn't show them the fine points that he understood, other barbers ruined their reputations by burning men's scalps.

As I spoke with barbershop owners, I also learned that Orville was the most financially successful Black barber in Chicago. He was one of the stars of the Barbers Union. In several of the other unions, leaders intimidated people into joining. Some officials operated like hoodlums and conducted shakedowns for dues. Unlike employees of big companies, barbershop owners worked for themselves. With no powerful employer to negotiate against, what was the benefit? Almost all the Black barbers on the South Side were in the union. Guys felt afraid and succumbed to the pressure. The union officials lived pretty good.

Most barbers were cutting hair for $1 or $1.50 a head. Orville was doing the process and charging $5.

The Barbers Union may have loved Orville, but I did not hear one good thing about him at any barbershop I visited. Just a few days of selling left a bad feeling in my spirit.

The good news was, everyone wanted to try Ultra Wave.

When the next Wednesday came around, Orville hadn't gone out again.

"What happened this time?" I demanded.

"I had to handle some business," he told me. "You know how it goes."

"What I know is that we have an agreement. I make the product, and you go out and sell it."

"I know what our agreement was," he replied with a slight

edge on his voice. "I'll pull my weight. Be patient, man, and get off my case."

Patience was one thing I didn't have. With a wife and two children at home, bills to pay and no other income, the pressure was on. For the next ten days, I hit every barbershop I could find.

I went to shop after shop. This was my chance to get out of poverty.

Fortunately, it didn't take long for word of Ultra Wave's good results to travel the grapevine. Soon, when I walked in to introduce myself, a guy might say, "Oh, I've heard about you! How much Ultra Wave you got?"

At the end of two weeks, I had earned $750 — more than $8,500 today. It was $250 more than I needed to recover our costs, and enough to order ingredients to make more product. Thank goodness Chicago was one of the largest markets in the country. While I was out pounding the pavement, Orville had used most of our first batch.

We'd been in business for a month. By the middle of March, Orville had only gone selling once. I fell behind on my bills, and was feeling the pinch at home.

"I know the company's going to work out. I need you to go out and earn some money," I told my wife, Joan.

"Okay," she told me, with a willing spirit. "While I work, maybe one of the older women in the building or my mom could help out with the kids."

A couple years earlier I had volunteered as a precinct captain, helping get out the vote in our neighborhood. The role gave me an inside track when it came to finding work. Every precinct leader could access a certain number of jobs for their community's residents. Until now, I'd only helped other people. And since I worked at Fuller Products, I never once considered taking advantage of any of these opportunities. But at this point, I needed to help myself.

I went to our ward chairman, Doc Whittey, and told him that Joan needed a job. Doc got her a position at the criminal court appeals division. Joan started out with a nice salary— she made more money than I did at Fuller Products. She loved the work, and it took a lot of the pressure off. Joan's income sustained us until we could climb out of debt.

As Ultra Wave's reputation and sales volume grew, my friend Ernest Lafontant told me he thought I had a responsibility to tell Mr. Fuller what I was doing. Ernest and I had become close while working together at Fuller Products. Mr. Fuller had brought Ernest to Chicago from Birmingham, Alabama, where Lafontant worked for the Black multimillionaire A. G. Gaston, who founded the Booker T. Washington Insurance Company, Smith and Gaston Funeral Directors, the Booker T. Washington Business College, and countless other businesses, including Citizens Federal Savings Bank. When Ernest arrived in Chicago to become Mr. Fuller's purchasing agent, he already owned a brand-new Chrysler. Chrysler hadn't yet produced many cars. The fact he purchased one of the first meant he was already fairly prosperous. Ernest and I clicked from the beginning, and I took his advice.

I knocked on Mr. Fuller's office door.

"Come in, George," he said, looking up from some papers he'd been reading.

"Mr. Fuller, I've started a company, Johnson Products!"

"Oh, that's great," he replied. "What kind of product have you got?"

I showed Ultra Wave Hair Culture to him and explained how it worked, expecting him to be excited for me.

"You're not gonna get anywhere with barbers," he warned. "Barbers are the worst payers in the world."

"Well, I'm gonna try and see how it goes," I responded. "When it gets to the point that it impacts my position, I'll let you know. I'll give you ample notice so you can put someone with me, and I can train my replacement. That way, they'll have the benefit of all the techniques I've learned and improvements I've made, so there will be no difference in products." I'd done a lot of little things to refine Mr. Fuller's products and processes, and that expertise was in my head, not laid out on paper.

Unfazed, Mr. Fuller put his head back down and continued his work. I think about the fact that I said *when* it impacts my position, not *if.* Even though I was struggling, the thought never crossed my mind that I might not make it. I moved forward with Johnson Products. I may not have had any money, but I believed in our product.

It slowly began to dawn on me that when I'd calculated my costs, I hadn't included the value of my own time, energy, or labor. In other words, my cost structure didn't cover my overhead. The deal I made to sell to Orville at my cost meant there was no profit in the business. I was donating all my energy and labor to him, and the only money coming in was what I sold on my own. Whatever revenues were generated were produced by my efforts. My so-called partner was benefiting wildly from me, but I wasn't benefiting from him. Adding insult to injury, I learned that on a couple of Wednesdays when he should have been out selling Ultra Wave, he opened his barbershop.

I felt like I was Orville Nelson's slave. This deal could not continue.

"We agreed that I make the product and you sell it," I

reminded him one night after he closed his shop doors and was straightening up. "But in the entire time we've been in business, you've only been out selling twice."

Orville kept sweeping the floor and didn't respond.

"I can't afford to do business like this," I continued, as he pushed hair into a dustpan and emptied it into the trash. "We are far behind the schedule I had envisioned, and I can't afford to progress this slowly."

I didn't seem to be getting through to him.

"This is just unreasonable," I announced, feeling pissed. "I'm not gonna keep on carrying your weight. I want to dissolve our partnership."

Orville stopped sweeping and turned to me with a deadpan look.

"If that's what you want," he said, "that's okay with me."

I didn't know what I expected, but it certainly wasn't this type of response.

The next day I obtained a well-connected lawyer to help me file a motion to dissolve my partnership with Orville. Charles Armstrong was a friend and my former assistant precinct captain. When I went into business, I resigned and named him my replacement.

On June 15, Charles and I met at the courthouse downtown on LaSalle Street.

Orville was represented by a well-built high-yellow guy who had slicked-back "good" hair, and was chomping on a cigar.

"George is the head of the Barbers Union," Orville said to me with a smug look on his face.

"This is my attorney, Charles Armstrong," I responded. "Charles is a state representative and politician in the Democratic Party."

"Oh, good choice," George said, unable to hide that he was impressed with Charles, who was a bit darker skinned, medium build, and with "nice" hair as well.

The fact that George knew that Charles was formidable made me feel confident. No matter what stunt Orville tried to pull, I had power on my side.

Charles and I stood opposite Orville and George in front of the judge.

"You take what *you* brought to the partnership," the judge said, looking at Orville; "and you take what *you* brought," he said, motioning to me.

I brought the formula for Ultra Wave to our partnership, and my name was on the door. It meant the names Johnson Products Company and Ultra Wave both belonged to me. That was our settlement. The separation of Orville Nelson and George E. Johnson had only taken four months—it had to be one of the fastest separations of business partners ever. We walked out of the courtroom. Orville went his way, and I went mine.

Word about Ultra Wave's effectiveness had been spreading. Barbers had begun coming to Leon's beauty supply, looking for our product. Some guys were even driving in from out of town, sometimes from small places I'd never heard of. Other than perhaps from our shipping label, I had no idea how they found us.

I started working as hard as I could to manufacture enough product to meet the demand. Many nights I didn't leave for home until long after midnight, Mr. Fuller's voice in my head:

You have to have a burning desire . . .

Thankfully, Leon let us put Ultra Wave out in his store for barbers to purchase it retail.

It was around that time I bought my first car, a green Ford station wagon. It was time to head farther out from the city to start selling. Clearly, the demand was there.

That's when a chemist friend on the West Side gave my coattail a pull.

"I got a call from Orville Nelson's wife today," he told me. "She was inquiring about some of the ingredients I sell you, but she was kind of evasive. I think he might be trying to knock off your formula."

Orville's wife had been paying our bills. The invoices clearly listed the ingredients we used, including the emulsifier Doc and I had searched for high and low. It dawned on me that almost as soon as we created our own partnership, Orville had started working against me behind my back.

Then I started hearing other unsettling rumors out in the streets.

"Your friend Orville came through here the other day," one barber I'd made friends with greeted me.

"Oh yeah, what's he talking about?"

"He's out here selling his own conking product."

"His own product!" I exclaimed. "I own the formula—he can't do that."

"He's calling it Wavo."

Doc and I had created a proprietary product.

Orville may have known what was in Ultra Wave Hair Culture, but it didn't mean he knew how to formulate the product. Wavo was better than the conk, but inferior to Ultra Wave.

There was nothing I could do. Orville was Orville; he ran scams. I could only focus on what I was doing.

To increase my sales revenue, I needed to increase my

production volume. I couldn't continue to work all day at Fuller's and then at night at Leon's. The next day, I told Mr. Fuller that I would probably leave his company soon and would let him know at least thirty days in advance. He seemed distracted as I talked to him, so shortly afterward I sent him a message that it was time for me to start training my replacement. I wanted to show whoever would come after me how I'd finessed and improved upon Mr. Fuller's processes and formulas.

My mentor didn't respond.

My mother thought the risk of leaving Fuller Products was too great. "You have a lifetime job, and you have a wife and two kids," she told me. And she was right. From her perspective, that was too much risk. I was making $85 a week and it wasn't sufficient now that I was married. I'd earned only a $20 raise over the past ten years. I wanted to eat better, splurge on some Miller High Life, and get to work without having to borrow from my mother.

Another month rolled around. I told Mr. Fuller that Johnson Products' sales were increasing rapidly. "Demand is growing to the point I'm under a lot of pressure," I told him. "It looks like I'll have to leave."

To my surprise, he still didn't put anyone to train with me. I knew he cared about his business and I was trying to create a smooth transition, but his behavior confused me.

I remember just like it was yesterday. The third week of July in 1954. A typical Chicago summer late afternoon, hot and sweaty. I walked into Leon's place, and the August issue of *Ebony* magazine was sitting on the counter. When I saw the cover, I almost hit the floor. There was a photograph of Nat King Cole, probably the hottest artist in the country at that time, sitting in a barber's chair, hair conked and finger-waved, with Orville Nelson standing beside him. Above the picture a white headline read "Beauty Shop for Men."

I rifled through the issue to find the cover story, a feature about men and the process. Apparently, Orville was Nat King Cole's personal barber and had been conking the famous Chicago crooner's hair. The article claimed that Orville was the number-one guy conking hair in the country.

Barely a month had passed since we dissolved our business. Orville knew this article would be coming out in advance. No wonder he was willing to dissolve the partnership. After the issue was published, the postman told me Orville started receiving droves of letters. The mailman delivered Orville's mail in sacks.

I felt powerless—he'd gotten me.

But I kept my head down and continued doing what I was doing.

By the time August came around, my business was still doing pretty well, despite all of Orville's publicity. I reached the point where I could pay my bills with the money I was earning selling Ultra Wave Hair Culture. I asked Joan to leave her job at the court to work with me. I needed someone to handle clerical work and fill package orders.

"I don't want to leave my job," she responded. "I like it, and I make a lot of money."

The money Joan was earning was helping her accomplish some things she always wanted for herself. My wife had gotten into buying clothes, and it was clear that she possessed an impeccable eye for style.

"I am grateful that you helped me get out from under all those bills, but I don't need your money anymore," I told her. If the *Ebony* situation had taught me anything, it was that the number-one Black barber in the country approved of and used my product. I felt unafraid.

"Well, I want to keep working at the courts," she said. But eventually she quit and came to work with me, at first reluctantly. I taught Joan most of the things we had to do, and we worked long hours together. Her mom often came over to help us take care of the kids.

"I have nothing to lose," I told my mother, and I meant it.

Then I turned my attention back to Mr. Fuller.

"I'm grateful for my time with you," I told him. "But I've reached the point I have to leave."

Mr. Fuller finally put his brother-in-law with me for the next two weeks. It wasn't enough time to train him well, but I'd given my mentor plenty of notice.

The day I left Fuller Products felt bittersweet. I couldn't have become who I was without him, but it was time to go.

A couple of months after the *Ebony* article came out, I was in the back of Leon's place making my products when Orville Nelson darkened my doorstep.

"Hey man," he greeted me, dressed to the nines, sporting his Quo Vadis and grinning like a Cheshire cat. "Come on outside and take a look. I want you to see my new Cadillac."

I didn't have time for Orville, but I didn't protest. I set my work down and followed him out front. Already people were crowding around his car, a canary-yellow Cadillac Coupe DeVille convertible, parked along the curb.

"It's beautiful," I told him as I looked over the red-and-cream leather interior, whitewall tires, fins, and chrome bumpers and trim.

Orville beamed ear-to-ear as people complimented him. When he turned back toward me, a cloud passed over his face.

"I really came by here to tell you that a year from now you won't have a dime," he sneered. "I'm going to run you out of business."

Taken aback, I paused for a moment. "Well, you go and do what *you* can do," I told him. "I'm going to do what *I* can do."

I turned away, walked through Leon's door, and went right back to work. I pushed what he said right out of my mind.

4

Our Reputation Made Us

THE SKY WAS still dark when I pulled my new Ford station wagon in front of Millard Frazier, standing out in front of his apartment building in the predawn hour.

"Hey man, good to see you," I told him as I got out, shook his hand, walked around to the back of the car, and used my key to open the trunk.

"It's good to be seen!" he answered, laughing, as he carefully placed his suitcase inside, walked to the passenger side, opened the door, and got in.

I stood outside and took a quick puff of a cigarette, watching the ashes glow as I pulled on it.

"Mind if I turn on the radio?" he asked.

"Go right ahead."

Millard scanned the dial, found Ray Charles's "I Got a Woman," and began to sing along.

Today was an important day. It was time to begin building my business by turning around the damage Orville was causing, starting with Indianapolis.

Right after he appeared on the *Ebony* cover, Orville did what he hadn't done with Ultra Wave—he hit the road to sell Wavo. But between hawking his inferior product, lying, and being selfish, unethical, and unreliable, Orville was leaving a trail of pissed-off barbers in his wake all over the Midwest. My former partner turned business rival was destroying his own possibilities.

I viewed Orville's screwups as an opportunity for me. My intuition told me I could build Ultra Wave sales by following Orville into a market, cleaning up after him, and flipping the situation around by offering barbers both my high-quality product and free education on how to use it. I looked forward to meeting the challenge.

I approached Millard about helping me implement my plan. I had him in mind ever since I first started selling him Ultra Wave at his Chicago barbershop. Millard was a really good barber. In fact, I started going to him to cut my hair. Millard was also a dedicated man. He didn't conk hair quite as quickly as Orville, but he did the process and finger wave well. The process soon became his major offering. The combination of strong skills and a good guy was exactly what I needed.

"We can educate barbers on Wednesdays, when you and other barbers are closed but a lot of guys still come into their shops," I told him when I approached him.

"Oh, I got it," he replied. "I could run my business the rest of the week."

"That's right," I said. "If you're interested, we will start with Indianapolis. We will drive down together, and I'll convince one owner to let us use his shop to train his barbers and whoever else in the community wants to come. I'll pay you to come down with me the first time, then I'll fly you back down there on however many Wednesdays it takes to educate whatever barbers are interested. You'll leave early in the morning but will be home in time for dinner."

"So we will go out together at first, you will do the selling, and then you will pay me to go back by myself to train the barbers—"

"Exactly," I replied. "And to sweeten the pot, I will give you free Ultra Wave to use here in your own barbershop."

"I like how you're talking, Johnson," Millard said. "You've got a deal."

Being dressed in my best, sitting behind the wheel of my new car, and having Millard at my side for the first time was quite a satisfying feeling. By the time the sun began to shine on the rows of green cornstalks that seemed to stretch from the highway to eternity, he had nodded off.

After about three hours, I could see Indy's skyline. I followed the road signs toward downtown, keeping my eyes open for the telltale railroad tracks leading to the Black side of town. Once I found them, it was easy to locate the main avenue running through the Black community. I parked the car, and we began walking down the street in search of a good-sized barbershop with an owner who might sign on to work with us. Educating a number of barbers at once would justify the expense of flying Millard back to Indianapolis to train them. The busier the barbershop, the quicker I could recover the investment I was making in educating them.

I knocked on the door of a shop where I could see the owner inside sweeping and pushed it partway open.

"Come on in," he said, looking up while still handling his broom, wearing the customary tan barber smock, the news on the radio in the background.

"We've driven here from Chicago this morning to offer you a free opportunity."

"You drove down here from Chicago?"

"Yessir, we woke up bright and early!" I replied.

"Well, why would anyone do that?" The guy laughed. "How can I help you fellas?"

"I've created a new product, Ultra Wave Hair Culture, that will allow you to process men's hair successfully and safely without burning their scalp."

"You say you can straighten a man's hair without it burning him?" he said, one eyebrow raised. "That would be a miracle. I'd like to see it!"

"We have scientifically formulated Ultra Wave Hair Culture to do just that," I informed him. "We'd like to teach you how to use our product effectively, and I'm offering to do it for free."

"Well, we don't really do much hair straightening," he answered. "We do more straight-up barbering."

"We'd like to help you change that," I responded, knowing the economics worked in my favor. Financially, I could help most barbershops become much more profitable. A haircut typically cost $1.25. I told him processing hair could generate $5 in revenue and be performed more quickly than the typical haircut.

"I'm from Missouri, brother. You've gotta show me!"

"I'd like to, if you will give me the chance," I said. "We're not here to *sell* you something, we're here to *give* you something. Ultra Wave Hair Culture is the first scientifically formulated hair straightener on the market. We'd like to host a demonstration in your shop to educate barbers on how to do the process safely and effectively. At no cost to you, Millard will fly in to train you, your barbers, and whoever else you invite. We'll do it on a Wednesday, when everyone's already off."

"What's the catch?"

"There is no catch."

"Well, there's always a catch," he said. "Have you ever met that cat, Orville Nelson, the guy on the cover of *Ebony* magazine?"

Here was my chance. Mr. Fuller taught us to look for the advantage in any disadvantage; to look for the opportunity in the problem.

"What's the minimum?" the barbershop owner asked.

"What do you mean by minimum?"

"Orville made us buy $1,200 in product." That would be $13,000 today.

Orville also required each shop owner to guarantee that ten additional barbers would attend. He was supposed to be teaching, but he gave one, and only one, demonstration that moved slowly enough that barbers could observe his technique. After that, he picked up the pace quickly and worked as fast as he could. Using the same product he sold to the owner, Orville behaved as though their shop was his own and straightened the hair of as many of the barber's customers as possible, charging each man $5. Having witnessed Orville's speediness with my own eyes, I knew he could talk fast, work his comb fast, and finger-wave fast as lightning.

By the end of the day, Orville both used up a good bit of the barber's straightener *and* made a mint processing the barber's clients' hair. When he stepped back into his shiny yellow Caddy to return to Chicago, he also drove off with a good bit of the revenue the shop owner would otherwise have earned that day. Worse, the barber still didn't know how to use Wavo. When they tried on their own, barbers often screwed up their customers' hair. Now they had upset clients threatening to leave them for another barber.

"Johnson Products Company doesn't operate like that," I told barbers Orville had run his racket on. "Millard here is one of Chicago's best barbers. He's got a shop of his own, and he understands how important it is to satisfy your customers. At no cost to you, he will train your people to do the process right. He will come back and keep teaching, week after week, until every one of your guys knows what they're doing."

"You say you're going to train us for *free*?" The business owner's eyebrows rose.

"Yessir," I answered. "And offering your clients the opportunity to get their hair straightened will create a line out the door. You'll do very well."

"Okay, when can Millard come?"

As we walked around, talking to barbers, Millard and I found some others who were willing to work with us. The next week Millard traveled to Indianapolis alone. He spent Wednesday teaching barbers how to apply the product, get the hair nice and straight, and create the finger wave. He returned home that same night. Back in Chicago, I persuaded a lot of barbers to hang around Millard's barbershop during the rest of the week to get trained on how to use Ultra Wave. Over the coming months I also had Millard go around Chicago to do the same things as he did in Indianapolis. Our work in Chicago produced the money that allowed us to hit the road.

Millard returned to Indianapolis for five or six weeks to develop the market. We decided to stay with that first barbershop until both his guys and the barbers he invited in from other shops were competent. It didn't necessarily take a barber six weeks to learn how to use the product, but we wanted barbers to teach each other how to use our product correctly. Plus, it might take several sessions for some barbers to tighten up their finger-wave skills.

With Indianapolis up and running, I took the money we made in Indy and developed the next market: Cleveland. In Ohio, I had to do the same thing—clean up after Orville. His bad behavior was making me successful. I felt grateful.

My goal was to educate my customers, and moving slowly, market by market, was the best approach. Six months after I bought my first car, I'd driven thousands of miles and needed to replace it. I purchased my second Ford station wagon.

In city after city throughout the Midwest, the process I followed was always the same. I identified several barbershop owners willing to invite other barbers into their shop. I drove or flew in to set things up and then flew Millard in on Wednesdays. Mind you, people weren't flying like they are today. But you couldn't necessarily drive to a city, do all the work, and drive back to Chicago in the same day. Investing in air travel was expensive but necessary. While Millard conducted the training program, I returned to Chicago to produce more inventory. After we left a market, we returned if problems came to our attention.

It didn't take long before these educational sessions produced results, and the money was coming in fast.

As word traveled, more and more barbers became interested in learning to use Ultra Wave.

"What are you using? Where are you buying it?" they asked one another. At that point, I needed to stay in Chicago to make enough product to service our markets.

Throughout our venture, I began to discover that when

you do the right things, people have positive conversations about you. Rather than running my wheels off searching for barbers, barbers began calling to invite me to their areas.

When Johnson Products sold Ultra Wave Hair Culture to barbers, there were rules we had them follow. For instance, we didn't sell Ultra Wave to anyone until they had attended at least five demonstrations.

"What do you mean?" one of them asked, incredulously, when we turned down his money. "You can't run a business that way!"

"I have to teach people how to use our product correctly," I responded.

"Ain't nobody else thinking about all this education you want us to do," another barber told me. While trying to implement this program, I was up against more competitors than just Orville, and none were requiring education or skills. Orville was selling Wavo; in New York City we encountered the George Posner Company; a product made by an entertainer out of Los Angeles had quite a following. Another, called Conkalene, was being sold retail. And teaching barbers how to use Ultra Wave simultaneously improved their skills with my competitors' products.

"You're going to invest all this time and money teaching, and they're just going to turn around and buy from someone who will undercut you on price," some barbers warned me.

One even laughed, "You're just fattening frogs for snakes!"

It was essential that I treat people the way I wanted to be treated. Educating my customers was the right thing to do. However, it came at a cost.

Still, Johnson Products moved forward, one market at a

time. The money I made in Chicago, I invested in Indianapolis. The money I made in Indianapolis, I invested in Cleveland. The money I made in Cleveland helped me open Detroit. City by city, I planted roots in the barbering community, and we educated barbers until they were proficient with our products, which soon included a black rinse neutralizer that Doc Martini developed to keep the hair from turning a little red after the process, as happened sometimes, and Ultra Wave Hair Cream Oil, to maintain the hair and keep it soft and shiny.

Shop by shop, we built a good name for the Johnson Products Company. City by city, and town by town, our reputation made us.

As I had conversations with shop owners across the Midwest, I began to discover firsthand both that love is the fundamental spirit of how life operates and that it's inexhaustible. I learned that the more love I showed to others, the more fulfillment I experienced, and the more joyful and successful my life became.

My family was an important part of the business. During those early months of Johnson Products, Joan wore many hats. When I was on the road, she handled the books, took over production, poured and labeled the jars, and helped with shipping. There were even times when she loaded product onto trucks alone. She did all the things I couldn't afford to hire someone to do. Sometimes Joan even sat out front in Leon's shop and sold product to barbers looking to buy Ultra Wave, wholesale. Joan's involvement and skills were vital to me and allowed me to get out to build the market. I couldn't have gotten the company up and running without her.

My brother Robert lived in Washington, DC, with his wife and two children. When he and his wife separated, when he was about twenty-six, Robert returned to Chicago. I gave him a job and taught him how to make and package our products. Without telling him, I also started sending his ex-wife a little money every week.

Robert wasn't as serious about work as John and I, but he and I had a good relationship. I showed him a lot about the business and depended on him. When I was on the road, he and Joan produced Ultra Wave, filled and labeled the jars, packaged the product, took orders, filled out bills of lading, and loaded the trucks. Before long, he even got his hair processed.

Around that time I also hired my brother-in-law, Edris Ford, the husband of Joan's sister, Gwen. Having my family around me was a big relief.

One day while I was manufacturing Ultra Wave, I received a phone call from out of the blue.

"My name is Don Robey," the voice on the line said. "I'm calling you from Houston, Texas."

"Houston?"

"Yessir!" he exclaimed. "Home to the oil capital of the United States, the best barbecue sauce you've ever had in your life, and Duke/Peacock Records, of which I am the owner. I manage Big Mama Thornton, Bobby 'Blue' Bland, Johnny Ace, the Dixie Hummingbirds, the Mighty Clouds of Joy, and a bunch of other gospel and R&B music artists."

"That's quite impressive, sir," I replied.

"I just got through trying Ultra Wave Hair Culture, and it's the best product I've ever used," the man exclaimed.

"Why, thank you!"

"I've used straighteners all my life," he continued. "Ultra Wave Hair Culture is the mildest and the easiest. I'm just in love with it!"

"That's music to my ears!"

"I am calling to make you a proposition," he set forth. "Mr. Johnson, I'd like to become your exclusive distributor for the entire state of Texas."

"All of Texas?"

"That's right!"

"The entire state?"

"Yessir, Mr. Johnson!"

"Mr. Robey, I'm flattered, but I'm not sure we can do that."

"Well, I'd like to invite you down to see what we've got going on." He needed product and wanted us to see the possibility. "Once you're here, I'll show you the opportunity, we can talk face-to-face, and you can think about it. I want to become Ultra Wave's biggest distributor."

I turned this surprising opportunity over in my mind as I filled jars at Leon's facility that night. Who didn't know the groups he managed? Big Mama Thornton had recorded "Hound Dog" first, but at that moment singer Johnny Ace was burning up the charts with his remake.

When I slid into bed later, I talked to Joan about the proposition.

"If I went to Houston, I'd be away from you and the boys for several days."

"I can handle things here," she said sleepily. "I think you should go. Sounds like a great opportunity."

I contacted Millard. He told me about a mutual friend, Jerrell Rodgers, who could go with us to conduct all the trainings and demos Robey was going to set up.

The night before we left, I threw my wife a twenty-sixth birthday party.

I'd never had enough money to throw a party in my

entire life, but now I could afford to purchase champagne. I invited my mother, Joan's aunts and uncles, and mine, several of my cousins, and our friends from growing up and from Fuller Products. Joan was thrilled, and she loved the festivities. All of us enjoyed the champagne, but I drank too much. The champagne made me drunk.

After the party was over, Millard, Jerrell, and I loaded a lot of merchandise into the back of my station wagon. I knew Robey would buy a lot of product, and I took the amount I wanted him to buy. I preferred Black-owned hotels when I traveled in the North. Traveling down South required Black folks to get more creative. With three drivers, we planned to travel straight through. Since I was in bad shape from drinking, I lay on the back seat, sleeping it off. I remember stopping somewhere to get some soup to help sober up, and I think I threw it up. I slept for quite a while, but at some point the car shook hard enough to wake me up. Jerrell had nodded, drifted off the road, and swerved back onto the highway. Fearing for life and limb sobered me up quick. In addition to not wanting to die, I was worried about all the merchandise in the back—I couldn't afford for anything to happen to it. I took the wheel and drove from there.

We pulled into Houston a little before midnight about twenty hours later. We found a hotel, and I slept long and hard. By ten the next morning, we were up and ready, and found our way to Duke/Peacock Records. Don Robey strode out to greet us, wearing cowboy boots and a ten-gallon hat, and chomping on a big fat cigar.

"Welcome to the Lone Star State," said this man, light-skinned enough to have passed for White. As he stuck out his hand, I noticed a huge diamond on his finger.

The guys stayed outside while Robey took me into his

recording studio, where we talked business. Then he drove all of us around, showing us the Gulf of Mexico, Galveston Bay, oil rigs, and other sights. He also took us by a number of barbershops, where he introduced us to lots of barbers interested in learning how to use Ultra Wave. In fact, he'd already scheduled Ultra Wave demonstrations. Right away, I could see that the opportunity was incredible. We agreed that in addition to the educational sessions they conducted this time, Millard would return to Texas and perform a bunch of additional demonstrations.

Since Texas was such a big state, I hesitated to give Don the exclusive rights.

"Maybe this will help you decide," he said, peeling off twenty-one $100 bills and placing them in my hand, one at a time. That would be about $24,000 today. "I'm going to need enough product to get started," he continued, giving me a long look and grinning. "What do you think?"

I kept my cool, but $2,100 was the most cash I'd ever held in my hand at one time.

"Let's start with Houston and go from there!" I said, shaking his hand.

Millard and Jerrell stayed in Texas to teach barbers and conduct demonstrations. I had to rush back and make product. I left them with my car.

Later that day, Don drove me to the train station in his big Cadillac, strode up to the White ticket counter, and bought a one-way sleeping car ticket. Then he boarded like he was some big-time White guy who had me in tow. He led me to a sleeping car, put me in a bedroom, and had a side conversation with the Pullman porters.

"Mr. Johnson is not going to come out of that sleeping car until after the train passes St. Louis," he told them, knowing Black people weren't allowed in the sleeping car until north of the Mason-Dixon line. "Be sure to bring him his food and take care of him," he said, slipping some cash into their hands.

"Yessir!" they said, as they slid the money into their pockets.

Joan's stepfather was a Pullman porter, one of the Black men who served the luxury Whites-only sleeping cars of Chicago businessman George Pullman's trains. It was one of the best jobs a Black man of that era could find. The job involved carrying baggage, shining shoes, setting up and cleaning the sleeping compartments, and cooking and serving passengers food and drink. Some were required to sing and dance. The downside was that men had to be away from home for weeks at a time, working the mandatory four hundred hours a month, often sixteen to eighteen hours a day, on trains they could not ride as customers because of their race.

I was anxious about being in the sleeping car. I watched the countryside roll by as the train rumbled north to Dallas, east to Longview, north to Texarkana, then up to Little Rock, then Poplar Bluff, stopping at all sorts of small towns along the way.

From time to time the porters knocked on my door to take my order and bring me meals. Between meals, I held my breath every time I heard someone walk past. I didn't breathe a sigh of relief until we pulled out of St. Louis and didn't completely relax until I saw the Chicago skyline.

After I arrived back home, I worked twenty-four hours straight. Two days later, Joan and I began shipping Don Robey his Ultra Wave.

Out on the road, once we crossed the Mason-Dixon line, Millard and I had to get creative with our lodging. Cities like

Memphis, Nashville, and Kansas City were a problem. A little farther away, Little Rock, Arkansas and Miami posed challenges.

The day Jerrell nearly drove us into the ditch, we'd almost learned the hard way that it didn't make sense to travel to Houston all in one shot. We started breaking up the trip at Little Rock. There was no hotel where Black people could stay. Fortunately Millard had a contact at Philander Smith College, a historically Black college. Turns out the only room was in the women's dormitory. There's no telling where we would have slept if school had been in session and the students had been in town. In Nashville, we stayed at Fisk University in a men's dormitory, which was one big, wide-open room with lots of beds. Neither the showers—nor even the toilets—had separation between them. In other cities, we found a church and asked if they knew anyone who would rent us a room in their home. As we traveled, we compiled a list of places where we could stay.

Finding lodging wasn't our only challenge. Once on our way to Florida, we stopped in a small town in Georgia. We saw two Black men standing out in front of a fast-food restaurant, vigorously waving patrons to come to their drive-in stations.

Millard and I were famished. We pulled into the parking lot and started to turn into one of the waiter's stands.

"Y'all colored," one of the men announced as we rolled down our windows.

"You know damn well we're colored," I answered.

"We don't serve colored here," this Black man told me, of the restaurant which was certainly White-owned.

"*Man*, we are *hungry*."

"Well, I'm going to see if I can bring you something in a sack," he conceded.

"Yeah, well, bring two Cokes with it," I told him, annoyed.

83

A few minutes later the waiter returned with two hamburgers and two Cokes.

"Y'all can keep the bottles," he said. "We don't want the bottles back."

Thankfully, we didn't face these indignities in Atlanta. A family who owned a popular soul food restaurant also ran a hotel where it was safe to stay. Even trying to fill up your tank down south, the service-station attendants' attitudes were terrible. They looked at our brown faces, saw our Illinois license plate, and serviced White people's cars before they filled us up. Eventually they got around to pumping our gas. We paid politely and got out of there without much of a problem.

Florida was a much larger, and much hotter, state than either I or my car imagined.

"Doggone it," I said, looking at the steam suddenly rising from the hood, somewhere outside Sarasota. With our car engine hissing, we had to find a service station quickly and hope it would help us before we ended up stranded on the side of the road.

We neared a small gas station just a mile or so down the highway. We could see a bus pulled into the service area and a group of Black men milling around. It was a good sign the station might serve us. Millard correctly identified the carrier as a tour bus.

"I wonder who's in it?" he asked. As I headed inside to speak with the mechanic, he walked over to talk to the guys standing by the bus.

"B.B.!" Millard shouted and began belly laughing.

I turned around and saw a familiar-looking, brown-skinned man grinning ear to ear

"Maaaan, is that you?" he chuckled, and headed over to give Millard a hug. "Of all the places to run into each other."

While my car was being repaired, I found myself talking to the great blues guitarist B. B. King. Turns out, Millard processed B.B.'s hair whenever he came to Chicago to perform. We had a nice conversation with him and his musicians.

"Hold on," I said, before they loaded back up. I headed over to our car, grabbed a case of Ultra Wave out of the trunk, and put it in the back of his bus.

Once we arrived in Miami, we stayed at the Lord Calvert Motel, which was converted from all-White to Black. Compared to everyplace else we had to stay, it was pretty fabulous.

We traveled the region during some dangerous times. It was the summer Emmett Till was lynched, mutilated, and dumped in the Tallahatchie River. I later learned Emmett lived across the street from Joan's mother and played with our sons a bit when they were little.

There were also joyful occasions, such as the success of the Montgomery bus boycott. In Clinton, Tennessee, a group of Black high schoolers also became the first students to integrate a public school in the South. These students were courageous. They were called the Clinton 12.

Fortunately, Millard and I were blessed to travel the Deep South without experiencing any physical violence.

Johnson Products ended 1955 with four employees and $18,000 in sales, about $200,000 today. With the business growing extremely quickly, I needed help with sales and began to pay close attention when salesmen walked into the shop. One in particular caught my eye.

"My name is Hilton Tregg," he said. "I'm here to talk to you about a mimeograph service."

"A mimeograph service?" I asked, puzzled.

What in the world would I need a mimeograph service for?

"Our service will help you make copies of your paper-work," he continued confidently.

"No disrespect, but I don't need a mimeograph service, man," I told him, taking note of the yeoman's effort this charismatic young fellow gave to sell this uninspiring product. He had a great personality, the gift of gab, and my instincts told me he was sincere and honest. He impressed me. Having spent much time around Mr. Fuller's agents, I knew Tregg had the potential to be a good salesman, but he wasn't quite where he needed to be yet.

"Listen, I like you," I told him. "My business is growing and I'm going to need salesmen in a year or so. You're the kind of guy I want to hire. Have you heard of Mr. S. B. Fuller or his company, Fuller Products?"

"Who hasn't?"

"I think you should go work for him," I advised, knowing that Mr. Fuller could develop his spiritual background and character. "He can provide you with the training you'll need to succeed. Let's stay in touch, and after you work for him for a while, I'd like you to come back, and we'll talk about you working for me. I will contact you when I can afford to hire you."

I didn't know all the details, but Mr. Fuller was putting some of his high-potential sales agents into some sort of training. It was a correspondence program associated with Napoleon Hill's book *Think and Grow Rich*. To his credit, Hilton Tregg went to work at Fuller Products.

By 1956 I needed a network of distributors to keep up with the rapidly growing demand. Well-established distributorships already existed in several cities. In Detroit, Melvin

Jefferson, owner of Superior Beauty Supply, was one of the first Black distributors to carry JPC products. Selling Ultra Wave helped him increase his business dramatically. In Cleveland, we helped Joe Bailey grow Bailey's Beauty Supply. But not every distributor served Black clients, and because most banks refused to loan money to Black people, I realized that if I needed a distributor, I might have to put him in business myself, even though I was just getting JPC on its feet. Either I practiced the Golden Rule and extended credit to new distributors, or I couldn't grow my business. The choice was easy.

One day in an Indianapolis barbershop, a policeman wearing a pompadour introduced himself.

"I see you're new in town doing business," he said.

"Yes, we're training barbers to make sure their clients get the best process results."

"I tried Ultra Wave, and I really like it," he continued. "I don't make a lot of money as a policeman. I'm always working more than one job. I'd like to sell Ultra Wave Hair Culture on the side. I'm honest—people will tell you that—and I guarantee I'd move your products fast."

"So what are you proposing?" I asked.

"Well, I don't have the cash to buy it from you, but if you stake me with some products, as soon as I sell them, I'll get the money right back to you."

By this point, I was developing a sixth sense about people. I felt like I could trust him.

Just a few months earlier, my suppliers had taken a chance on me. This man was asking me to do the same with him. Orville had taken advantage of me—but if I wanted to make progress, I had to continue to take risks. Believing in a police officer seemed like a safe bet.

"Okay, I'll extend you credit," I said.

I shipped him some products, and he kept his end of the bargain and paid me quickly. I increased the amount of products, and he sold those fast as well. Over time, I raised the amount of credit I offered him. Eventually, he opened a store and became my Indianapolis distributor to help me better serve the market.

I put Black distributors in business in Cincinnati, Louisville, and Chicago, as well.

Chicago was our largest market. There I worked with Chico Foote, who had been working for a local distributor until they had a falling-out. Chico told me he wanted to represent Ultra Wave.

As I did with the other distributors, I gave him enough merchandise to generate some cash for himself. He sold it, he paid me, and I gave him some more. In time he opened his own beauty-supply company, and it became one of the biggest in the city. To grow our own business, JPC had to take a chance and put other Black people in business. We did this in a lot of cities. I put the sons of a man who worked for me into business. Then one of my early salespeople, in Louisville, Kentucky, had the last name Bright. We put Bright Brothers into business. Los Angeles also became a strong market. As we gave Ultra Wave to these distributorships, it really bumped up their business.

I was manufacturing products at Leon's when a guy showed up after driving all the way from Kansas City. He wanted to buy some Ultra Wave. I came from the back of the shop to help him.

"What's wrong with this stuff?" the guy asked, looking puzzled.

"What do you mean, what's wrong with this stuff?" I felt indignant.

"There must be something wrong with it," he insisted. "You make it, don't you?"

"Yeah . . ."

"Why don't you use it?"

I thought for a moment about what the guy said. I hadn't used Ultra Wave because I was busy either making product till all hours at night or driving all around the Midwest. I hadn't had time to even think about getting the process. But his comment rang a bell in my head. *I am selling a product that I'm not using.* The same evening, I went over to Millard's shop and asked him to process my hair.

After a couple of years, Johnson Products outgrew Leon's facility. In 1956 I rented a storefront a couple of miles away, at 6631 South Ashland, in the Englewood neighborhood. I began to set up shop, just three blocks on the other side of the color line between the Black and White communities. At that point, Englewood was sparsely populated with Black people.

I began moving our equipment in and starting to fix up the place. Apparently, that was fine as long as the White patrons of the tavern next door believed I was a worker and not the owner.

One morning, I pulled up and looked at my establishment.

"I'll be damned . . ."

My big plateglass window was broken out, as was the window in the door. I looked through the broken glass. There was a big rock on the floor. I unlocked the door and surveyed my equipment, glass crunching beneath my feet. None of it had been damaged, but I needed to call the cops. I hadn't installed a telephone yet, and I walked into the tavern next door.

"Do you mind if I use your pay phone?" I asked, referring to the public telephone people could make calls from for a nickel. "I need to call the police. Someone broke out my front window."

"Someone broke your front window?" said the tavern owner, a White man. "I've never heard of anything like it."

"Yeah, well, it happened."

"Do you know when?"

"I was here until well after dinnertime. They must have done it last night."

"I'm shocked!"

"Yeah, well, they got me. I need to call the police."

"By all means," he answered, a nice guy.

Two police officers drove right over. I told them what happened. They weren't surprised. In fact, they determined the person who threw the rock was probably a customer of the tavern, which had an all-White clientele. I got the place boarded up. After that, I needed police protection. The police stationed a patrol car in front of the building during the daytime and sometimes in the back as well, at night. The security was expensive. For my family to eat, I had to make products, and I needed to get back on the other side of the color line.

I found another storefront about a mile to the northeast, at 1146 West Sixty-Third Street, and relocated. It cost me a lot of money to get out of my original lease. At that point, the business really took off. I typically worked until I had to stop from exhaustion, doing whatever was required to move the company forward. This phase of rapid development was wonderful, but it took a lot out of me.

In 1957 a lump appeared on the right side of my rib cage, and it grew until it stuck out by about an inch. Before long, it transformed from annoying to painful. My doctor performed a scan that showed something unusual wrapped around my rib. He told me I needed an operation. While I was under the knife, my surgeon cut out a tumorlike piece of flesh as well as the tip of one of my ribs.

"You have extrapulmonary tuberculosis," he told me after I came out from under anesthesia.

"What's that?"

"Tuberculosis that somehow involves organs other than the lungs," he explained. "You have to stop smoking."

I didn't want to risk my ability to provide for Joan and our sons, and I certainly didn't want to die. He gave me some medication, which I took for about two weeks, until I began to question his diagnosis and discontinued it on my own. I struggled with my physician's warning to kick the habit. I'd been smoking for almost fifteen years and reached for a cigarette first thing each morning after my feet hit the floor. I was up to smoking a pack and a half a day. I attempted to quit, but cigarette hunger tortured me. It was a struggle, but I persisted and eventually stopped.

I bought Joan a brand-new yellow 1956 Chevy convertible for $600, and a '57 Mercury station wagon for myself. One day shortly thereafter, while I was out of town, Joan drove her Chevy to a busy barbershop on the West Side to collect on a past-due bill.

"I don't have the money to pay you," the barber told her, dismissively, because she was a woman.

"Well, I'll just sit right here and wait till you do," she said. My wife wasn't gonna let this guy get away with pushing her around. "You're gonna pay me." She sat right there reading *Ebony* magazine—a recently launched publication focusing on Black lifestyle published by John H. Johnson, who once

91

worked for Supreme Life Insurance — as the men in the shop debated whether the boss of Chicago's Democratic political machine, Richard J. Daley, who was running for office, would be a good mayor for Black people. She patiently played a crossword puzzle as they talked about how Nat King Cole had been assaulted by White supremacists during a concert in Birmingham. They took pride that he was the first African American to host a prime-time television show, *The Nat King Cole Show*, on NBC. Joan raised her eyebrows and shook her head as one fellow engaged in bawdy talk in an effort to rattle her. Joan Johnson stayed put until the barber had cut enough heads to hand over her money. Standing up to that man in his own barbershop made her famous in certain barber circles.

With JPC growing larger, I found myself in need of a mixing machine. I located a used one that could handle eight times the volume of the barrel I had been using to mix Ultra Wave by hand. I went to South Side Bank, where I'd been banking for two years. A respectable amount of money had flowed through my account, and I had never overdrawn it.

"I am running a business, and it's growing so quickly that I need to borrow five hundred dollars to purchase a used mixing machine."

"You want *what?*" asked the loan officer, a White man wearing a shirt and tie.

"I want to borrow five hundred dollars to buy a mixing machine that will increase the production of my business," I said, prepared to talk to the man about my company.

"Ha-ha-ha, a business loan?" The officer laughed.

Seething, I stood up, walked to a teller, withdrew all my money, and went to Chicago City Bank, where I deposited my funds. From there, I drove over to Mr. Fuller's office and told him my dilemma. He cut me a check right on the spot. I bought the machine, and it tripled my business. I paid Mr. Fuller back a few months later.

I could not count on banks and I began to realize that my mentor was right—JPC could not depend on barbers. Not only did we encounter many competitive products, but back in Chicago, during the late 1950s, Jack the Barber started selling a hair straightener he called Deluxol. Jack owned a busy barbershop on Fifty-Fifth Street. Millard had trained him to use Ultra Wave Hair Culture, and for some time Jack bought Ultra Wave from us. Suddenly from nowhere, he came out with Deluxol. Jack and Leon were friends. I knew I'd accidentally left Ultra Wave's formula laying around Leon's shop a couple of times. Jack became my first coattail rider.

Even though JPC entered markets to teach barbers how to use Ultra Wave and show them how to improve their bottom line by switching clients from traditional hair straighteners, when a competitor came along with a less expensive product, far too many barbers went for the cheaper, inferior stuff. A lot of barbers stayed with JPC, but a lot didn't. They were price-conscious, but not quality-conscious. But that did not influence our commitment to bringing the best product possible to the marketplace.

5

Moving On Up

IN 1937 A realtor named Carl Hansberry—a founder of Lake Street Bank, one of Chicago's first Black-owned financial institutions—intentionally attempted to purchase property in the all-White, racially segregated area near Sixty-First Street and Rhodes Avenue. Several realtors who believed in racial integration and were Mr. Hansberry's allies conspired to help him secretly buy the home. Once neighbors learned about Mr. Hansberry's ownership, a White mob surrounded his house and threatened his family. One gang member threw a brick through the window that narrowly missed Mr. Hansberry's eight-year-old daughter.

When challenged in the legal system, Illinois's supreme court upheld the racially restrictive covenants—enforceable legal agreements many property owners signed, agreeing not to sell their house to a particular group of people, usually Black. In Chicago, restrictive covenants helped confine Black people to certain areas of the South Side and block them from moving into others. As a result of the ruling, the Hansberry family was forced to move out.

In 1940 the US Supreme Court reversed the lower court's ruling. In *Hansberry v. Lee*, that decision, widely publicized by the *Chicago Defender*, opened thirty blocks of the South Side to Black residents. And while it didn't end racially restrictive covenants at that time, it became one of numerous important actions that eventually brought them to an end.

Mr. Hansberry's daughter, Lorraine, the little girl who dodged the brick, became a writer. In 1950 her play *A Raisin in the Sun* became the first by an African American woman to be produced on Broadway. The play also became the first by a Black person to win a New York Drama Critics' Circle Award.

In 1957 I turned thirty, and housing was still primarily segregated in Chicago. I learned more about the situation when Joan and I made the big decision to buy our own home.

A Black real estate agent took us house-hunting. We especially liked the leafy Chatham area of the South Side, a soundly middle-class community filled with bungalows, most built during the 1910s and '20s. The neighborhood also had more recently constructed ranch-style homes and the occasional well-kept three-story apartment building. Chatham's schools were good, and the neighborhood had been known for upholding strict property standards, a discreet way of saying that there had been an effort to keep Black people out. The middle-class Black people moving in took pride in maintaining their property.

A three-bedroom, two-bath tan-brick bungalow with a gable roof caught our eye. The home had a den, an unfinished basement, and a lush green yard. I began to imagine 8412 South Michigan Avenue as a place I could create a comforting environment for my family. JPC had turned consistently profitable, but our family had been living modestly. I hadn't been paying myself a salary, and I was only taking out of the company's profits whatever amount we needed to live on.

I struck a deal with the owner, a Jewish man who owned a moving business. I paid some amount of cash to compensate him for the market value of the house, then we took over his mortgage, eventually paying the remainder he owed, $30,000, about $335,000 today. Suddenly we were living the American Dream.

Being the first member of my family to own a home was a source of great excitement among my relatives. My mom was especially proud that we could afford a house with such a large mortgage. I reflected upon all the Fullerites who I'd seen buy their own homes, but it wasn't easy back then. First, your job had to be paying well enough that you could save money. Even then, banks didn't write mortgages to Black people. They drew red lines around entire Black neighborhoods and refused to invest in the communities or the people, while White Americans and many recent immigrants were able to obtain loans. Later, I learned that many Black Chicagoans were unwittingly agreeing to housing "contracts," where they made monthly payments toward ownership but would lose all their equity if they missed even one payment.

But owning a home meant even more than becoming middle-class. After moving often during childhood, I had a stable home for my wife and our sons. Also important to me, after living apart from my father and longing to be with him for much of my life, was having the nuclear family I strongly longed for.

Beyond that, I wanted them to avoid some of the horrible things that happened to me during my childhood in neighborhoods such as Bridgeport and Uptown, where White hoodlums attacked Black people on the street, and others bombed homes and businesses.

Once, when I was thirteen, a friend and I were riding our bicycles near South Parkway, where lots of cars parked in the large open space at Twenty-Second Street. I stopped to roll up my right pants cuff to prevent it from interfering with the chain. I placed my foot on the running board of a car for balance.

"Hey, you niggers!" a man's voice thundered. "You're breaking into these cars!"

"No sir!" I answered, my eyes landing on the tall White man wearing a white shirt and black pants. "I'm just rolling up my pants."

"I'm going to call the police!"

My friend and I took off riding as fast as we could. Suddenly I found myself sliding headlong across the pavement. I'd been hit by a car. The driver got out to check on me. I tried to get up, but my right leg couldn't push. Blood was staining my pant leg, and the muscle above my ankle had been sliced almost down to the bone. Somehow I ended up at Michael Reese Hospital, six blocks away, and someone tracked down my mother. She held my hand while a doctor stitched the wound. Turns out the car's bumper had clipped me about my right ankle, cutting the muscle in my lower leg.

The Spirit blessed me to be among the growing numbers able to escape the limited opportunities to which Black

Americans historically had been confined. Buying a home marked just how far the Lord had brought me.

I was born in Richton, Mississippi, a small town about twenty-seven miles outside Hattiesburg, on June 16, 1927, to Priscilla Dean Johnson and Charles David Johnson. My mom was from Heidelberg, about halfway between Hattiesburg and Meridian, born in 1912, the fifth of six children. She made it to the sixth grade, as was typical of that era. Underestimate her intelligence or her wisdom at your own risk. My dad was about five years older than her, born in 1907, somewhere in Alabama. Somehow Daddy obtained some college education. It was rare back then for any American, but it was remarkable for a Black man in the rural South, particularly someone brown-skinned. My mom and dad married, and they had John, Robert, and me by the time my mom was eighteen years old.

Many Black folks in Mississippi sharecropped for White landowners, renting small plots of land in exchange for a portion of their crop at the end of the year. This arrangement kept Black people extremely poor, in debt, unable to afford their own land, and lacking in basic human and civil rights. What little money they made could be wiped out in an instant by drought, flood, a failed crop, or an unscrupulous landowner. Almost all of the landowners were unscrupulous. The threat of racial violence also hung over their heads. Even today, almost a hundred years after we left, Mississippi remains one of the worst places on almost every indicator of a Black person's quality of life.

My mother's older siblings had already escaped the state. They joined what became known as the Great Migration, the roughly fifty-year period beginning in 1910 when more than six million African Americans fled the South's exploitive labor relationships and racial violence, seeking better jobs, greater freedom, and more opportunities in the North. My aunts and uncles wrote frequently, sending Mama money and begging her to bring her husband, children, and his parents to Chicago, where they settled. My mother tried to convince Daddy that the Windy City was better, but my father wasn't working the fields. He had a good job at a company that made pressed wallboard. Certainly his parents didn't want any of us to go. Complicating matters, many Black people were leaving the South, and White landowners and employers were spreading stories about how badly Black people were being treated up North. They weren't always wrong, but their motivation was to convince their Black laborers to keep working their land for next to nothing.

Apparently my mother agreed with my father for a year or so. Eventually she made up her own mind and decided to leave. Mama possessed a lot of courage to say goodbye to the man she loved and the only place she knew in order to travel north with John, who was four; Robert, only five months old; and me, a two-year old. When she left in August 1929, she was merely a teenager. Her younger sister, Evelyn, accompanied us.

I imagine we took the Illinois Central Railroad, which ran from New Orleans to Chicago. Around the time we arrived, the vast majority of Black Chicagoans lived in a seven-mile-long by one-and-a-half-mile-wide strip of land on the South Side that ran from Twenty-Second to Sixty-Third Street and from State Street to Cottage Grove, just a stone's throw from Lake Michigan. Many Whites once disparaged this community as "the Black Belt," "the Black Ghetto," or "Darkie Town." Black people saw the neighborhood differently. For decades, many called it Bronzeville. It was one of few places where Black Chicagoans could live safely away from the racial violence that shocking numbers of the city's White residents historically enacted.

When our family arrived, we lived in one room on the second floor of a rooming house near Twenty-Ninth Street and Ellis Avenue, which one of Mama's siblings must have acquired before we arrived. Mama, my brothers, and I shared a single room and one bed. We shared a communal kitchen and bathroom with the other tenants. The bathroom was down the hall, and water always stood on the hallway floor. The dark corridor to get to our quarters scared me to death. One night I got out of bed and peed on the floor to avoid racing down that frightening hall.

About a week after we arrived, my mother started working at Michael Reese Hospital, about a block from our rooming house. Funded by the fortune of a deceased Jewish businessman, it was a rare place where all people could receive treatment, no matter their race, ethnicity, or class. Mama started out as a cleanup girl in the dietary department. She worked hard. Her job didn't pay much. Thank goodness she had it before the Depression hit that October, when massive numbers of people were thrown out of work. During the Great Depression, there was some shame associated with being on government relief. People saw it as something you took not because you wanted to but because you had to, you couldn't do any better. We greatly appreciated that we weren't on relief. That said, we weren't much better off than the other impoverished families around us.

My mother was kind, caring, and warm. She wasn't huggy-huggy, but she hugged us enough and made us know that she loved us. We felt protected. She took us to Olivet Baptist Church near Thirty-First Street and Vernon Avenue early on. I recited an Easter poem there when I was only three or four. I enjoyed the music, the choir, the feeling I got being among many people, and the devotion. Each night before bedtime we prayed together on our knees with Mama, leaning forward on our cot.

For several years we moved from place to place, living with relatives. We were staying with my mother's sister, Aunt Lucille, and her husband, Uncle Chip, when the snowstorm of 1930 dumped almost twenty inches on the city. By the time I was five, our family had moved again, this time to share an apartment with Mama's brother, St. Elmo Thigpen—we called him Uncle Saint—and his wife, Aunt Earlene, on the third floor of a building on Forty-Second Street that had about twelve apartments. Aunt Earlene had converted Uncle Saint to Catholicism, and we started attending St. Elizabeth's Catholic School at Forty-First Street and Wabash Avenue, along with their children. I suspect we were able to afford the tuition because Uncle Saint, who had a jitney service, drove a limousine. Mom left for work early, Aunt Earlene got us ready, and Uncle Saint dropped us off at St. Elizabeth's in his limo.

I wanted my sons to get a strong education like I received at St. Elizabeth's. It gave me a great appreciation of learning and a good start academically. My cousin Evelyn and I were strong pupils and would often be invited to join a group of young students who visited the older children's classrooms, where we were quizzed about the catechism to embarrass and perhaps motivate them. By the time we left St. Elizabeth's, I possessed an understanding of the Spirit and the spiritual world. While I already knew about God, attending St. Elizabeth's deepened my knowledge of the Spirit.

When I was about nine, we boys and Mama moved again. I transferred to the Stephen A. Douglas School at Thirty-Second Street and South Calumet, followed by Doolittle Elementary School at Thirty-Fifth near Cottage Grove Avenue, where my very first Black teacher expected a lot from his students.

Most of my childhood took place near Thirty-Fourth and Vernon Avenue, where my mother obtained her own apartment. It was a residential area filled with three-story apartment buildings and several commercial establishments — the laundromat, the Greyhound maintenance station, an A&P grocery store, several markets, and so on. Most of its residents were striving for a better life; Black people's racial and socioeconomic challenges were evident in our South Side neighborhood. Parts of our community looked decent and well kept. Other blocks were not nice. During the 1930s and '40s, the city didn't pick up trash or plow snow in Black neighborhoods as it did in White communities. On Vernon between Thirty-Fourth and Thirty-Fifth, the butcher, the chicken store, and the grocery store all threw meat, chicken feathers, and poultry guts into their trash bins. Some residents threw their garbage into several vacant lots; many superintendents burned the trash from their buildings. This combination stank and attracted huge brown rats, some seven or eight inches long, not including the tail. John and I saw a couple of rats so frequently we named them. A few blocks away was Thirty-First Street, called the Bucket of Blood. You would be ill advised to walk down Thirty-First between State and the Lake at night. There was a lot of drinking and carrying on. People carried switchblades, and sometimes fights broke out.

Though I lived in a ghetto, some of our neighbors did well. I paid particular attention to the good livers. Next door to our three-story redbrick building was a two-story brick row house where an independently wealthy woman who had a Rolls-Royce but didn't work lived with her sister. The schoolteachers on our block seemed to be doing just fine. Being a postman was a well-respected and dignified job that also offered security, which most jobs available to Black people did not. Postal workers also owned nice houses.

There was an enclave a block away—on Thirty-Fourth between Rhodes and Cottage Grove—where several doctors, lawyers, ministers, nurses, entrepreneurs, and other professionals lived a lot better than we did. In fact, Dr. Maurice Shaw, Reverend McGee, and my best friend Bill's father, Mr. Simmons, seemed to be prospering. Mr. Simmons was an executive at People's Gas, whose headquarters were over at Thirty-Ninth and Wabash. Of course, the Jones Brothers and other people in the "policy racket"—the numbers—lived extremely well. And a brick home on the corner of Thirty-Second and Vernon had a yard and its own tennis court. Watching Black people have such a wonderful time hitting that ball back and forth fascinated me.

When Mama took us farther along South Parkway, I saw countless redbrick and stone mansions, some with pillars, marble stairways and entrances, and ornate wrought-iron fences. Many were a source of community pride. People pointed out the home of a famous singer named Etta Moten Barnett, the first Black woman to perform at the White House. She later played the lead role, Bess, in George Gershwin's opera *Porgy and Bess*. Around Forty-Fifth Street was a mansion owned by a woman people referred to as Madame Malone. Her hair and beauty school, Poro College, took up several lots on the block. Annie Turnbo Malone was a chemist, Black beauty mogul, millionaire, and philanthropist who got her start working with Black hair care entrepreneur, activist, and philanthropist Madam C. J. Walker, the first American woman to become a self-made millionaire.

Ours was a harmonious community, and the presence of people we called "good livers" made a deep impression and helped me understand that not everyone shared the same economic situation, and not all Black people were impoverished. Our family may have been poor, but the good livers' children had skates, bicycles, nice wardrobes. They had all the things we didn't have but wanted. I saw that a Black person could achieve a more prosperous life. Even though I was always hustling for money, knowing that gave me hope.

Racial segregation created many disadvantages, but Black people also experienced benefits from living together. While much of mainstream society didn't even view us as human, our proximity helped us to support, encourage, patronize, create art for, and respect each other. To make ends meet, my mother took in a roomer, a middle-aged man named Mr. Pierce. He slept in the bedroom, Mama slept in the dining room on the pullout couch, and we three boys slept in the living room on cots we folded up and put into the closet during the day. Business owners had a built-in market they could easily cultivate. This was especially true of those who sold products or services for African Americans. Our people took pride in supporting and patronizing Black enterprises as part of our efforts to advance the race. Citizens and shop owners conquered the odds together, and the South Side birthed numerous successful entrepreneurs.

A vibrant community of artists and intellectuals flourished. Creative geniuses like musicians Louis Armstrong, Mahalia Jackson, and Quincy Jones; writers, artists, and activists like Ida B. Wells, Richard Wright, Gwendolyn

Brooks, and Margaret Burroughs; and choreographer Katherine Dunham are among many luminaries who grew up and developed their craft there. Just walking the street, you might hear a trumpet wailing, a saxophone playing, or a group of singers vocalizing on the corner. The athletic achievements of Jesse Owens, Joe Louis, Ralph Metcalf, and other legends inspired our community and gave us hope. Free arts organizations like the Abraham Lincoln Center and the South Side Community Art Center were both hotbeds of activity.

Chicago's South Side also became a symbol and metaphor for African Americans' possibilities in the face of oppression, during an era of racial transformation beyond anything our nation had known. During my early youth, for many people the nickname Bronzeville symbolized Black people's ingenious ability to hustle their way out of deep poverty, improve their life's circumstances, create vibrant culture and a spirited community, and even join the Black middle and upper classes in experiencing the American Dream. Many people also used the phrase "the Black Metropolis" to describe both the physical and metaphorical characteristics of Chicago's South Side, an amazing city within a city. By the mid-1940s, if Bronzeville had been its own city, it would have been the second largest Black community in the United States, after Harlem.

I felt blessed both to have come from this vibrant community and to now be in a position to provide better opportunities for my family.

I also felt strongly about wanting my kids to grow up with their mother and their father living in the same home. My parents had divorced and lived hundreds of miles apart. While we lived with our mom, our father made sure we knew he was thinking of us. Each month the postman delivered a letter from him that made us jump up and down as we opened it. Daddy wrote about how much he loved and missed us and sent each of us one dollar. His letters and dollars made us feel good about him, though several years had passed since we'd seen him. We also had a few black-and-white pictures of our father. One showed him standing alongside a double-wing, single-engine airplane with an open cockpit. For years, my knowledge of Dad came from his letters and those photographs. I knew he loved me, but a space lingered in my heart because he wasn't with us. Sometimes my brothers and I felt sad about it. Most of the other kids' fathers lived with them. I saw the kids who had both a mother and father as lucky, and believed we were not as fortunate. I didn't want my own children to have these kinds of feelings.

Thankfully, when I was ten, my mother told us she wanted us to know our father and grandparents. She was going to put us on the train to Mississippi, and we were going to stay there for a year, she said. At Hattiesburg, we stepped off the train expecting our father to greet us. But he wasn't on the platform or inside the little wooden depot. We were all upset, but I was *really* upset—just frightened to death. As the oldest, John attempted to keep us calm. Turns out our father had been at a different station and needed to borrow a car to get to us. Few Black people had cars, and this took a while. When he finally pulled up, we raced toward him.

"*Daddy, Daddy!*"

He swooped us up, kissing and hugging each of us. It was like we had never been apart. Daddy was on the petite side and a couple of inches shorter than my mother. He was quite handsome, and in his face, I could see my big eyes. As we drove off, I sat in the back seat studying his dark-brown skin, his hair cut a little shorter than mine, and the round bald spot atop his head. Being with Daddy in person was much better than looking at some dog-eared photo. Meeting him opened the door to an entirely new experience of life, the one I would have lived had Mama not been courageous and come north.

Our father drove us to Runnelstown, halfway between Hattiesburg and Richton. We pulled up in the yard of a white two-story wood-frame house with a great big porch wrapped around the front and several shade trees alongside it. An older woman came out the door wearing a dress and an apron, then pointed to a pen full of chickens with a wood-board fence around it.

"Go out and catch that pullet right there," she instructed, gesturing toward the chicken she wanted before even saying hello. We didn't know that a pullet was a hen that's less than one year old, too young to have started laying eggs. The pullet the woman wanted was white, as were most of the other chickens, but they were larger. John, Robert, and I all gave it our best. We flew around the yard chasing the bird she pointed out as it escaped between the other chickens, and they all ran from us.

"Catch that pullet right there!" the woman hollered as she darted around the pen with us. Chickens raced in every direction, squawking, feathers flying—it was a mess. Before long we were all worn out. We didn't catch the pullet, and neither did this small, wiry woman, who turned out to be our grandmother. Our reward for all our efforts was our grandmother walking out to the garden, gathering three weeds, plaiting them together, and giving us a spanking. Our Mississippi beginnings had gone from bad to worse. Getting stripes on our butts was a helluva hello. Not only that, at first I struggled to understand everyone's accent. *What are they saying?* Sometimes I needed them to repeat themselves several times. They struggled to understand me, too.

Turned out there wasn't enough space for us at Daddy's place. He lived in a boarding house in a different town. My brothers and I stayed in my grandparents' three- or four-bedroom house, along with six or seven cousins, stacked up no fewer than three to a bed. Each morning our grandmother woke us up mighty early and instructed us what vegetables to gather from the long rows of beans, tomatoes, peppers, carrots, greens, collards, and okra in her garden.

Grandma was a heck of a good cook. For breakfast she made the fresh vegetables we picked, along with pork—not bacon, but something like it—and eggs, which were plentiful since the hens laid all the time. Her biscuits were flaky and buttery, and she prepared a great gravy. Even today I remember how tasty the biscuits were. I mean, *whew!* When you ate at her table, you were happy to be there. Every meal became a scramble between us children. My cousin Sonny was younger and smaller. One day breakfast disappeared more quickly than usual, and he lamented with his Southern accent, "I would eat some mo' but I don't see no mo.' I would eat some mo' but I don't see no mo.'" Sonny verbalized what I was thinking because I would've eaten some mo', too, had we not wiped out breakfast in no time.

Our grandparents lived on a sharecropping farm. We sharecropped with them from June through August. By the break of dawn, we went out in big fields with long rows. On day one, we picked green peas, string beans, and cotton. If we were out picking beans, my grandmother and grandfather were picking beans; if we were picking tomatoes, they were picking tomatoes; or watermelon; or cotton; or whatever it was. We wore straw hats because they covered our heads but also let some air through. There were woods all around but not a lick of shade.

My grandfather only grew a little cotton, but he hired us out to pick it on other people's farms. Picking cotton was particularly miserable. If I didn't get my fingers inside the cotton boll right, its sharp point tore up my fingers and fingernails and they bled from underneath. When we picked for other people, we made money. It wasn't much, but being paid inspired us. Picking cotton earned a penny a pound; most days I made 75 cents, about $16 today for a very long day's work. It took a hell of a while, but one day I picked 104 pounds. I wrote my mother to tell her to bring us home.

In August, after the cotton fields were picked clean, we said goodbye to our grandparents, and Daddy drove us over green rolling hills to live with him in Laurel, about fifty miles from the Alabama state line. He found us a nice little house that sat atop stilts, and when the land flooded our home did not. The landlady stayed in the back, and we occupied the front. As the oldest, John slept alone on a cot. Robert, Daddy, and I all crowded into the same bed. Each night before bedtime, we said prayers together on our knees.

My entire fifth-grade school year, we lived with our father. I attended Southside School, a two-story brick building educating about twenty students in each class, in the third through fifth grades. All our teachers were Black. There was a girl in my class named Leontyne. She went on to become the first internationally known Black opera singer, Leontyne Price.

Like Mama, our dad was a spiritual man. We went to the Baptist church down the street, and Daddy had us baptized.

He also loved to sing and play the guitar. In college he sang with a group of blind singers called the Blind Boys, well known throughout the South. During the middle of each week, he sat on the floor and serenaded us with spirituals and songs he'd written. Daddy took us to the swimming hole. We went fishing and rabbit hunting for the first time. I also got to meet my father's brother, my namesake, Uncle George. He and his wife ran the household of a well-to-do White family and lived with them in their large one-level brick home.

Near Christmas, our mother came to Mississippi and stayed with us over the holidays. It was the first time I remember she and our father being together — and it's one of my favorite memories. Mama stayed for about a week, and she and Daddy were jolly and happy. We had been having a wonderful time with our dad, and Mama's visit was icing on the cake.

While it was a joy to spend all that time with my father, nothing could have prepared us for life in the South. Daddy sat us down and told us how to talk to southern White folks.

"Say 'Yes sir' or 'No ma'am,' " he instructed. "If you have a cap on your head, take it off. And no matter what they say, don't give them any backtalk, just keep going."

As we moved around town, we heeded Daddy's advice. Anytime I went to the store, if I asked the man behind a cash register for my change, he would hardly respond — and if he did, he would be nasty. I also experienced some cruelty in the all-White neighborhood where my father got me a paper route. I quit the route, got a wagon, bought bundles of kindling wood, and sold them in our neighborhood at a profit. In my own community, I was treated well, and I made money.

Whites' poor behavior followed us to the swimming hole. On one occasion I was with a group of kids laughing,

110

jumping, and diving into the water from an elevated rock. Suddenly a loud and menacing voice sliced the fun like a hot knife cuts butter.

"*Hey, you niggers!*"

All the kids froze. My hair stood on end.

"*We're* going swimming," a man's voice thundered in such a threatening tone I can still hear it today. "Y'all get out of there!"

The local Black kids scrambled out of the hole, jumped into their clothes, and took off running. My brothers and I followed their lead. If they were in a hurry to get out of there, we were, too.

Another day, Daddy sent me to get a tub of butter at a store up the block. When I pushed the door open, I saw the store owner and his wife leaning so far over a radio that the crowns of their heads were facing me. The radio's volume was high, and I stopped to listen. At that age, everything coming out of a radio seemed like the voice of God to me.

"If you elect me, I'm gonna pass a bill to send all the niggers back to Africa," a man's voice shouted.

Oh, my God! I started imagining all the elephants, lions, tigers, and gorillas I saw in the *Tarzan* movies. I ran out of the store crying and screaming, "Daddy, Daddy!"

"What's wrong, son?" my father asked when I arrived back at the house.

"Daddy, they say they're gonna pass a bill to send all the niggers back to Africa!" I cried, repeating the racial epithet I somehow already knew applied to me.

"Oh, that's nobody but Bilbo," he said, smiling and calm. "Don't worry about that, he's trying to get reelected."

Theodore Bilbo had been Mississippi's US senator. During the 1940s he admitted that he belonged to the Ku Klux

Klan, engaged in supremacist rhetoric, and encouraged White men to employ violence to keep Black people from voting. Bilbo's Senate colleagues investigated and found him guilty of violating both the United States Constitution and federal election laws.

There was the Saturday when John and I discovered the movie theater in the small business district downtown and went there with Robert. We bought our tickets from the cashier out front and started to walk inside.

"Where are you boys going?"

We turned to see a White man standing behind us.

"To see the movie," we answered.

"Well, just hold up now. You see the corner here?" He pointed.

"Yes . . ."

"Go and make a right turn, and you'll see a fire escape," he instructed. "Climb up that fire escape and you will be in the movie."

Why do we have to go up the fire escape? I wondered, as we walked to the corner to see what in the world he was talking about.

"I'm not going to the movies," I told my brothers. I didn't understand what was going on, but as I looked up those steps, I knew his treatment of us was wrong. I wasn't going to let anyone do that to me. That was it. I never went to another movie in Mississippi. John and Robert never went back either.

Before long the school year drew to a close, and the time came to return to Chicago. I loved Daddy before we visited Mississippi, but I'd learned to love him deeply while we were on that trip.

"I'm never coming back to the South," I told him. "If you don't come to Chicago, you will never see me again."

Back home, I was glad to be in my community again. I felt proud to be among the growing numbers of Black folks who were able to better themselves no matter the obstacles they encountered.

Three years later Daddy moved to Joliet, about an hour southwest of Chicago, down Interstate 57. By then he had married one of my mother's cousins and become a waiter on the Santa Fe railroad line. At some point, he worked the Burlington railroad.

By the time our family moved into the Chatham home, White people were fleeing the area in droves. They did not want to live next to Black people. In 1950 the neighborhood was 99 percent White; by 1960, it was 63 percent Black. White flight was common across Chicago.

The irony was that many prominent Black people lived in our solidly middle-class community. They included business professionals, ministers, entrepreneurs, and educators. Quite a few were more established and better educated than the White people running away from us. Among the most well-known was Dr. T. R. M. Howard. In 1956, Dr. Howard moved to Chicago from Mound Bayou, Mississippi, after the Ku Klux Klan ran him out. The Klan became angry with Dr. Howard after he transformed his home into a command center for folks investigating and reporting on Emmett Till's lynching the previous summer. In Chatham, Dr. Howard established Friendship Medical Center, which provided medical services, including abortions before they were legal. He also helped found the Chicago League of Negro Voters and, later, Operation Breadbasket.

The acclaimed gospel singer Mahalia Jackson lived in our community. A decade earlier her song "Move On Up a

Little Higher" became the highest-selling gospel single in history. In 1956 she performed on *The Ed Sullivan Show*, one of the first times a Black artist appeared on a television variety show. Not long before we moved to Chatham, she performed for Montgomery residents following the success of their bus boycott. In a few years, she would sing both at John F. Kennedy's inauguration and before Dr. King spoke at the March on Washington.

Cook County probate court judge Richard Gumbel lived in the neighborhood, as well. Judge Gumbel and his wife, Rhea Alice, had two sons, Greg and Bryant, who became famous TV announcers. The Robichaux family owned Baldwin Ice Cream. One neighbor was a pharmacist; another a policeman; still another worked for a Los Angeles talent agency; many women were educators. We became friendly with Melvin and Doris Young, a policeman and a teacher whose two children were John and Eric's ages. There was Wilson Frost, who would temporarily be named mayor right after the death of Richard J. Daley (the first Mayor Daley). Fred Rice would become Chicago's first Black police superintendent. One of our next-door neighbors was White. He was one of the few who stuck around for quite a while.

We think about family life differently today; back then most people believed that the husband should be the family's primary breadwinner. If a man could obtain a good paying job so his wife could stay home with the children, she did. When women could afford to stay home, that was seen as the ideal. But life was expensive, and it was extremely difficult for Black men to find good work. If a man didn't make enough money to cover the family's lifestyle, his wife would get a job to supplement her husband's income. In reality, most Black women worked.

At this point, Joan could afford to stay home and raise our sons. But Joan loved JPC. I hired a housekeeper, Gloria, both to help around the house and to help with the kids. This freed Joan to devote more time to JPC. She loved to come to the office.

For the first time in my life, I experienced weekends off. I bought baseballs and mitts and taught Eric and John how to pitch and catch in our backyard. We pretended we were Roy Campanella, Roberto Clemente, Bob Gibson, and Willie Mays—some of the Black and Afro-Latino stars integrating Major League Baseball during that era. Other times we'd go to our neighbor Melvin Young's home to play basketball on the court in his backyard. From time to time I put a movie screen on the front lawn and invited neighborhood kids to sit on the front steps and watch. I built a barbecue pit out back, where I loved to grill steaks and pop open a beer. We invited family and friends to come over to eat, enjoy our home, and pick fresh peaches straight off our tree.

6

Blessings and Faithfulness

AS MILLARD AND I rolled out Ultra Wave and conducted demonstrations, I noticed that for every barbershop I walked into, I passed by two beauty salons. Clearly, the hairdresser market was larger.

Doc Martini and I began to conduct research.

Mine consisted of walking into beauty shops, surveying the situation, speaking with the owner, learning how hair salons work, and trying to figure out what women wanted to do with their hair. When I entered a salon, all eyes would turn to me, since I was typically the only man in the place. Shopkeepers already knew all about Ultra Wave and told me I needed to offer something like it for women.

The salons had an interesting setup. Whoever owned the

lease owned the shop. She would sublease to other beauticians, charging them rent to operate in her salon. The stylists were independent and did their own thing. There wasn't a lot of standardization; each hairdresser seemed to have their own set of products as well as their own ideas about how best to serve clients.

The one thing that was consistent, no matter the salon, was that each one had an exhaust fan to blow out smoke. Something about hairstyling was generating lots of smoky fumes.

Curious, I asked what was going on. Shop owners told me the process of straightening women's hair produced smoke.

"Will you show me what's happening?" I asked.

I learned that the stylist first applied a lubricant—some used petrolatum, called "grease"; others used mineral oil— to protect hair from being burned. Then she heated a gold- or silver-colored metal comb atop a hot plate or flame burner. The stylist pulled the hot comb through a section of hair to stretch the hair. This straightened it. The heat from the comb burned the lubricant off the hair. That's what produced both the stench that I smelled and the ubiquitous smoke.

On top of that, there was another problem. If the comb was too hot, the hair would burn. If it remained too cold, the hair wouldn't straighten. But the hairdresser couldn't control the comb's temperature. If the hairdresser wasn't careful while trying to straighten the edges of a woman's hair, she might burn her client's ears, the nape of her neck beneath her "kitchen," or even her forehead. The lubricant also left women's hair greasy and heavy. The more I learned, the more I understood the challenges beauticians encountered.

For the client, hair straightening gave them a look they desired, temporarily. At the first sign of rain or even humidity, though, the hair could revert to its naturally wavy, curly, frizzy, or kinky state, leaving the woman unable to style it like she could right after straightening. Many Black women repeated this process every two weeks, in an attempt to keep their hair "presentable"—that is, acceptable to White people, particularly employers.

I reported my findings to Doc Martini, who was still working at Fuller Products. Together, we came up with several goals he said he'd help me pursue on the side. We wanted to better everyone's working conditions by improving the air quality in the salons, and we wanted to enhance the process beauticians used to straighten their clients' hair.

Doc's quest began with research on how to get rid of the smoke. To do this, he began to explore ingredients that could replace the grease that stylists used. He also wanted to create a substitute for mineral oil. Removing these lubricants from the ingredients that stylists used required him to use his skills as a scientist to formulate a new brand. He experimented with many ingredients, including, surprisingly, water. Doc also tinkered with other components, such as tocopherol (vitamin E) and other antioxidants, with the goal of helping to improve the condition of a woman's hair. Ideally, we wanted to create a product that didn't merely straighten a woman's hair but also left it in better condition as well. We certainly didn't want anybody getting burned or losing hair.

Around the same time, Don Robey began pressing me to sell him a women's product that straightened hair permanently, as Ultra Wave did for men. Doc and I decided to explore how we could expand Ultra Wave to women's hair.

We produced an experimental product, picked out the name Silk-O-Cess, and had new labels printed. Not surprisingly, Robey wanted me to bring Silk-O-Cess to Texas. I figured I'd use the state as our test market. If everything worked out, I'd sell Silk-O-Cess exclusively in Texas. We also experimented with Silk-O-Cess using hairdressers in Chicago, where beauticians were generally more proficient than in other parts of the country.

Millard and I drove to Texas, where Robey pulled together a small group of hairdressers for Millard to train. With our Ultra Wave business growing quickly, Millard didn't have a lot of time. We instructed a small group of beauticians, with the idea that they, in turn, could teach others. I stayed in town while Millard conducted the first demonstration. The next day, I headed back to Chicago.

I felt excited on the long ride home. I was racing up a two-lane highway at eighty-five or ninety miles per hour when a herd of cattle suddenly began crossing the highway ahead of me. Certain I was a goner, I threw on the brakes as hard as I could, and prayed I didn't crash into a herd of eight-hundred-pound cows.

Boom!

I heard the sound before I realized that the front of the car had collided with the tail of the last cow that crossed the highway. The very last one!

I had no question the Lord was with me.

I hardly made it back to Chicago before we started having problems in Texas. Some of the women Millard trained hadn't paid enough attention. Eager to offer Silk-O-Cess to their customers, they went back to their salons before they could apply the product both safely and competently. Millard immediately stopped the demos and attended to these

119

hairdressers. As soon as I heard about the problems, I shut down the whole program. I didn't want bad things snowballing out of control. It would have horrible ramifications for JPC. I took back all our product and stopped Robey from selling it.

Doc Martini and I returned to the drawing board.

Suddenly, Silk-O-Cess knockoffs began flooding the market. I wasn't surprised to see Orville's poor imitation. Henry Bundles, a member of Madam C. J. Walker's family, sold Hair Straight, one of the biggest copycat brands. I was told he obtained a loan from some White Indianapolis bankers and connected with a man whose last name was Childrey. Childrey used to work for Orville, making Wavo for him. Bundles and Orville Nelson followed a business model that emphasized selling, rather than educating hairdressers to use the product properly. Bundles's people demonstrated Hair Straight on two or three models in front of an audience of several hundred hairdressers, many of whom were not paying close attention. Sometimes the women were chatting; at other times these events included vocalists, musicians, and other entertainment. After the models' hair was relaxed and styled, they walked through the audience. Hairdressers oohed and ahhed over their straight tresses, styled into the looks of the time, such as a beehive, bouffant, or straight bob.

Orville, Bundles, and others typically sold a lot of product quickly, but once they returned to their salons, beauticians often received inconsistent and even unsatisfactory results. Some clients' hairstyles didn't come out as they had hoped, and far too many hairdressers made their clients unhappy.

Our competitors had jumped ahead of us again. Of course, I didn't let the pressure rush me.

Back at Fuller Products, some people were blaming Doc Martini because I left. Doc got tired of the gossip. Fortunately, his annoyance coincided with my need for his help. I invited him to work for JPC. It was expensive to hire him, but he was worth it. For his convenience, I built a lab for him near where he lived.

As Doc developed various product improvements, we arranged for beauticians to test them in their salons. They gave us advice about how they worked. With each piece of feedback, Doc tweaked the formulation. His first scientific research led Johnson Products to launch a haircare brand we called Ultra Sheen. I chose the word *ultra* because our products performed above and beyond all the existing brands, and *sheen* because they left the hair shiny.

The first product, Ultra Sheen Cream Satin Press, revolutionized the way hairdressers pressed hair, eliminated the need for high heat and grease, and eliminated smoke. Doc formulated Cream Satin Press with expensive ingredients that allowed us to cut in half the amount of heat required to straighten the hair. The product also rejuvenated hair. Together, these steps offered a significant innovation, dramatically reducing the stress on Black women's hair, leaving it with a beautiful sheen. Women walked out of the salon with better straightening results, and because the hairdresser had only used half the heat, she would have staved off the damage caused by a traditional hot comb.

Most beauticians were grateful to have a high-performing product that also allowed them to improve the air quality in their shops. But with its pale-yellow color and thick, creamy consistency, Ultra Sheen Cream Satin Press looked different from the grease, mineral oil, and petrolatum hairdressers were used to. We were surprised to discover a group of beauticians who were reluctant to give up their grease and wanted to understand why.

"I don't know," some stylists said. "How does a woman keep her hair moisturized between appointments? I'm going to keep selling her grease, so her hair doesn't look dry."

We came up with a product to address that need, Ultra Sheen Hair and Scalp Conditioner. It was a fantastic formula that gave the hair a healthy glow, left a light coating on the scalp, and required only one-third as much product as traditional grease. To clean all these products from the hair and scalp, we created Ultra Sheen Cream Shampoo.

While our products were superior, they weren't enough. Turns out many Black women imagined not having to straighten their hair as frequently. In their desire for longer-lasting results, women began clamoring for a high-quality hair relaxer. As local hairdressers gave us feedback, we reduced the alkalinity of men's Ultra Wave Hair Culture to a level that would straighten women's hair safely and effectively. We named this new product Ultra Sheen Relaxer. I began to consider how to launch into our pipeline this innovative women's hair relaxer.

Mr. Fuller taught me that you have to pray for wisdom, and if you're worthy, you'll receive it. I needed a lot of wisdom. In search of it, my morning meditation lasted about twenty-five minutes. I read the Bible, prayed for others, and then asked God for wisdom, knowledge, vision, and understanding. After that, I listened for God's response.

The time had come to begin building my sales force. I called Hilton Tregg, as I told him I would after he'd trained at Fuller Products for about a year and completed the Napoleon Hill Development Program. When we spoke, it was clear that Hilton had become an excellent salesman. I knew people would trust him.

Over the next couple of years, I began to hire more salespeople, imitating Mr. Fuller's example of being discerning and careful about who he accepted as an agent and entrusted with the black bag full of merchandise. I first ascertained whether there was a spiritual side to the person. My goal was to hire employees who embraced and respected my spiritual values. I needed honest and principled people who understood and were committed to the doctrine on which I founded Johnson Products: Do unto others as you would have others do unto you.

After Hilton, I hired Jim Middlebrooks, another Fullerite; then one of my high school buddies, Pat Johnson. Next, I brought on Andrew Bright.

As I read from the Word, I tried to inculcate into my sales team the ideals I was learning. We gathered in my office and read together. I talked to them first about believing in God and the spirit of God in all of us, and to recognize God as our heavenly father.

Joan and I also invited the salespeople to our home to hang out with us. We held barbecues and built a lot of camaraderie. A couple of our distributors stayed with us when they came to town. Melvin Jefferson and his wife came from Detroit, and Don Robey visited a couple of times. We also hosted quarterly meetings and an annual dinner for the entire company.

"What do you do to train your salespeople?" distributors asked. "They're the only ones I can find out here in the market after six p.m."

"I keep talking to them about the Lord," I answered.

Everything I taught JPC's salespeople had a spiritual meaning. As the Lord inspired me, I inspired our people as much as I could. I had to motivate Jim Middlebrooks almost all the time. I regularly called him up to see how he was doing.

"Cleveland is just a graveyard with lights," he told me one night. I knew that kind of attitude wouldn't get us anywhere. I kept him on, and over time mentored him into a better leader.

One day my mother called me out of the blue. By now, Mama had joined the legions of people drawn to work at Fuller Products. She was now the company's floor lady.

"I just fired someone," she told me. "She's very smart, she catches on quickly, and she's a good worker."

"Well then, why did you fire her?"

As I listened to my mother's explanation, I realized that these two strong women had clashed.

"She would be a great help for you," my mother said.

Right away I hired Vera Williams to be in charge of production. She became one of the best employees I ever hired.

By 1958 the growth of the women's market caused us to outgrow our West Sixty-Third Street location. Johnson Products paid cash for a three-story factory building at 5831 South Green Street.

We were nearing the 1960s, but a Black worker earned just 53 percent of a White worker's wage, down from 60 percent back in 1950. Compensating for the inequity, JPC gave away Thanksgiving baskets containing an eighteen-pound turkey and other typical foods people ate for the holiday. On top, we added several jars of our products. Vera helped us fill these gift baskets. My neighbors Doris and Melvin Young supplied us with the names of needy people. Doris taught in the heart of the Black community and knew many struggling families. The program grew until the late 1960s, when it became too big to manage.

Around that time, Max Holzman — the man who brought me six cases of jars when I started the company and who continued to supply JPC with glass — told me the owner of Murray's Superior Hair Pomade was trying to sell the business. Murray's was a good company, and I thought it would fit well with Ultra Wave Hair Culture. The product was easy to manufacture, and I could gain sales and profit. I would love to own it, and I gave Mrs. Murray a call.

When I drove out to her office on South Chicago Avenue to meet her, Mrs. Murray invited me in. She was an older woman, seated, and I believe she used a cane. She didn't get up the whole time I was there.

I made an offer at $125,000, the full price that she was asking for. I offered to pay cash. I also made an absolute promise that everyone would retain their jobs. In addition, I would keep their building on South Chicago Avenue.

"Well, I don't know about that," she told me. "Your hair straightener is affecting our business."

"Yes, I understand, Mrs. Murray," I told her. "I'd like the products to complement each other, not compete."

"Our sales are down, and your company is responsible," she said. "I don't see how I could ever sell to you."

"Please, Mrs. Murray, I promise you — "

"Mr. Johnson, I can't do it."

"Murray's Hair Pomade is very popular with men. With your approval, I'd love to have the opportunity to make a wonderful product even better," I told her. "I give you my word, I won't lay anyone off, and I will not sell your building."

"I won't do it."

"Please," I begged her, almost in tears. The fact that she misunderstood my intentions and didn't trust me really hurt. "I have no intention of putting Murray's out of business. I want to keep the jobs and the business in the community."

"I'm sorry, Johnson. I'm not going to change my mind."

Instead of selling her business to me, Mrs. Murray sold to a White-owned manufacturer in Detroit. The buyer was the brother-in-law of one of my best distributors.

"Oh, you've got to be kidding me!" I cried in anguish when I found out. "She sold the business out of our community, and the guy didn't keep her people. All those Black folks lost their jobs and he didn't even pay her cash!"

Mrs. Murray just didn't want me to have it. And from the late 1960s to this very day, all the owner has done is milk Murray's hair pomade for profits. I wished every Black person shared my concern for the development of community and the race.

As JPC grew, I grew, and my sense of what we could accomplish grew. In 1960 we rented a ballroom above several storefronts at Sixty-Fourth and Cottage Grove, and invited beauticians to a catered event to introduce Ultra Sheen Relaxer, Ultra Sheen Neutralizing Shampoo, and Ultra Sheen Rinse-N-Set to the market. I invited Mr. Fuller to be our speaker. By then everyone knew him as the richest Black man in America. His success was the talk of Black Chicago.

On the night of the event, the hall was packed with hairdressers, dressed to the nines. Mrs. Jackson, our caterer, served fried chicken dinners, and everyone had access to an open bar. Maybe there was too much liquor. When it came time for Mr. Fuller to speak, some of the women were a bit unruly.

"Excuse me, excuse me, please," I said in attempt to get their attention. They finally quieted down a little as I began ringing a spoon against the side of a glass. "I'd like to introduce you to one of the greatest men our city has ever known. He's a well-known businessman who believes in God, believes in our people, and who believes in doing good. A man I am pleased to call my mentor. The man who helped me get on my feet and launch my own company."

Everyone applauded, and the room grew silent as Mr. Fuller stepped to the podium.

"Good evening, ladies and gentlemen," he began. "I'm excited to be here to support this wonderful young man, George Johnson, who worked for me for about 10 years."

That night he shared a motivational message, conveying some of the same themes he imparted to his sales agents. After his speech, models walked among the beauticians, showing off their Ultra Sheen–relaxed hair as the beauticians clamored to touch their soft and shiny tresses.

Overall, the night was an amazing success, and now Chicago hairdressers knew us. Quickly thereafter, we built a relationship with a distributor. Right away, our Ultra Sheen products showed increased sales. Ultra Wave Hair Culture may have gotten Johnson Products onto our feet, but from this point forward the beauty products market became the biggest contributor to our growth. The professional products for women that we sold to beauticians began to outsell the products we created for men. These changes required me to shift my business model to focus on the beauty salon market.

We began training hairdressers in Chicago, instructing beauticians on how to use our products by holding clinics in rented spaces or on the premises of a distributor already selling JPC brands. Clinics took place on Monday, the day beauty shops were closed so that beauticians were able to attend.

"We will teach you how to use our products and we'll teach you at no charge," we told hairstylists. "But you have to commit to attending the clinics until our demonstrators award you a certificate guaranteeing you are able to use Ultra Sheen Relaxer successfully and safely. You will not be allowed to buy the product until you earn a certificate."

No company had ever required anything like this before. We received a lot of pushback.

"You can't run a business like that. You're limiting the sales of your own product!" distributors who were not in our program told us.

I understood the limitation, but it was a risk I was willing to take.

"The certificate will give your clients peace of mind, knowing their relaxer will be applied without damaging their hair," we responded.

Johnson Products representatives took our clinics to one market at a time, similar to how we did with barbers. In each location we selected one distributor, typically the city's largest, at the risk of making other distributors unhappy. For a limited time we offered that business the opportunity to be the exclusive seller of Ultra Sheen Relaxer. This exclusivity bought us some measure of protection. We held this distributor accountable for making sure that only the hairdressers who earned certificates purchased our product.

"After we educate enough hairdressers to handle Ultra Sheen Relaxer properly, I will open up sales to other distributors," I explained.

Our competitors didn't care whether hairdressers knew

how to use their product. They thought we were not smart for the same reasons barbers thought we made a mistake with Ultra Wave. The same training we offered stylists for free also taught them how to use competitive brands more effectively.

The process was slow, but we kept the program going for almost three years, determined to teach beauticians to use our products safely and successfully.

Not surprisingly, by the time we showed up with our Ultra Sheen Relaxer training program, we were a step behind Orville and other competitors. As happened with Ultra Wave, we often had to clean up after them. But from a business standpoint, the results of this tortoise-and-the-hare approach were fantastic. The certified hairdressers were successful with their clients and helped other stylists perfect their skills.

There was a significant additional upside for beauticians. For generations, the beauty industry had given Black women a way to earn an independent and dignified living no matter the community's social condition. It provided them control over their own destiny, and the ability to earn good wages. Before the women's liberation movement hit in the 1960s and '70s, opening the doors of economic opportunity to greater numbers of women, the hair industry had given many of them economic salvation. JPC had a plan to improve upon that.

Traditionally, a hairdresser's prices were higher than those of a barber. Ultra Sheen Relaxer created a significant financial upside. The kit cost about $5 and contained enough product to relax two clients' hair. JPC suggested that stylists charge between $12 and $15 per relaxer. This allowed them to substantially increase their income. Many professional beauticians' earnings skyrocketed from $120 to $500 or more per week, and from roughly $6,200 to more than $25,000 per year. That's $65,000 to $260,000 today. The changes we helped create in the economics of a beautician's business did wonders for many Black businesswomen's pocketbooks, families, and quality of life. Of course, some of our competitors would undersell us in an attempt to get hairdressers to switch to their brand. Some stylists did, but most remained loyal to us.

The more I traveled from city to city, the more I saw something else that bothered me. There was a lack of uniform operating standards in the salon business. If there were five hairdressers working in one establishment, there were essentially five different businesses. An owner might have both highly experienced and inexperienced hair stylists working under her roof. Each bought their own supplies and could use products of any quality. There were no consequences if they made mistakes, other than possibly losing a client.

"Don't you worry this might give you a bad reputation?" I asked.

"Oh, no, everyone has to start somewhere," owners answered. "If her customers are dissatisfied, that's on her."

I heard similar comments about stylists' attendance. Every hairdresser worked her own schedule. She came in whenever she wanted, she took breaks when she wanted, she went home when she wanted. All a stylist had to do was pay her rent, and the shop owner seemed to be happy.

To me, this didn't make good business sense.

I wanted every shop to carry JPC products—and ideally, only our products. Whether women wanted to wear bombshell waves or beehive styles, I wanted them to associate Ultra Sheen Conditioner and Hair Dress, Ultra Sheen Relaxer, and our other products with professional stylists.

I envisioned helping hairdressers become more profitable, and the industry more professional. I observed that each stylist essentially had a captive audience for ninety minutes to three hours while they washed, relaxed, rinsed, put rollers in, sat women under the dryer, removed their rollers, and styled their clients' hair. In my view, beauticians could also use this time to sell haircare products for clients to use at home. In addition to hair products, they could also sell other beauty-related items, like lipstick, skin creams, and perfume. I started imagining JPC helping salon owners to run a more profitable business overall.

To contribute to this goal, JPC opened the Ultra Sheen Model Beauty Salon in a small storefront in Chicago. My intention was to show beauticians how to create a state-of-the-art beauty salon with only a modest financial investment. I wanted to establish standards for how a salon should operate professionally and profitably, to teach hairdressers industry best practices, and to instruct them how to run a more successful and professional business.

Our Model Salon was state of the art and aesthetically pleasing. We hired an interior designer to create a warm, welcoming, and bright space. A receptionist greeted our clients, seated them, made them feel welcome, handed them something to read while they waited, and scheduled their next appointment. We imported state-of-the-art circular operator stations with mirrors all around them, a hair dryer that stylists pulled down from above, and modern and comfortable swivel chairs.

Unlike a traditional hair salon, the Ultra Sheen Model Beauty Salon did not rent booths. Instead we hired hairdressers to work for the Model Salon full-time, from 8:00 a.m. to 6:00 p.m, six days a week. We paid them on a commission basis—45 percent to the operator and 55 percent to the salon. We offered hairdressers benefits that included paid vacations, health insurance, and sick days off. We provided attractive uniforms, and all the product the stylists needed.

We also hired a well-known and successful stylist from Baltimore, Carolyn Murry. She trained the hairdressers how to use JPC products, improved their hair-relaxing skills, taught them how to run a salon, and helped them set up their books. We offered financial incentives for beauticians to increase their number of clients. We even invited stylists who did hair from home or salons elsewhere in the community to observe how Model Salon hairdressers used our products. A sleek glass display case contained JPC's retail brands, as well as beautiful jewelry and cosmetics that clients could purchase.

But beyond that, I wanted Black businesses to succeed. Hair salons as well as barbershops were economic engines in our communities. If a hairdresser or barber did well, that meant business for the beauty-supply distributor who sold our product, as well as combs, aprons, hand mirrors, and so on. Before their appointment, a customer might drop off their clothes at the laundry or dry cleaners. On the way home, folks might order a meal from the neighborhood soul-food restaurant, or run through the grocery store. They might go to the clothing boutique and purchase a new shirt or a dress.

Unfortunately, we had a tough time. Beauticians were set in their way of doing business, and were not interested in transitioning to the state of the art. The Ultra Sheen Model

Beauty Salon failed. I learned an important lesson. Even when you run a successful business, not everything that you try works. The setback did not discourage me from trying to help them improve their businesses.

We kept the hairdressers engaged. In the summer of 1961, we held our second Ultra Sheen dinner at a union hall on Forty-Seventh Street and South Wabash Avenue. We wanted to treat the hairdressers to a special evening featuring the best entertainment available. Trumpeter and vocalist Louis Armstrong and singer Joe Williams performed, adding an air of classiness to the event that allowed the attendees to experience the good life as well. We hired a Black caterer, Mrs. Jackson, to serve the six hundred hairdressers who attended. It was the largest catering opportunity she'd been offered. Mrs. Jackson did an incredible job. The event dinner was wonderful. It allowed us to spread the word about our products and add to our bottom line.

As the company grew and JPC generated more revenue, I could have paid myself handsomely, as a typical CEO would do. I chose not to. I also didn't want to pay myself a big salary and then return 60 to 71 percent of it in income taxes. Instead, I kept taking out of JPC only the amount of money I needed to live. As a result, money accumulated in the company.

In 1960, when I had seventeen employees, my accountants informed me that I could contribute 15 percent of JPC's before-tax profits to a profit-sharing plan that would allow our employees to participate in the company's financial gains. The way I looked at it, profit sharing would provide our employees a major incentive to stay with JPC and work hard in the company's interest. They helped me make the profits, and I thought I ought to share the profits with them.

Employees were surprised and ecstatic. Our employees had been doing well financially before the plan, and afterward, they became even more dedicated.

Some other companies offered their workers profit sharing; however, employer discrimination locked the vast majority of Black workers out of jobs with this type of benefit. In Chicago, the Sears, Roebuck and Company offered profit sharing, but during the 1960s Sears refused to racially integrate its sales, clerical, and managerial positions. Sears was immeasurably larger, but on a proportional basis, JPC's benefits were as strong as theirs.

By the end of 1960, JPC's gross sales totaled about $675,000, almost $7 million today.

Within a few years, our company completed the slow and painstaking education phase and rollout of Ultra Sheen Relaxer. By then, we owned 45 percent of the professional relaxer market.

JPC also introduced Ultra Sheen Conditioner and Hair Dress to the retail market, which primarily consisted of individually owned drugstores. (Supermarkets, mass merchandisers, and specialty shops didn't carry haircare products.) Except for Ultra Wave Hair Culture and Murray's Superior Hair Pomade for men, few Black hair products were sold retail at all. Those retailers who did sell Black hair products, almost all of whom were White men, kept them in drawers behind the counter. A customer had to ask for them.

"You're losing out by keeping our products under lock and key," my salesmen and I repeatedly told retail store owners and drugstore owners. "You're holding your own business back from making real money."

"Well, Black people steal," they replied.

"Every race has people who steal, but most Black people aren't thieves," I told them, feeling a moral responsibility to defend against these ingrained racist beliefs.

"Well, what if the products don't sell?"

"Just put them out and see what happens," I challenged. "Believe me, you'll sell them."

JPC had to fight to create room on the shelves for our products. In the process, we learned about the many deals that companies cut to get distribution and shelf space. Once we secured shelf space, retail sales were soaring.

In the middle of all this success, I suddenly became conflicted as I read the Bible. Scriptures like "The love of money is the root of all evil" and "You can't love money and serve God" confused me. I suddenly found myself wondering whether I should give up my business to enter the ministry.

I made an appointment with my pastor, Dr. William J. Faulkner, at Park Manor United Church of Christ. It had once been all White, but it didn't take long before White folks moved out and it was an all-Black congregation. We attended regularly, and Joan and our children were involved. Dr. Faulkner was formerly the dean of students at Fisk University. I told him about my successful business.

"Praise God!" he exclaimed. "The Lord is really blessing your faithfulness."

"Yes, He is, Reverend Faulkner, and I've been feeling called by the ministry," I confessed.

"I guess that shouldn't surprise me. You're a very faithful young man."

"Thank you, sir. But I'm confused. I love Johnson Products and feel responsible for my employees," I told him. "If I'm supposed to be a minister and serve people, I don't want to make a mistake and miss my calling."

"What you're doing right now is helping a lot of people, George."

"But running a business isn't as important as the ministry. And I don't want to make a mistake and pursue the wrong career."

"Well, George, providing employment and sharing money rather than hoarding is very important," Dr. Faulkner replied. "A good man with money can do a lot of good for people. In fact, he can do as much good as a minister can."

It was as if God had sent a thunderbolt of enlightenment from heaven. Being assured that there was no conflict between making money and doing good set me free.

During our meeting, Dr. Faulkner handed me a little-bitty navy-blue book, *Pathways to Spiritual Power: A Pocket Devotional Guide to Spiritual Living*, by Thomas S. Kepler.

"I also want you to find the book *On Being a Real Person* by a New York minister, Dr. Harry Emerson Fosdick," he told me.

Until then, the Bible had been the only spiritual book I read. *Pathways to Spiritual Power* helped me to think positively. I read it over and over, keeping it near me, in my hand, my desk, or my breast pocket. *On Being a Real Person* challenged me intellectually, emotionally, and spiritually.

"Life consists not simply in what heredity and environment do to us but in how we respond to what it does to us," it said.

Hmm . . .

I continued to read.

> Fate slew him, but he did not drop;
> She felled—he did not fall—
> Impaled him on her fiercest stakes—
> He neutralized them all.

Every Black person I knew was struggling with the fate of being born into a racist society. They were trying to survive and, if possible, build a meaningful life within. I didn't know quite how, but the possibility that a man could "neutralize" Fate's fiercest stakes intrigued me. I continued reading . . .

"We are not responsible for our heredity; but if it is true that a third factor enters into the building of personality— the power to face life with an individual rejoinder—then we are responsible for *that*."

The more I read Dr. Fosdick's thoughts about a person's individual power, the more I embraced them.

Working together, these ideas helped me understand that I was not responsible for the deprivation I experienced growing up. Neither were the members of my race struggling all around me. Yet and still, I had within me the power to choose my responses, whether to racism or to other forms of adversity I experienced. I felt drawn to these ideas that I could *choose* my responses. These ideas stretched my sense of possibility, not just for me but also for all human beings.

I longed to become the "real person" Dr. Fosdick wrote of, a man who could respond to life's difficulties in a positive or in a spiritual way. I envisioned myself triumphing over challenges, especially those I faced as we grew the business.

Dr. Faulkner and I continued to meet. He also introduced me to the writings of a Quaker minister, Rufus Jones. Among his many ideas, Jones believed that spiritual people should do more than merely study the Bible. He believed they should "help build a better world for unborn generations." Though this challenged some of the religious orthodoxy of the times, it made sense to me. "Keep your feet on the ground and get something done," he wrote. "A true and noble life must move on both these legs and not a single one of them alone."

Ideas like these helped me figure out what having money and being a good man could look like.

Dr. Faulkner also recommended Thomas R. Kelly's *A Testament to Devotion*. Dr. Kelly's work was one of the deepest religious books I ever read. It introduced me to a state of mind he called "simultaneity," when you are conscious of the Spirit and of the world—all the time and at the same time.

All day every day, I tried to remain conscious of both my relationship with God and my ability to apply my faith to our community and our people. I felt free of any conflict between having money, and even wealth, and being a good man. They could exist together.

7

The Black Side of Paradise

EARLY IN OUR marriage, I saved for two years to take Joan on a honeymoon. We traveled to a Black resort in Paradise Lake, Michigan. It was owned and operated by a woman known as Chick-Chick. Her lodge sat right along the lake and catered to working-class Blacks. Chick-Chick prepared amazing meals, one of the highlights of our trip. Waking up on the water and motoring around on the facility's twelve-foot boat helped open my eyes to ways we could live. There was a "Black side" of Paradise Lake. White folks were on the other side; the two never mixed. Still, the adventure planted the idea of owning a vacation home in my mind.

Seven years later, Johnson Products was doing well, and I was able to take time off and enjoy my family. I located a fourteen-acre property in Endeavor, Wisconsin, a little over two hundred miles north of Chicago. The grounds included a white three-bedroom frame house and a log cabin heated with a potbellied stove, next to the beach along Buffalo Lake. I could afford to invest in a place where we could get away, have fun, and be together.

It took four or five hours to drive to Endeavor. We typically spent long weekends or week-long vacations there. Members of our extended family, our neighbors Doris and Melvin Young, and their children, Pam and Stephen, enjoyed visiting. I invited my aunt Evelyn to bring her children. My mother loved to stay in the log cabin with Evelyn, the sister who accompanied her on our family's journey north from Mississippi. I heated and air-conditioned the cabin for comfort. Eric and John, who were about six and eight when I bought the property, invited friends. Every visit, the cool pine-scented air filled my lungs, and I relaxed in a way I didn't at home. We slept late, ate breakfast outdoors at the picnic table, spent afternoons on Adirondack chairs in the sand, and watched the kids swimming and boats bobbing. Joan enjoyed her cigarettes, and we sipped drinks and listened to Ray Charles sing "Georgia on My Mind."

In Endeavor I also bought a fantastic new invention in boating, a twenty-one-foot inboard jet boat that sucked water from beneath it into the engine and then thrust the water out the rear for propulsion. Eventually we added a swimming pool. I was grateful to be able to afford it all. Excited by our new motorboat, I subscribed to *Yachting* magazine. One issue featured the seventy-two-foot yacht owned by Charles Walgreen Jr., the heir to his father's Chicago-based drugstore chain.

"Would you look at this," I said, whistling in admiration. "Joan, there's a kitchen, living room, bedrooms, and bathrooms in this yacht."

"It's really nice. It would be great if we had one," she replied.

I didn't say it out loud, but in my mind, I set a goal that I would own a boat like that someday. And a mere few years later I could finally afford to place an order for the seventy-two-foot Burger yacht. I added a three-foot cockpit to the stern to fish in Lake Michigan.

My wife and I aspired to an ever more comfortable lifestyle and to experience more of life's luxuries.

"I want to live in a house like this," Joan mused to no one in particular as she sat on the living room sofa beneath the front window, legs curled beneath her. Reading *Better Homes & Gardens* magazine was one of our favorite activities.

"Let me see," I said, stepping away from JPC's books, which I was poring over at the dining room table.

"Look at these sliding-glass doors and floor-to-ceiling windows," she said, pointing to pictures of an innovative home with contemporary architecture not seen in traditional homes. "They let a lot of light inside."

"Oh, wow, that *is* beautiful."

"It's like you're warm and cozy inside, but the outside still comes in," she said. "It's almost like the garden is inside the house. What a beautiful home. I'd love to live like this."

"Maybe we can even have something better!" I added.

We had only lived in our Chatham home for a few years when I began imagining building a contemporary house like the one in the magazine. For $50,000, I bought a 50-by-125-foot lot from a certified public accountant named Arthur Wilson, next door to Chicago's first Black police chief, Captain Bluitt. Located on the street one block east of our house on Michigan Avenue, this lot at 8418 Indiana Avenue was twice as wide as most of the properties in the neighborhood. Fifty thousand dollars then is about $530,000 today.

I called Huebner & Henneberg, the architects who built the house we'd admired in *Better Homes & Gardens*. I made an appointment for Jim Henneberg to come look at the lot and discuss what we wanted to do. The fact that he didn't hesitate to come to the South Side told me he was a liberal, which made me feel comfortable. We discussed our ideas, especially the landscaping. I wanted maximum privacy and a circular driveway.

Jim showed us photographs of a number of homes he designed in this new modernist style, as well as some architectural drawings and three-dimensional models of unique free-form homes that didn't conform to traditional approaches to architecture. We liked the idea of a one-story L-shaped home with floor-to-ceiling windows, designed in the International Style, with its light-filled rooms. After several meetings he presented an artist's rendering and floor plan, featuring a kitchen, living room, and family room opening onto a central garden, and a basketball court for the boys. Late that year, we approved the architect's design and broke ground.

During the fall of 1961, just four years after we purchased the Chatham house, we moved into our Indiana Avenue house. The modern, free-form single-level home of beige brick was the first of its kind in our neighborhood. Right away, people began driving by to look at it. Some cruised by slowly; others stopped in the middle of the street and pointed; still others parked out front and stood on the sidewalk talking about it. People walked past slowly pretending not to look; some turned right around and passed by again from the other direction.

About 10 years later we wanted to upgrade even further,

when someone told us about a great property in Glencoe, Illinois, a small predominantly White village north of Evanston. We drove out to take a look. The home sat on an acre of land and had a huge pool and a lighted tennis court. Across Glencoe's railroad tracks, a Black community had formed almost 130 years earlier, along the Underground Railroad. Many of their descendants had been maids, cooks, and waiters to the community's wealthy Whites. Other residents owned their own homes. Some were working class and still others successful business owners. Many were sending their kids to college. But the house wasn't what we wanted.

Shortly afterward, our family went on vacation to Europe. Jim Henneberg called when we were in Madrid.

"We just found out about a property that's about to go on the market," he said. "It's on two acres right on Lake Michigan. The house sits on high ground, but it has steps leading down to the beach."

The listing sounded promising. We cut our trip short and returned to Chicago to look at it. Joan and I loved the old frame house, and the coach house out back with an apartment in it. Even though it was a fixer-upper, we made a full-price offer that the sellers accepted.

Until they discovered their prospective buyers were Black. At that point, they started hemming, hawing, and trying to renege.

"Tell them I'll sue," I told our realtor, as we strove to kick down the doors of residential segregation. "They'll also have to pay your full commission because they accepted our full-price offer."

The sellers changed their minds.

Joan and I decided to tear down the old house, and we asked Huebner & Henneberg to design a new one. They started drawing up plans right away, but then Jim Henneberg traveled to Japan to work on a different project.

One month went by, then two months. I started getting anxious. At the rate the architects were moving, there wouldn't be time both to build the house and to get the kids in school by September. We decided to see if the previous house in Glencoe we passed on was still available. It was. We bought it from the owner, Chicago real estate developer Jerry Wexler. In September, we put the kids in school and put the Lake Michigan fixer-upper back on the market.

Not everyone was pleased to see us doing well.

In February 1962, Joan and I flew to Florida. The CEO of the company that sold glass jars to JPC, Berman Brothers, was friends with the owner of the Casablanca Hotel on Miami Beach. The owner made a reservation for Joan and me.

Heads snapped in our direction as Joan and I walked through the lobby, filled with well-dressed White people.

"Good afternoon," I said as I strode up to the front desk. "Reservation for George Johnson, please."

The reservation attendant, who was White, looked shocked. "Are you playing here?" he asked in a condescending tone.

"*Playing* here?" I asked. "No, I'm not in the band. I have a reservation that Mr. Meyer Lansky made for me."

The man's eyes grew as big as saucers and his face turned beet red. He looked through the register and saw our names. Looking flustered, he checked us in, gave us a key, and pointed us toward the elevator. The bellhop took our luggage and led us to a beautifully appointed room.

Miami Beach was racially segregated. Black people could not live in the city, and were not allowed to stay in its hotels, swim in the ocean, or use most of the beaches. The police required them to have a "pass" to be in Miami Beach after 6:00 p.m. Yet Black artists could stay at the city's hotels while they performed. We were probably the first Black nonentertainers to integrate the hotel.

That evening, Joan and I headed to the dining room for our dinner reservations. When we walked in, time stopped as a wave of faces turned toward us. Joan looked particularly gorgeous as she strode through the dining room dressed to the nines. She held her head high.

"George, what the hell is happening here?" she asked, smiling through clenched teeth, as we tried to ignore the curious and uncomfortable stares. My wife knew full well what was going on. She didn't want to give anyone the satisfaction of knowing they'd upset her.

"That's their problem, Joan," I told her, faking a smile. "Let's just order our meal, have a nice time, and not let them affect us."

I felt uneasy and out of place as the only Negro in the room. It was a feeling I'd never experienced before.

"Can you believe this shit?" Joan asked through her teeth as she ate and attempted to look pleasant.

"I'm sorry I brought you here," I said, trying unsuccessfully to interest myself in whatever I ordered for dinner. "Let's just finish eating and get out of here."

A woman several tables away said something rude, barely loud enough for us to hear. I saw a dark look pass over Joan's face. My wife could be feisty. Her chest began to swell. I'm sure a storm cloud of angry thoughts started forming inside her head. I knew what was about to come next, and I would have to finish whatever she started. I put my napkin on my plate, slowly stood up, and calmly extended my hand to my wife before she lit somebody up.

The next day, we were just as uncomfortable when we lay by the pool on a chaise longue. The morning after that, we went for a boat ride from Miami to Fort Lauderdale along the Intracoastal Waterway. When the boat docked, we headed into the cafeteria for lunch, picked out what we wanted, and took our trays to the cashier.

"They say you can eat in the kitchen or leave the tray," said a Black man who had rushed in from the kitchen.

Before I could respond, Joan's body puffed up. I reached for her hand and began pulling her away. "Please, Joan, not now."

"I don't know who he thinks he is," she said so the guy could hear.

"I know, but not now," I told her in a low voice. "We don't need their food. Let's just walk away. Please, don't say anything."

"I just cannot believe," she began, the volume of her voice rising.

"Please, Joan," I said. "Let's leave. Let's leave."

I got us out of there quickly before she made a bad situation worse.

Black life in Chicago came with its share of indignities, but we'd never experienced this level of hostility. The racism we endured was incessant.

"This city will *never* get another dime of our money!" Joan said. "We will never put up with this, ever again!"

The wealth and blessings of our family were growing in many ways. On May 23, 1962, our family welcomed our third child, George Ellis Johnson Jr., born at Michael Reese Hospital, where my mother once worked. I was excited to have another child. Our housekeeper, Gloria, sometimes brought her three-year-old daughter to work. Her daughter tried to call our new baby "sweetie pie" and it came out "petey pie." The name stuck, and everyone started calling George Jr. "Petey."

Ed Hughes, our Louisville salesman, visited us with a young boxer, a nineteen-year-old man named Cassius Clay. Ed and Cassius were wandering through our house when they came upon the nursery. Cassius picked up our newborn and put him to his chest, kissing Petey, patting him on the back, and cuddling him for a good half hour.

"Will you sign your autograph for me?" my son Johnny, who was then nine, asked Cassius.

"Why not?"

Johnny brought him a fifty-page pad.

"Will you sign every page?" he asked him.

"No, you just get one autograph, son," I told Johnny.

"But I want to take them to school and sell them," he said.

"Oh, I don't mind," Cassius replied, as everyone laughed. He patiently autographed every single page. On Monday, Johnny took his pad filled with autographs to school but returned crestfallen; none of his classmates at his predominantly White school knew who Cassius Clay was. Two years passed before this gifted boxer shook up the world by defeating Sonny Liston to become heavyweight champion. By then Johnny's notebook full of autographs was long gone.

In June 1964, Joan gave birth following a surprise pregnancy.

I was sitting in the waiting room nervously when the nurse came in with the good news.

"Your wife has delivered, Mr. Johnson," she told me. "It's a girl!"

I stood up and started pacing.

"I don't believe it, I have to see her!"

Joan and I were both ecstatic to finally have a daughter. We named her Joan Marie and called her Joanie. And not only were we thrilled to have a daughter, we loved that we had a second set of children. Eric and John, who were now thirteen and eleven, felt excited as well.

As I traveled to visit JPC's markets, there was an occasion when I was sitting in first class on a flight to Chicago from Miami. The only other passenger in first class was also a Black man.

"Excuse me, sir," I introduced myself. "Do you want to sit together and talk?"

"That would be good, man," the gentleman replied. I noticed an accent.

"Where're you from?"

"Kingston, Jamaica," he told me.

"Jamaica!" I exclaimed. "What are you doing way up here?"

"Yah, man, it's too cold." He laughed, introducing himself as Pat Stevens. "Back home, my mother and I own a cement block factory. I'm on my way to meet with a company that makes the machinery that forms cement blocks."

"That's interesting," I told him, and we chatted about business. "I've never been to Jamaica. What's it like down there?"

"You should come!" Pat answered enthusiastically. "We just earned our independence from Great Britain. Come see the new nation we're building. You'll get some sun, swim in the ocean, and enjoy yourself."

He began educating me about what had been going on

in his country, politically. It reminded me that the freedom struggle against colonialism taking place in Ghana, Senegal, Mali, Congo, Nigeria, and many more African nations was also happening in the Caribbean.

"If I get a chance to have a vacation in the future, I'm going to think about Jamaica," I told him. After our Miami experience it was an easy choice.

Our first vacation in Jamaica was quite a turnaround from the United States. Between the turquoise-blue sea, the warm winter trade winds, and the green mountains in the distance, I fell in love with the country right away. And unlike in the States, where Black people lived in fear under White people's authority, in Jamaica everybody in charge was Black.

This is how Black life is supposed to be!

During just four days, I experienced a sense of possibility I'd never had back home.

For our next vacation, we took the whole family to Ocho Rios, where we had a house in the development Paradise. We stayed for a month. I wanted our sons to experience the freedom.

"Remember I met that Jamaican guy in first class on the airplane?" I asked Joan as we sat poolside.

"Yeah, I do."

"I'm gonna call him."

Pat Stevens invited us to Kingston, where he lived. He showed me the community, introduced me to some government officials, and took me to an area called Runaway Bay. I came upon a two-acre property for sale three-quarters of a mile from the Caribbean. From it, you could see both the beach and the sea. I bought it for $15,000 (about $156,000 today), right on the spot. We prepared to start building. I'd read a story about a fictional Tibetan valley, Shangri-La, where you remained young as long as you stayed there. I named our villa Shangri-La. The first year after the house opened, our family traveled to Jamaica thirteen times, mostly for four-day weekends.

Back then, not a lot of Americans visited Jamaica. Before all the resorts were built, a trip to the islands was a luxurious thing. In addition to enjoying Shangri-La with our family, I also used Shangri-La to build relationships and encourage distributors to pay attention to our brand. JPC set promotional goals for our distributors and offered all-expense-paid week-long vacations to Shangri-La as incentive.

8

Fire!

THERE WAS A time when Posner Products was a fierce competitor, particularly in New York. Its founder, George Posner, was quick to cut his prices in his hometown. We sold a case of twelve jars of Ultra Wave for $12. Normally, he priced a little higher than ours, but on his home turf he would drop the price in half in an attempt to keep us out of the market. And price-conscious New York barbers were not the most loyal. Posner even bought Ultra Wave from barbers and replaced it with Posner Hair Straightener. Eventually, Posner cut his prices in half in Chicago as well. This caused us to struggle a bit in two major markets.

To keep our business growing, it meant traveling farther and more often to develop new markets.

On one trip to New York City, I went to meet with an international business consulting firm to discuss what they could do for us in the European market. While I was there, a secretary burst into our eleven a.m. meeting.

"Mr. Johnson, there's an emergency call for you!"

"George, the plant's on fire," Joan shouted through the phone. "Robert just called and told me that flames are leaping out of the roof. It looks to be a total loss! The fire department has been there for thirty minutes."

I grabbed my coat and briefcase, rushed out of the office, got on the elevator, and ran out into the street, where I flagged a yellow cab.

"LaGuardia Airport!" I said to the cabbie. There was no time to check out of my hotel.

I caught the next flight to Chicago.

I smelled the smoke as I pulled up. Bright red fire trucks surrounded our building. The fire seemed to be out. There was a hook-and-ladder that reached to the roof, and a fireman pulled Pat Johnson, our sales manager, out of a third-floor salesroom window.

"Mr. Johnson, Mr. Johnson," one of our employees cried as he ran toward me in tears. "We did everything we could, but George Fulton didn't make it."

My knees buckled. "What happened?"

"An electrical fire, sir," one of the workers told me. "We told George it was safer to jump out the second-floor window with us, but he ran downstairs, and we never saw him again!"

"Oh my God! Is there anyone else?"

"Everyone else is okay. Just a couple of sprained ankles from dropping out the window."

"Are you the owner?" a fireman asked.

"Yes, I'm George Johnson, the company president."

"I'm the fire marshal," he said, shaking my hand. "The

fire seems to have traveled from the basement up the elevator shaft. It looks like it ignited some materials from there. The gentleman who perished got trapped at the bottom of the steps. The door was locked." He went on to explain how George had unknowingly run toward the smoke and the fire as the stairwell behaved like a chimney flue, sucking the flame and smoke upward.

As I stood viewing the devastation, I descended into a deep state of shock.

There was a gas station on the other side of the alley. We had safety concerns about the potential of someone coming in from the gas station and going into the basement unseen. But by that hour, the door should have been open.

After the last fire truck left, I slowly walked through the ruined manufacturing facility. Water stood on the floor. The sound of it still cascading from the roof tormented me. Through the burned-out rafters, I saw the gray sky. The smell of smoke mixed with Ultra Wave and Ultra Sheen almost made me nauseous. Some of the machinery was still usable. Little of the purchased packaging was salvageable.

I imagined George rushing down the stairs, encountering a locked door, and perishing as he tried to escape. My head spun, and fiery images and disturbing thoughts played over and over in my mind.

I hadn't known George Fulton personally, but I felt grief-stricken at his death. I visited his family and offered my condolences. I was especially devastated to discover that he was such a young man, and he and his wife had recently had their first child. I vowed to do everything necessary to take care of his widow and infant.

"We will keep him on the payroll," I promised his wife. "When JPC gives out raises, George will get a raise. Whatever benefits he would have received will be available to you and your child."

There was no way to undo the tragedy, but I hoped our gestures helped relieve some of their suffering. I wanted to make them as whole as humanly possible.

The date October 19, 1964, will be etched into my memory forever.

Almost exactly ten years after we began, our manufacturing plant was in ruin, I'd lost an employee, and Johnson Products Company was hopelessly out of business.

Where am I going from here?

The following morning the telephone awakened me from the most anguished sleep of my entire life.

"Naked I came from my mother's womb, and naked shall I return," said a familiar baritone voice through the telephone handset Joan handed me as I lay in bed.

"Hello, Mr. Fuller," I whispered.

"The Lord gave, and the Lord has taken away; blessed be the name of the Lord," my mentor continued. "Why don't you come on down to my office and let's talk?"

"Yessir," I said, still smelling smoke in my nostrils. If there were more words to say, I didn't know them. My mentor's offer of comfort propelled my feet toward the bathroom. In the shower, hot water soothed my body, but the sounds that normally comforted me now reminded me of the water dripping from the roof into the burned-out ruin of my manufacturing plant.

I don't know how I made it to Fuller Products that morning. I vaguely remember taking the elevator to the third floor, walking into Mr. Fuller's office, and sitting with my head between my hands.

"We are all tested by the Spirit," my mentor said before

quoting the biblical book of Job: "Then Job answered the Lord and said, I know that you can do all things, and that no purpose of yours can be thwarted."

I struggled to focus as images of fire trucks in front of our soldering building, gaping holes in the roof, and boxes of blackened supplies replayed in my memory.

"George, Job had trouble, but his faith never faltered," Mr. Fuller continued. "My business isn't as busy as it used to be. There's a lot of space in the building, and I have excess capacity in the plant. If there is anything we have you can use, you are welcome to it."

"Huh?" I asked, slowly raising my head and returning my attention to the present.

Did I hear Mr. Fuller correctly?

"There is a lot of space for materials, and a lot of room in the production schedule," he continued. "You can bring in your people and use whatever you need."

"Do you mean use your plant?"

"Yes, George."

"My God, thank you, Mr. Fuller," I whispered, my voice cracking and barely able to speak.

I snapped out of deep shock and depression in that instant. My spirit lit up. God had solved my trauma within hours.

I'm going to make this lifeline work!

Every experience in my early life to that point prepared me to meet this challenge of rebuilding a business from scratch. The hard work it was going to require to do this all over again was in my blood.

I learned about hard work during the Great Depression in the 1930s. When I was four, an uncle who worked in one of

Chicago's slaughterhouses paid my cousin and me four cents a day. Our job was to run soap and water into the bathtub, stand in the tub with our bare feet, and stomp on the overalls he wore that day, to get the blood and the dirt out.

Two years later, Mama sat John and me down at the kitchen table. She had a job at Michael Reese Hospital, but we weren't much better off than the other impoverished families around us.

"I make just enough money to keep a roof over our heads and food on the table," she told us. "If you want to do fun things that some of the other kids do—if you want to buy candy, go to the movies—you'll have to make money to get them yourselves."

"You don't need to buy candy for us, Mama. We can get jobs," we told her. At about six and eight years old, John and I started a little hustle in our apartment building. We walked up and down the back stairs and dug into the garbage cans to pull out the newspaper, pull out the milk bottles, pull out the rags, pull out all the salvageable things we could find. We sold them to the junkman in the alley.

"I'll pay you a penny for four milk bottles," the junkman told us. "I can also give you a penny for every pound of paper you bring me."

We also collected cigarette packages, especially Lucky Strikes. The boxes had a tinfoil lining that kept the cigarettes fresh. You separated the tinfoil and created a ball that, weeks later, weighed a couple of pounds. Aluminum foil paid better than anything. We called our trash-picking "junking." Junking was my first business. Contributing financially to my mother meant the world to me.

Mama needed us to help at home. John and I rushed from school to make the beds, wash dishes, and sweep and mop the floors before she returned. I rubbed my knuckles raw on the tin scrub board while some of our friends were playing marbles. When I was eight, I could iron shirts almost as well as Mama could. John and I were never idle (Robert was too young to keep up).

The wealthy woman next door who owned the Rolls-Royce hired me to take a brush, a bucket of water, and some Big Ben soap and scrub her large kitchen floor on my knees for a quarter. I don't know how she got her money, but I could see it wasn't policy—the numbers—or prostitution.

When I was about nine, Aunt Bessie gave me a wooden shoeshine box and enough money to buy supplies. A friend and I walked to the Illinois Central train station at Twelfth and Michigan looking for work. We waited on the sidewalk and tried to catch people before they entered the station.

"Shoeshine for a nickel, mister," I shouted, trying my best to attract some customers. "I'll have your shoes looking as good as new!"

Around that time John began delivering a Randolph Hearst newspaper, the *Chicago Herald American*, published each weekday afternoon and on Sundays. It was a much better proposition than junking or shining shoes. I commenced what would become a pattern in our relationship. I got the same job as he had, right after him. I served about sixty *Herald American* customers during the week. On Saturdays, I hawked the Black-owned *Chicago Defender.*

Most of my *Herald American* customers were Black except in the Woodland Park and Groveland Park areas, near Lake Michigan, which were predominantly White. I also trudged up the stairs of the eighteen-story redbrick Ellis Building at the corner of Thirty-First and Ellis, dropping off papers as I climbed.

People depended upon the newspaper to find out about job openings, weekly grocery specials, department store sales, local politics, the society news, arts and entertainment, and more. I learned to be reliable no matter the weather. I didn't want to disappoint anyone. The snow started falling in November, and every time it snowed, even more piled up. You ended up with a snowpack four or five feet high at the curb on most streets. The wind was so strong I leaned into it to avoid being knocked down when I was carrying my papers. Even though I delivered through rain, sleet, snow, and hail, some people took advantage of little paperboys.

"I can't pay you; I don't have any money," they said when I came to collect.

"But I already delivered the paper to you."

"I'm sorry, kid, but I just don't have it."

"I have to pay the *Herald American!*" I argued.

"I told you I don't have any money!"

If the customers didn't pay, it wasn't the company that suffered the loss. I only got to keep what was left over after I paid the newspaper company. All too often that was nothing. Fortunately, the newspaper offered a lot of incentives and prizes, like dishes and candy. I gave these gifts to my mother. For every new subscriber I retained for two months, I received a check for seventy-five cents. I would write up lots of new customers and make my money when those checks came in. I put whatever earnings I had into Drexel National Bank.

Though it was difficult working while my friends were playing, I benefited greatly from being a paperboy. I had to learn the neighborhood, sell my services, remember customers' names and where they wanted their paper, deliver during Chicago's brutal winters, practice my math, and collect money and save it. These responsibilities helped organize my mind, teach perseverance, hone basic business skills, and deepen my work ethic. I even learned a bit about managing profit and loss, or P&L. I experienced a lot of L, but that turned out to be a great teacher. I developed confidence in my ability to earn money. For a young Black boy, $4 a week (about $85 today) was good money. I made enough to contribute meaningfully to our household. That meant everything to me.

My interactions also gave me the opportunity to see how when I did something nice for someone, they did something nice back. Even when I wasn't present, customers said good things about me to other people. That gave me a good reputation that helped me get new customers. I grew my route to about one hundred customers.

I also learned essential lessons about trusting my intuition. For instance, the Ellis Building was located on 31st Street, called the Bucket of Blood. Sometimes gang members stuck up the residents. At times, I experienced a sort of extrasensory perception that I was in danger. If I was heading downstairs, I might walk back up. If I was heading upstairs, I might head back down. At other points along my route my instincts occasionally cautioned me. I stepped into a doorway or vestibule or took other steps to feel comfortable until the sensation passed. This happened often enough that I learned to pay attention to the feeling. Everybody in that newspaper branch, including John, was robbed multiple times. I was never robbed. I learned to listen to my hunches and this instinctual part of myself.

After I stopped delivering papers, I got a job setting bowling pins at an alley on Wabash downtown. Whenever a hot record came on, the bowlers, who were all White, encouraged me to dance. I didn't know how to dance, but whenever

159

they egged me on, I started moving. They threw coins on the floor, and I picked up as many nickels, dimes, and quarters as they threw. If they wanted to throw their money around, I would gladly collect it.

When I was fourteen, John got a job pressing clothes at a dry cleaner's shop. I started working in the back, cleaning men's and women's hats. The benzene and other chemicals made me dizzy, but the job paid more than my paper route. I opened the back door for ventilation to avoid getting sick.

When I was sixteen, I escaped the dangerous dry cleaner's shop and started bussing tables at the College Inn at the Sherman Hotel, a large, swanky downtown establishment. The College Inn was the most famous nightclub and restaurant outside of New York City and the hottest spot in town. Its location on the hotel's lower level contributed to its cool. All the top entertainers performed there—Louis Armstrong, Tony Bennett, Tommy Dorsey, Billy Eckstine, Michelle Lee, Louis Jordan, Stan Kenton, Frank Sinatra, and others. They were broadcast live on radio stations all around the country. This was before television. The Inn's customers were White, and all the waiters were Black. I found myself surrounded by White patrons with money, who always showed up stylishly dressed. I'd already been paying attention to the ways of the well-dressed. I also walked around our neighborhood studying and being influenced by what the good livers were wearing. I wanted to fit in with their kids. I was exposed to the fashions of the affluent.

Bussing tables at the College Inn was brutal. I was only about five-six and maybe 130 pounds. That made me one of the youngest and smallest people working a job usually held by mature men. Each waiter served three or four tables, wearing blousy pants and turbans with a ten-inch feather, as though they were from Arabia. I changed the tablecloth, refreshed the silverware, and took dishes away, quickly and invisibly, for two waiters. The Inn's protocol required us to carry our tray on one hand at shoulder level. Physically, the job beat you to death. Sometimes the waiter would pile an unmerciful number of dirty dishes on my tray. Depending upon who I was working with, he might stack the dishes high on purpose. I carried my tray with my right hand, leaning far left for balance. Between that and carrying newspapers, I developed scoliosis, a curved spine.

I made around $100 per week bussing tables, more than $90,000 per year in today's dollars. This was an unheard-of amount for a Black person, particularly of my age. The performers gave waiters gratuities to deliver water backstage or to their dressing room. My eyes opened even wider to the types of experiences wealthy White people enjoyed. My mother's boyfriend rescued me from the Inn's brutal labor by getting me a job in the washroom at the Drake Hotel. I handed men white cotton towels to dry their hands. I brushed down their clothing and wiped their shoes to a shine. Every night the quarters, nickels, and dimes the Drake's patrons tipped me made the pockets of my white staff jacket sag. Come the end of the week I might have $100 or $150 in change.

The work ethic, resilience, and nimbleness I developed during my youth always carried me. Working hard was nothing new to me, and it would never get old.

I called Joan to tell her about Mr. Fuller's generous offer to use his manufacturing plant. Joan called Robert, and they got on the line with our employees. In the critical moments after the fire started, my executive assistant, Dorothy McConnor, had the presence of mind to gather all the receivables, books, and important records and lock them in the safe. We took the documents we needed to Fuller Products; others I took home for safekeeping.

Right away, I met with Mr. Fuller's plant manager, Kenneth Pennington, to find out what machines they had and the production schedule for the machinery I needed.

Next, I figured out when and how to slot our people in. I called all our employees to Fuller Products. They arrived grim and worried they might lose the job they loved, the best job many ever had.

After I told them the news, joy and relief spread across everyone's faces. I laid out the plan. Some employees joined me to pick through the burned-out building and figure out what equipment, packaging, and raw material we could salvage. All our boxes burned; the jars didn't burn but some had smoke damage. Thieves got into JPC's plant quickly. They cleaned out all the copper in the building, including the parts that operated the elevator. I caught a guy taking apart a big automatic filling machine to try to steal it.

I got on the phone with the people who supplied us glass jars, caps, raw materials, and machinery, and I asked for their help. People like Max Holzman, the salesman who had helped me start JPC by bringing me six dozen jars. I tracked down George Fineburg, a Jewish man who had been working with me since our early days. George had built the conveyors.

"We will do whatever you need to help you get back in business," they told me.

Then there was the matter of my brother, John, who I felt I needed more than ever. Every time I went to the Big Apple, I also worked on my side project of trying to persuade my big brother to come work for JPC. I wanted him to be the head of all of sales, but John and his wife, Naomi, were doing extremely well for themselves. John basically had his own business running the Brooklyn branch of Rose Meta.

"I need you!" I begged John. "Please come help me rebuild."

"Okay, George," he told me. "I need a little time to talk to Naomi and set her up to run our business here. But I'll figure it out."

Knowing John would be coming gave me a lot of additional confidence. He was an extremely capable leader.

For many weeks, my employees went overboard.

"Excuse me, when are you going to be through with that kettle? Whenever you're free, we want to get in there," I heard, as they interspersed themselves between Mr. Fuller's people and worked whenever we had packaging, raw materials, and line time. If a conveyor belt was full of Mr. Fuller's products, they wouldn't touch it. But the Fullerites left at five p.m. Our dedicated employees worked around the clock. Sometimes our people would show up at two in the morning.

Whether it took coming in at all hours, or waiting around until a line was vacant, or making do with whatever supplies we had, our personnel did whatever was necessary to keep Johnson Products in business. From our suppliers to our distributors, our customers, and our employees, many people went above and beyond to keep us on our feet. Everybody got busy and kept busy. JPC people kept Mr. Fuller's conveyor belts humming.

During this time, I stepped more deeply into my faith and spiritual support system. I took both my prayer life and communication with God to a higher level, asking for vision, provision, and encouragement. I read from the Bible intensely, jumping back and forth from the Old Testament to the New Testament. It was the source of my strength.

I leaned more deeply into simultaneity, and I attempted to turn my life into a living prayer. I worshipped God in every moment, which gave me an ongoing sense of connection to the Spirit.

I also tried to lean into Dr. Fosdick's idea that life consists not just of what your heredity and environment do to you but also of how you *respond* to what happens to you. If there was ever a time to act upon this premise, it was now. I started to feel the spiritual power to determine my response.

Mr. Fuller was always encouraging me, too.

"Don't give up, George," he told me. "The Lord is with you. Do whatever it takes to get your business back up and running. Seek and ye shall find; knock and the door will be open to you."

Reverend Faulkner stood in my corner, as well, reminding me that each challenge was preparing me for the next one I'd face.

"The struggle of climbing brings the growth," he heartened me.

I progressed through this catastrophe by using a stairstep approach. When I reached one level, I could see the next. When I stepped onto that level, I could see the upcoming one and in time move beyond it. As I accomplished one thing, God gave me the provision to take the subsequent action. If I followed the Lord, I didn't have to know all the steps. I just needed to know the step in front of me, and take it.

I remained grateful and upbeat. I worked my butt off for long hours, but somehow I didn't feel it. I knew I was being blessed, and I kept counting my blessings. I had the Spirit to guide me.

The Lord endowed us with favor in the midst of our trials. By their sheer will, our employees helped save the company. Day by day, I witnessed the goodwill JPC put into the world through the Golden Rule come back to us in ways I couldn't have ever imagined. I hadn't envisioned needing our employees to rescue JPC when I provided strong benefits and profit sharing to them. But in the middle of this crisis, I witnessed just how much their jobs at Johnson Products meant to them.

One of my biggest blessings was that Joan had my back. My wife's support during that period of crisis meant the world to me. At work and at home, Joan did anything and everything the situation required. I wasn't particularly attentive during those months. Many nights, I didn't get home until after the kids were asleep. Until we got JPC back on its feet, I just needed Joan and our housekeeper, Gloria, to handle things, and they did. On the nights I was able to get home early, seeing Joan and the children's bright smiles, hearing their laughter, and feeling their hugs gave me an enormous amount of strength.

JPC's products were number one in the hair relaxer and hair spray categories. Our biggest volume was sold through beauty salons. But if a beautician needed a relaxer or shampoo and the distributor was out of our product, she had a half dozen other products she could easily substitute. And if a manufacturer couldn't supply a retail store's demand for even a short period, they could lose shelf space they'd fought months to obtain. Our competitors expected to experience big benefits from the JPC fire.

To their chagrin, JPC began shipping merchandise within ten days—so quickly nobody in the haircare industry believed we had even burned down. We filled all our orders, and no out-of-stock situations developed anywhere. Our company experienced zero financial problems.

Johnson Products Company controlled 45 percent of the professional relaxer market, and the companies that had jumped out in front of us found themselves far behind. By the end of 1964, sales were strong and JPC crossed the $4 million sales mark, despite the fire.

In early 1965, Johnson Products moved into a temporary facility at 2700 South Chicago Avenue.

Around that same time, my brother John Edward Johnson came onboard as our vice president of sales. Before my big brother arrived, I was a jack-of-all-trades. Having spent twenty years in Mr. Fuller's system, John was much more experienced than I. He understood salespeople and how to encourage and inspire them. After twenty years spent heading a sales force in Brooklyn, I was excited to have John bring his finely tuned skills to lead and motivate JPC's sales team.

John was an extrovert and a charmer. He had a warm smile, a magnetic personality, and a way of meeting and extending himself to people. He made everyone feel at ease. From the managers in the office to the sales force, everyone was crazy about John. He was a straight shooter who liked to help people. He also had a great sense of humor. My brother spent a lot of time talking to our employees over coffee or lunch, whether or not they worked in sales.

"You've gotta be hungry," he told them. "You've gotta want it."

John stuck closely to Mr. Fuller's philosophy and read inspirational texts with his team. He galvanized our employees and increased their professionalism. His presence was a huge lift for me.

Initially, John commuted between New York and Chicago. Naomi stayed in Brooklyn, running the business they'd been building for more than two decades. For a while, he was both JPC's VP of sales and branch manager for Rose Meta. He worked in Chicago for three weeks, then returned to New York for a week to ten days. It didn't take long, though, until JPC consumed him. Naomi took over as Rose Meta's leader. John kept JPC's sales force motivated through all the changes and challenges. He excelled at structuring and organizing the department and all the related activities.

Now that John had my back, I was free to think about a permanent location for JPC.

I knew about a massive stretch of vacant land at Eighty-Fifth and Lafayette that the city of Chicago had been using as a dump. As I drove by to look at it carefully, I saw huge blocks of concrete and asphalt sidewalk and pavement piled nine feet high. I couldn't believe the mess. But the property was located along the Dan Ryan Expressway, the main thoroughfare between downtown Chicago and the South Side, which meant it would be easy for employees to get to work and for trucks to come in and out for shipping.

I discovered the owner was a man named Harold Green, the president of South Side Bank, where the loan officer had laughed in my face ten years earlier. The irony didn't escape me; nor did the opportunity. In mid-January 1965, I called Green and asked if he might be interested in selling two acres of property. We then met at his office to discuss it. I wanted the land, and I wanted it in a hurry. I knew I needed to be careful and decided not to dicker much. I definitely didn't want to lowball him.

"What do you want for it?" I asked.

"One hundred ten thousand," he answered, setting the

base for our negotiation at a little over $1 million in today's dollars.

"That seems a bit high," I responded. "The property is a mess. It has to be cleaned up."

"That's prime real estate!"

All of Black Chicago knew about the tragedy JPC had experienced. As I talked to Green, the thought crossed my mind that this was the perfect location for JPC to resurrect itself. I would build my plant there, where the Black community could witness our rise, and see evidence that something great was possible for people like us.

"Maybe so, but I'd have to excavate all that concrete," I told him. "I'll give you a hundred thousand"—roughly $950,000 today—"for two acres."

"George, you've got to be kidding," he answered. "The property's right on the Dan Ryan. Everyone will want it."

"Not in that state they won't."

We settled on $105,000, and I paid him cash.

"If you're smart, you'll use this money to excavate the rest of the property," I told him. "You're never going to sell it with all that crap piled on it."

I wasn't ready now, but I had a vision for that land, and I wanted it cleaned up on his dime, not mine.

Addressing the land I just purchased, I reached out to Louis Huebner and Jim Henneberg and asked for their help with designing the new facility. Within several weeks they returned with renderings of a permanent thirty-thousand-square-foot manufacturing facility, a beautiful, modern two-story brick building with lots of large glass windows and a dramatic front entrance. The facility would be a helluva lot bigger than we'd ever had, and would handle the growth I sensed was imminent. I took out a $250,000 mortgage—almost $2.4 million today.

Once JPC's new headquarters began going up, I walked the construction site many times. I overlooked all the stages—digging the foundation, erecting the I-beams, and raising the walls and the roof. People from the community were walking the site, too, wanting to know what was going on.

Less than two years after the fire had almost put us out of business, Johnson Products Company took a brief hiatus in production and relocated our equipment. In October 1966, we officially moved into our new facility at 8522 South Lafayette Avenue.

9

Independence

FOR MOST OF the twentieth century, people relied on local banks to provide loans to people in their neighborhood. A bank is important to the economic development of a community. But if mainstream banks won't write you loans, as the Black community experienced, it's darn near impossible to grow and prosper economically.

S. B. Fuller's story speaks to this well. There were several occasions in his career where a single business loan would have helped him achieve greater heights. One such instance occurred during the late 1950s or early 1960s, when the southern supremacist group the White Citizens Council (WCC) discovered that H-A Hair Arranger and Jean Nadal Cosmetics were produced by a company owned by a Black man. The WCC started a boycott of these brands, which accounted for more than 60 percent of Mr. Fuller's sales. Many drugstore chains throughout the South pulled the products off their shelves.

Even though Mr. Fuller owned the largest Black-owned manufacturing company in America, had been in business for more than thirty years, and the company was generating multi-million-dollar revenue, he couldn't obtain a loan from a bank. In 1961 my mentor came to me to ask me to lend him money. It was the first time Mr. Fuller had asked me for anything. Given all he had done for me, helping him was an easy decision. I loaned him $135,000, about $1.4 million today. This was an example of how Black businessmen relied on each other.

When I worked for him, Mr. Fuller preached to us many times that he aspired to build the Fuller Products Company into a $100 million business. Back in 1949, not long after I returned from New York to Chicago, he took a step toward that goal by buying Boyer International and moving into its six-story building at 2700 South Wabash Avenue. Taking over an operation that large was a bold and absolutely ground-breaking move.

Banks would not loan money to Black businesses to start a company, upgrade or improve it, or grow. Mr. Fuller did what Black business owners of that era did: he convinced other members of the Black elite—doctors, lawyers, ministers, electricians, grocers, other entrepreneurs, and so on—to lend him money. To compete for their investment, he had to outbid the interest those professionals might earn depositing their money at a commercial bank by paying them an inordinately high interest rate of 10 percent. As a result of this and additional disadvantages, he and other Black-owned businesses had higher operating costs than White-owned companies. Paying higher interest rates made the businesses' profit margins smaller, which in turn hampered their ability to improve their products or services and finance their own growth.

Many Black entrepreneurs joined the National Negro Business League, an organization Booker T. Washington started to support Black businesses and the community's economic development. Mr. Fuller founded and served as president of the Chicago Negro Chamber of Commerce, whose slogan was "For economic emancipation, trade with your own." The fact that White shop owners often treated Black people poorly encouraged shoppers to patronize Black businesses. Black entrepreneurs worked to help each other make it. They shared their experiences and advice with those who were less informed. This included business strategies or suggestions on how to negotiate, ideas about where to buy things less expensively, referrals to good suppliers—anything that might help someone out.

Later, in 1963, there was another predicament where S. B. Fuller could have used some financial resources. It started with my mentor becoming the first Black man inducted into the National Association of Manufacturers' Hall of Fame. I wasn't there, but I was told that during his speech he stated that Black people could raise their socio-economic level if they merely worked harder to get a good education and showed more initiative in business and industry. I don't know whether any of Mr. Fuller's comments were misquoted, misunderstood, or taken out of context. I do know he remained a Republican when the party was defending segregation, and many Black people were becoming Democrats. He was always helping Black people do better; however, I believe he kowtowed to the Republican theories of economics and didn't hold them at all responsible for Black Americans' condition. He was also not an MLK enthusiast. Some Black business owners weren't MLK supporters because segregation helped their business. In an integrated society, it's not always easy for Black businesses to compete with well-financed White companies.

White Republicans applauded Mr. Fuller. But many Black people, including Dr. King and Bill Berry, were upset.

"It is most unfortunate that a man who's risen to such heights financially could reveal himself so insensitive to the plight of the very people who have helped make his success possible," Dr. King responded.

Some people felt that Mr. Fuller was looking down on them because he was successful. I knew he was always trying to inspire. As shopping malls developed and retail shopping expanded, many elite and college-educated Blacks also became put off by Mr. Fuller's door-to-door selling methods. Some called it "peddling." A handful of civil rights activists began to boycott Mr. Fuller, and it hurt his bottom line.

Fuller was ambitious and would not be deterred. Eventually, he attempted to shift his business to brick-and-mortar retailing. He and John Sengstacke, the owner of the *Chicago Defender*, led a group of Black investors to purchase Chicago's South Center Department Store. This created the largest Black-owned department store in the United States, and the first to integrate its people and executive leadership.

Unfortunately, the overhead costs to operate this prime commercial property were high. The buildings were old and required a lot of capital investment. As this was happening, increasing numbers of Black people began patronizing White-owned businesses, as segregation and Jim Crow culture slowly loosened their stranglehold. By and large, White people did not patronize Black-owned businesses—and this pattern continues today. The tide of these massive historical shifts pushed against Mr. Fuller. Short on money to operate his business, he attempted to obtain a loan. He was unsuccessful.

These scenarios show that even prosperous Mr. Fuller struggled because of his decades-long inability to obtain a business loan. I was very busy running JPC, and I don't know what Mr. Fuller was experiencing during those days. But in an attempt to solve his businesses' financial problems, Mr. Fuller sold promissory notes to Fullerites, church members, church congregations, and other ordinary people. They cost about $20. Apparently, he didn't redeem the notes in the time frame he had promised. Nor had he told investors about the financial condition of the company. After Mr. Fuller failed to pay on time, legally the notes transformed into long-term obligations. By law, he was required to report this to the SEC. Mr. Fuller didn't do that.

I'm not sure whether Mr. Fuller intentionally didn't tell the SEC, didn't know the law, or perhaps grew desperate. In any case, he made mistakes. Whatever money he asked for, I gave him. Still, in 1968, Mr. Fuller went bankrupt.

The Securities and Exchange Commission came down hard on my mentor. They convicted him of fraud. Mr. Fuller was given five years of probation and five years to redeem the certificates. He was able to redeem many, but he didn't generate enough revenue to get them all off the market. Some people made him out to be a con man.

I knew Mr. Fuller wasn't trying to take advantage of people. He was just trying to fund his business when mainstream banks wouldn't lend him money they would have gladly offered if he were White. But after almost forty years in business, most of it empowering Black Chicagoans, that's how they knocked Mr. Fuller down.

In about 1973, Ernest Lafontant and I organized a testimonial banquet to honor Mr. Fuller. My mentor had fallen on hard times. His reputation was tarnished, he had not been honored in the way he deserved, and he was experiencing health problems. We invited people like grocer Rick McGuire, *Ebony* magazine publisher John H. Johnson, and other community leaders to serve on the organizing committee. Our goal was to raise money to give to Mr. Fuller to live comfortably.

Johnson Products Company employees helped promote the dinner, and many people showed up that evening. Mr. Fuller sat in front of a banner that read "S. B. Fuller: Pioneer in Black Entrepreneurship." People gave testimonials about the vital role he played in helping Black Chicagoans thrive. At the end of the evening, we presented Mr. Fuller a hefty check for $120,000, about $700,000 today. We also gave him a bronze bust of himself created by the sculptor Jimilu Mason. I personally gave him two thousand shares of JPC stock, which was selling for around $73 a share.

Both with my mentor and in the community, I cared and wanted to make a difference. For generations, the racism that is so much a part of the nation's private institutions and government policies made it nearly impossible for almost all Black Americans to establish any savings. The money Black people should have accumulated from their labor during slavery enriched White America instead. During Jim Crow, the nation solidified Black people's second-class citizenship and locked them out of most well-paying mainstream jobs. Racism in the financial services industry made it almost impossible for Black people to obtain loans to start, grow, or invest in their businesses.

Government policies like the New Deal and the GI Bill were structured to contribute to the explosion of White wealth but froze the overwhelming majority of Black people out. Most mainstream banks redlined Black communities and refused to write loans of any kind. Black people were unable to secure loans to improve their homes or to obtain mortgages or move to the suburbs. As a result, they didn't benefit from the postwar housing boom and rising property values. They were deprived of the home equity many of our White peers tapped to start their businesses, weather difficult years, or implement improvements. We were also denied the equal education we could have leveraged to advance in life. Nor could we take out loans against our houses to send our children to college. I wanted to change all of this by opening a bank.

In 1932 the Great Depression wiped out Jesse Binga's bank at Thirty-First and State Streets, the only Black-owned bank in Chicago. For more than thirty years, there hadn't been anybody with the combination of funds and guts necessary to open a financial institution sympathetic and fair to Black people's efforts to get a car loan, mortgage, small-business loan, home equity loan, college loan, and so on.

In 1963 the Federal Deposit Insurance Corporation (FDIC) shut down Chatham Bank, due to some illegal activity. Chatham Bank was in the center of the Black community, but the entire time I banked there, I don't remember seeing one Black employee. I was one of a number of people whose deposits totaled more than $10,000 and had to wait for years to receive my money after it officially closed. As the FDIC collected the outstanding loans, they paid off their depositors. Chatham's loss created an opportunity.

A Black man named Henry Hervey, the president of Illinois Federal Savings and Loan, invited me to meet him at a restaurant.

"Members of our community are upset that Chatham Bank has closed," he began. "A couple other businessmen and I are trying to start a new bank in the Chatham Bank building. We want to know if you want to be included."

"Who all is getting involved?" I asked.

Hervey ran down a list of some of the area's who's who: Alvin Boutte, a pharmacist who owned several drugstores; Cirilo McSween, a local civil rights leader who owned a chain of McDonald's restaurants and was the first Black agent hired by New York Life Insurance; Daryl Grisham, the president of Parker House Sausage; Bob Bacon, a White man who owned a newspaper clipping service business; Morrie Polk, a White man whose family owned Polk Brothers, a successful furniture store that did business in the Black community; Bob Martin, who owned a construction company; Henry Fort, a businessman; Phil Kunstadtler, a liberal White man; and Andy Swish, president of Metropolitan Mutual Burial Association.

"That's an impressive list," I told him. "Well, this opportunity to open a Black-owned bank really appeals to me. I've had my own problems trying to borrow money."

"I didn't know that about you," Hervey said.

"Yeah, it's true," I replied. "I'm also worried that, without a bank, the community will decline. Sign me on to your cause."

We called ourselves Independence Bank because that's what we were striving for, financial independence. Our vision was for the community to have access to services that banks offer, such as checking and savings accounts, personal and business loans, and the like. We discovered that another group had formed to start a bank, Seaway Bank, as well.

To open, I believe we had to raise $1 million for our operating capital. The FDIC gave us the green light once we raised about $750,000, about $7.3 million today. I became a major sponsor, with one-third ownership. I invested $250,000.

On December 5, 1964, Independence Bank held its grand opening. The bank was packed. We served the neighbors hors d'oeuvres while making friends with them, and talked about the role we wanted to play in the community. A lot of White bankers came from downtown, especially from Harris Bank, the correspondent bank that backed us. But the FDIC, which had taken over Chatham Bank, continued to occupy half the location. Because that reminded us of the previous bank's cloudy past, the FDIC's presence took away from our excitement.

I became both chairman of the bank and chairman of the executive committee. The executive committee also acted as the loan committee, which approved or denied loans the bank's president recommended.

Before long we discovered that our president, the White man Harris Bank provided us, didn't have enough experience to do the job well. He also had a paternalistic attitude toward Black folks. We looked to him to evaluate people's ability to repay their loans, especially car loans. He was supposed to tell people no on the spot if their credit wasn't good or make a recommendation to the Loan Committee. This was one of his most important responsibilities.

Early on, our committee relied upon the president's expertise to guide us. Before long it became clear that some people who were unqualified for a loan knew how to read him and tell a good story to get over on him. He couldn't discern whose story to believe, and he trusted too many people. As a result, our bank made a large number of loans to deadbeats, which we discovered after people started missing payments. We ended up with delinquent loans. His replacement, a White man from a different bank, came with his own set of racial assumptions. We had to replace him as well, and the White man after him.

All three of the senior managers our correspondent bank supplied us were White. During the 1950s and '60s, White banks weren't hiring Black people into executive positions, and the White people they provided us weren't racially competent. It made it tough to help the community reach the independence we had in mind. Their inadequate management took some air out of our sails.

In 1970 Alvin Boutte sold his three pharmacies, took over as president, and brought stability to Independence Bank. Our institution served Chatham with pride. We helped Black people make the types of investments in their lives and our community that others of similar means had long been able to make.

After nearly thirty years of success, Al Boutte and I decided to sell Independence Bank in 1997. We sold to South Shore Bank, a White-led financial institution. Morally, I had no problem about selling to South Shore. South Shore had more money invested in the Black community than both Seaway Bank, the Black bank that opened the same month as ours, and Independence Bank, combined.

At that point, Al retired, and I did, too. We were proud of the legacy of Independence Bank. We trained hundreds of employees in the banking business, including three employees who became presidents of other banks. The bank lent money to thousands of Black Chicagoans, enabling them to become more self-sufficient. We had loaned people funds to buy safe and reliable transportation, purchase homes to raise their families in, start and support their businesses, and provide for themselves in a dignified way, and we had helped grow and stabilize the community so people were able to send their kids to college.

10

Love, Peace, and Soul

DURING THE MID-1950S, Johnson Products began advertising. We started by hiring a small White-owned ad agency, Allen, Anderson, Niefeld, & Paley back before there were any Black-owned advertising firms. The firm created posters and streamers to place in barbershop windows. In 1956 Vince Cullers, formerly the art director for *Ebony* magazine, opened his own advertising agency and created our first advertisement—a photograph of a handsome man whose hair had been processed into a pompadour, holding an eight-ounce jar of Ultra Wave Hair Culture. Vince's agency also created a poster we began displaying in barbershop windows.

Until then, JPC had only served the professional market, selling directly to barbers or distributors who served barbers. But Ultra Wave Hair Culture's success in barbershops created plenty of retail demand. The retail market presented a huge opportunity, and I moved on it. I began advertising to consumers in *Ebony*. It was an example of Black-owned businesses supporting each other.

Sales of Ultra Wave soared. Later we used the same method, advertising Ultra Sheen in *Ebony* magazine, and got steady results. One of the first successful ads for Ultra Sheen Conditioner and Hair Dress featured a popular Black model, Agnes Morris. We ran ads in other publications, including *Tone* and *Beauty Trade*, the only periodical that targeted hairdressers.

But in the 1960s color television was on the rise, and I began to think about how I could get TV advertising to promote our brands. Compared to magazines, television was an expensive investment. Airtime was sold based on the viewing area a station covers. A station covered the geographic area its signal reached. You couldn't direct content to specific populations by choosing say, BET, Lifetime, or Univision. When you purchased time in a market, you bought the entire area. If I had been selling a general-market product, that would have made great sense for me. But I was interested in reaching Black consumers, who represented about 30 percent of Chicago's population.

Racial segregation overwhelmingly restricted my demographic to the south and west sides of Chicago. Networks hardly made any television shows about Black people or featuring them, but as the civil rights movement propelled society forward, we began experiencing breakthroughs. In 1965 Bill Cosby became the first Black actor to star in a lead role, in the detective show *I Spy*. When *Star Trek* premiered in 1966, Nichelle Nichols starred as Lieutenant Uhura. In 1968 two Black sitcoms hit the air, the *Bill Cosby Show* and *Julia*, starring Diahann Carroll, the first to feature an African American woman. There were other shows but not many.

The fact that there wasn't an easy way to reach our market made the prospect of advertising on television an expensive gamble. Throwing away a lot of viewers meant throwing away a lot of money. Still, I wanted to explore the possibility. I could see how valuable TV was becoming. It was clearly the best form of advertising, and its effectiveness during those early years was astounding. I wanted to figure out how to make it work for JPC.

I met with our account executives at our ad agency Allen, Anderson, Niefeld & Paley, our mainstream firm. The best place to showcase the Johnson Products Company's brand would be a TV variety show, something akin to the *Ed Sullivan Show* or the *Dean Martin Show*. I wanted to create a one-hour variety special, where there would be music, comedy sketches, other entertainment, and a prominent host. The show would run in syndicated markets. In the process I would learn whether it was possible to get enough reaction to our products with television.

We called our first attempt at television *& Beautiful*, based on the phrase "Black and beautiful." *& Beautiful* aired in 1969. It starred Redd Foxx, a native Chicagoan and popular stand-up comedian. Though he went on to star in the sitcom *Sanford and Son*, this was Redd's first time on TV. On *& Beautiful* he played the role of a father. Gospel singer and popular recording artist Della Reese played Foxx's wife. She was already quite familiar with television. In 1959 she had a hit song, "Don't You Know?" After that, she occasionally filled in for Johnny Carson on the *Tonight Show*. For fun, the seven-foot-one NBA basketball star Wilt Chamberlain played the role of Redd and Della's son.

We produced *& Beautiful* in Los Angeles at Metromedia Studios, on Sunset Boulevard. The show was funny, snappy, and culturally relevant. The chemistry between Redd, Della, and Wilt was wonderful. Our plan was to show it in eleven markets in addition to Chicago, including New York, Los Angeles, Detroit, Cleveland, Houston, St. Louis, Atlanta, Memphis, Baltimore, Washington, DC, and Miami. Creating the show cost me more than $300,000; that's $2.5 million today.

For *& Beautiful* to succeed financially, we needed our retailers and distributors to buy loads of JPC product, expand our shelf space, and display our posters and in-store promotions. That's where the second challenge came in. Traditionally, when a product was going to be promoted on television, stores created large displays at the end of the aisle, stacked boxes of product in the aisle in front of the section, expanded shelf space, and ordered additional inventory to replace what was sold. There was no risk to the buyers. If the product didn't sell, they could send it back. At least, this is what they did for mainstream companies.

Our salesmen traveled to distributor after distributor, from drugstore to drugstore, supermarket after supermarket. Their goal was to convince drugstores and distributors to order larger-than-normal inventories. The majority of the outlets we called on were in Black neighborhoods. We knew they would experience huge demand from people coming into their store wanting to buy our products after our show aired. We called on account after account, but most White retailers didn't buy into our idea. Many were unable to imagine a Black company producing a television program. They definitely struggled to envision it being a success. Well, either they didn't believe it, or they just didn't want to do it. There was no way to tell. Many of the people our salesmen called on sabotaged our efforts by refusing to order. We hardly got any end cap displays at all.

JPC made *& Beautiful* anyhow. The special generated a lot of excitement, and within a day or two customers had picked most retail shelves bare of our products. Our jars of Ultra Wave Hair Culture and Ultra Sheen moved through the cash register and right out the door.

It was bad enough that the stores hadn't ordered extra inventory. Adding insult to injury, they didn't hurry to reorder once their shelves were wiped out.

As usual, Johnson Products was ahead of the times. Yes, we were frustrated and lost a lot of potential sales, but I saw the possibilities. We came right back and tried again.

& Beautiful II featured blues guitarist B. B. King and aired in 25 markets. B.B. and his well-known guitar, Lucille, tore it up. His hit "The Thrill Is Gone" was out. Even watching him on TV was electrifying. B.B. could really hit a lick! On this second go-round, we were a little more effective in getting retailers to order inventory. But they still didn't have enough confidence in us and ordered short. Our customers wiped out the shelves yet again.

Even though I lost some money, taking these risks taught me a lot about the power of television. Among other things, I learned how it operates as a business, and its ability to reach the Black consumer market. The Spirit told me to trust, even after these two disappointing experiences.

The era brought forth other new and important media firsts for Black America.

Johnson Products Company had been advertising in *Ebony* magazine since the late 1950s. We started out with one page and built up to four pages over time. In those days,

Chrysler was *Ebony*'s biggest advertiser, buying a couple of pages a month. *Ebony*'s owner, John H. Johnson, who I knew and was unrelated to, owned Johnson Publishing Company. He was on Chrysler's board.

In 1968 in New York, Edward Lewis, Clarence O. Smith, Cecil Hollingsworth, and Jonathan Blount founded Essence Communications. They intended to publish a lifestyle magazine for Black women focused on beauty, culture, fashion, and entertainment. I thought *Essence* was a great idea and committed to placing ads in it.

The first issue of *Essence* came out in May 1970. As happens with many start-ups, the founders had trouble funding it. This is especially true with Black-owned businesses because it's so difficult to pull together enough start-up cash. Hollingsworth came to me seeking financial support. I thought *Essence* provided a big opportunity to extend JPC's reach. I took a risk and paid them cash in advance to advertise. I don't remember all the specifics. I prepaid either two or four pages for twenty-four months in advance. This amounted to somewhere between $50,000 and $100,000, which would be between $400,000 and $800,000 today.

The same year, New York entrepreneur Earl G. Graves Sr. founded *Black Enterprise* magazine. We advertised in it as well.

During the middle to late 1960s, politics were beginning to influence hairstyles, and the "natural" hairstyle began to take off. It went far beyond Dr. King telling people to be their authentic selves; the Black Is Beautiful and Black Power movements sprung to life. In Chicago, the African Commune of Bad Relevant Artists (AfriCOBRA) and the Black Power Arts Movement were empowering residents, creating a new visual aesthetic, and painting positive images of Black people on buildings. Local cultural icon Bill Walker brought South Side artists together to celebrate Black heroes on the "Wall of Respect" mural on 47th Street. People were singing along to the James Brown song, "Say It Loud — I'm Black and I'm Proud." Aretha Franklin's "Respect" was an anthem for women, but it clearly communicated Black people's cry that American society treat us fairly and equitably.

Leaders like Angela Davis, Kathleen Cleaver, and Huey P. Newton were wearing Afros. So was the youth musical group the Jackson Five. Lots of women, JPC's primary customers, grew large bushes, as they were often called. Many young people, in particular, spoke negatively about relaxers.

Financially, Ultra Sheen and Ultra Wave had been JPC's heroes, but the writing was on the wall. We were going to lose some of our relaxer business.

"We need to develop a product to address this new need," I told Dr. Martini. He immediately went to work.

Doc started working on a chemical formula to create an aerosol product that made natural hair easier to comb or run a pick through. We also wanted it to create a nice sheen. Once he came up with the right formulations, we hired a private-label vendor. That way, we could launch more quickly than if we tried to manufacture the new product ourselves.

Our Black advertising agent Vince Cullers came up with the name Afro Sheen, which he trademarked and gave to JPC. He also lent his brilliant creative vision to our new brand. "I want to present Black people in a more positive light than the stereotypical images of us in subservient roles," Cullers told me. "We've seen enough Aunt Jemima, the maid wearing a 'do rag, and Uncle Ben, the butler."

I agreed. Times had changed.

Dr. King was dead. The Vietnam War was still going on.

Far too many Black men were returning home missing their arms and legs, suffering from PTSD, addicted to drugs, and in caskets. Many young folks, in particular, had lost patience with the pace of the SCLC's Christian-based approach to racial justice that emphasized integration and nonviolence. The Black Panther Party for Self-Defense had become popular, particularly with young and lower-income Black folks. The Panthers were demanding freedom, full employment, decent housing, education, a stop to police brutality, and an immediate end to the Vietnam War.

In other words, nobody wanted to see images of subservient Black people from our past.

When he designed our packaging, Vince created groundbreaking black jars and containers. The type was both colorful and in a trendsetting lowercase font. A brown-skinned Black couple with big Afros gazed lovingly at each other from the carton. The man wore muttonchop sideburns that were stylish at that time.

In addition to the unprecedented packaging, Vince proposed print ads with images that conveyed Black pride. He showed me layouts depicting Black men and women interacting with each other, proudly wearing blowouts and dashikis, and living positive lives. One ad had a Black couple looking lovingly at each other. Another showcased a Black mother gazing adoringly at her child. Yet another told the world Black people were "watu wazuri," beautiful people.

"These are powerful, Vince, I love them!"

We began running these pioneering ads in *Ebony, Beauty Trade, Essence,* and *Black Enterprise* magazines. Young people all over the country fell in love with the phrase "watu wazuri." The ad went on to win mainstream advertising awards.

In addition to Afro Sheen Hair Spray, JPC extended the

line by changing the packaging of Ultra Sheen Conditioner and Hair Dress and labeling it Afro Sheen Conditioner and Hair Dress. We also created the Afro Sheen Blowout Kit, a light relaxer that loosened some of the kink and left hair with texture, without straightening it. I read the signs of the times, as well. I cut off my process and started wearing my hair natural, shifting from using Ultra Wave Hair Culture over to Afro Sheen Hair Spray.

Unfortunately, Vince Cullers wasn't always easy to deal with. In the early 1970s, Johnson Products transitioned to a new Black-owned advertising agency, Burrell McBain. Tom Burrell was the first African American to work for a Chicago ad agency. He started out in the mailroom, but even in that low-level job, he dressed like an executive. Over time, Burrell worked his way up the ladder.

Our account exec Tom Kuehn at the advertising agency Allen, Anderson, Niefeld & Paley, the firm that worked on *&* *Beautiful*, called me.

"There's this TV show I think you should know about," Tom announced. "My friend Don Cornelius is a disc jockey at WVON radio station. He's created a Black dance show that copies Dick Clark's *American Bandstand*. It airs after school five days a week. I think it could be a great vehicle for you to advertise Ultra Sheen."

"Sounds interesting," I told him. "What is a DJ from a radio station that Black entrepreneurs advertise on doing on television?"

"I think Don is onto something. I want you to come with me to the studios and watch it live."

Tom explained that Cornelius filmed once a week on Channel 26 WCIU, which was airing locally, in black and white, on the old UHF frequency. But the signal was weak and didn't cover the entire market. By 1966, almost three-quarters of network TV was broadcast in color, but only about one-third of American households owned a color TV.

Tom and I went to WCIU's studio in the Financial Exchange Building one Thursday to watch the taping of the show. I will never forget the first time I met Don Cornelius. I arrived wearing a suit and tie. He showed up wearing an enormous Afro, a long bright-red coat with a huge collar, and thigh-high brown leather boots.

"Tom, what in the world?" I whispered under my breath, barely able to hold back my amusement.

"I know, George, but I need you to trust me," he answered. "I think it's exactly what you need."

And, boy, was Tom right!

From its now-famous opening "*Soooooouuuul* Train" to all of Don's wonderful DJing sayings—like "You can bet your last money, it's gonna be a stone gas, honey!"—*Soul Train* was a really wonderful show.

I saw young people doing the latest dances, dressed in bright dashikis, elephant bell-bottoms, miniskirts, crop tops, platform shoes, and other fashionable and colorful clothing. Though many of the young women wore relaxed hair, lots of these boys and girls wore naturals. A few had blowouts.

In person, the show was interesting and visually exciting. Don's appearance and attitude were pitch perfect. The way he ended the show—"Love, peace, and *soooooul*"—captured the spirit of the times.

But after witnessing the show live, the black-and-white video didn't pop. Without color, the images failed to capture the excitement of the live show. It didn't sizzle. It didn't knock me off my feet. *& Beautiful* and *& Beautiful II* sizzled. I wanted *Soul Train* to have that type of pizzazz.

"I think we should film a thirty-minute pilot in color," I suggested after considering it.

I bankrolled a thirty-minute color pilot, using Don's same concept and starring him as the host. In color, the show retained a lot of the energy of the live show. It was wildly entertaining and had great potential.

The Spirit hit me. I decided JPC would sponsor the show.

Don Cornelius and I agreed to go into business together. Don didn't have any money, but the show was his idea, he wrote the script, and he hosted it. To me, it was fair to give him 50 percent ownership in our venture. From a traditional business standpoint, it was a generous arrangement. Living by the Golden Rule, I saw Don's creative genius, and I wanted to support him. We also agreed that JPC would run three minutes of advertising during each show. Don could sell the other three minutes for his income.

Tom, Don, and I flew out to Los Angeles and met with my friends at Metromedia Studio. We negotiated a deal that Metromedia would tape four shows once month on a Saturday, when the studio wasn't normally operating. The union employees were all White and earned overtime to produce the show. Each taping cost more than $100,000. It was a lot of money, but I was excited about the opportunity to make TV work for JPC.

I also tried to strike a deal with ABC, CBS, or NBC. All three major networks turned us down. I didn't let that stop us. Johnson Products purchased airtime on independent stations in nine markets with large Black populations. There was Detroit, Cleveland, St. Louis, Philadelphia, Atlanta, Houston, Oakland, and Los Angeles—in addition to Channel 26 in Chicago. Buying time in these markets was expensive, and it set the stage for *Soul Train* to become the first Black nationally syndicated television show.

In addition to all these activities, I set up a meeting with Berry Gordy, owner of Motown Records. Motown was really hot at that time. Diana Ross's "Reach Out I'll Be There," Marvin Gaye's "Mercy, Mercy Me," and the Temptations' "Just My Imagination" were heating up the radio airwaves and playing in every beauty parlor and barbershop.

We were scheduled to meet with Berry Gordy, but when we arrived in Motown's reception room, I was surprised that a White man greeted us and invited us into his own office. We told him what *Soul Train* was all about.

"I'm not sure Berry would be interested in this," he told us.

"We'd like to speak with Berry, if we can." In doing business, it's important to have direct access to your peers. It's part of how power is built.

Turns out Berry was in a game room, playing pool.

"We will be filming a new show, and we need some acts," I told the music-business mogul. "This could be an opportunity for some of your artists to get more national exposure."

"Have you done this before, Johnson?" Berry asked.

"Yes and no," I told him. "We haven't aired *Soul Train* nationally, but JPC produced *& Beautiful* and *& Beautiful II* and our audience really responded."

"I don't know, it seems like a big risk," he said. "You haven't proven this concept yet. If it doesn't work out, it would be bad for my acts."

The fact that *Soul Train* didn't have a track record made it risky for Motown's prized talent to appear on our show. I was disappointed but I understood.

I hired my own entertainment for the first episode. Wilson Pickett had one of the hottest orchestras and a long list of hits. There was "It's Too Late" and "Hey Jude" and "Sugar, Sugar" and "Call My Name, I'll Be There." That's not to mention "In the Midnight Hour." I flew the group from New York to Los Angeles, put them up in a hotel, and paid them to perform. Don was helpful, too. As a DJ, he was in contact with entertainers and knew a lot of people who made records.

In addition to securing the artists, we hired a producer. Pam Brown became our director of personnel. She located and selected a group of high school students who were good dancers to appear on the first four shows. Pam was no-nonsense, compassionate, and fair. She organized the young people and instilled discipline, insisting on both good manners and appropriate attire.

I will always remember October 2, 1971, the first time the *Soul Train* cartoon chugged across the tracks.

"Hi there and welcome aboard," Don opened, wearing a white three-piece suit with wide lapels and a light-blue tie. "You're right on time for a beautiful trip on the Soul Train. If the sight and sound of soul is your pleasure, then what's your treasure? You can bet your bottom dollar we've got 'em, baby. And after a message from the Johnson Products Company, three of the most beautiful and talented sisters you've ever seen in your life are going to look you dead in the eyes, where your beauty lies."

Our first commercial aired at the top of the hour.

Then Don returned with the Honey Cones.

"Wanted: Young man single and free!" they sang. Then the kids danced to a James Brown recording, with many of the young women wearing vests, miniskirts, and hot pants and the young men wearing wide-collar shirts with high-waisted, flared plaid pants.

Shortly afterward, the Temptations' Eddie Kendricks

193

performed "I Did It All for You" as a solo act, singing in his trademark falsetto.

Later, Gladys Knight and the Pips performed "Friendship Train."

From Don's opening to the singing to the dancing to our ads, *Soul Train* overflowed with affirming images and messages in a unique way that had never been seen on color television before. The music, hairstyles, clothing, dance, and musical performances were not curated to suit mainstream audiences. Our musical guests didn't need to wear their best suit and tie. There was no pressure to straighten their hair or wear a pompadour. *Soul Train* conveyed contemporary Black youth hair, music, clothing, and culture. It was rising up from our community and organically conveying positive imagery and messages.

After we finished recording, we held a party for the dancers. Their performances thrilled me. The taping was terrific!

In the weeks before the show ran on television, many retailers ignored our advice to increase their inventory of Afro Sheen and Ultra Sheen. After the show aired, our ads put pressure on the retailers who refused our advice. There was such a huge demand from shoppers that retailers not only had to order more product but also had to increase their inventory and give us more shelf space. After seeing the initial impact of *Soul Train* on our viewers and our business, I never doubted the show would succeed.

The first few times we taped, I flew to Los Angeles on a Friday, watched the taping on Saturday, and flew back on Sunday.

Episode by episode, *Soul Train* showcased more and more popular acts. On the second show, Charlie Wright & the

Watts 103rd Street Rhythm Band sang the popular hit "Express Yourself." During episode three, the Chairmen of the Board sang "Give Me Just a Little More Time." By the end of October, the Staple Singers were performing "Respect Yourself," later followed by Bill Withers performing "Ain't No Sunshine" and "Grandma's Hands" and Al Green singing "Let's Stay Together."

Soul Train took off from there.

Early on, Don relocated to Los Angeles. He wrote the scripts, produced the episodes, and sold his three minutes of advertising. With Don, Pam, and the Metromedia crew covering Los Angeles, there was no reason for me to fly out to watch. After the first few episodes, I stayed in Chicago to run JPC. There were products to produce, advertisements to create, markets to open, distribution to improve, and people who needed jobs and benefits.

We hired a TV syndicator to expand our reach into more television markets. We progressed one city at a time. Some stations called us, seeking to air *Soul Train*. As our viewership increased, Ultra Sheen and Afro Sheen became such big profit makers for retailers that we were able to obtain four-foot-wide Afro Sheen displays in the haircare sections of a great number of retailers.

After advertising on *Soul Train* for just three months, JPC ended 1971 at $12 million in sales (about $94 million today), up 20 percent over the previous year. Between *& Beautiful* and *Soul Train*, I had to invest about three-quarters of a million dollars, and that was just the beginning.

As time passed, the young people on *Soul Train* danced in all sorts of creative ways and got their limbs to move into positions many of us had never imagined. The Breakdown. The Crackerjack. The Exercise. The Mechanical Man. The dance names and their moves seemed crazy, outlandish, and sometimes even weird. I witnessed the dancers get more innovative with each episode and had a lot of fun watching them compete to outdo each other. Within just a few episodes, these young people created the *Soul Train* line, which soon became central to American culture.

The fashions were also a reason to tune in. With each episode, their outfits became more and more stylish. To me, it seemed these young people wanted to be seen, act in the movies, and become stars. Their ingenuity challenged that of professionals. *Soul Train* made excellent television.

I appreciated and agreed with Tom Burrell's philosophy, "Black people are not dark-skinned White people."

Now that I had a more sizable advertising budget, I wanted to give him the chance I thought he deserved to portray Black people in an authentic way. Tom took the opportunity and ran with it, creating the uplifting and culturally conscious television and print media ads our community was starved for.

Our Afro Sheen commercials blew our viewers away. The trailblazing television ads he created showed Black women and men participating in careers in which we were rarely represented. One enacted a Black woman running for political office, in the vein of Shirley Chisholm. Another portrayed a Black female physician. In still another, a Black woman artist welded her sculpture with a torch. One featured an author; another, a flight attendant; yet another, a figure skater. The list went on.

In many of the commercials, a Black male newspaper reporter approached the women to interview them. Another Black man posed as a genie seeing the future in his crystal ball.

One of my favorites featured a mahogany-skinned Queen of Sheba with a large blowout, wearing a bright orange gown and sitting on a throne.

"Now out of the mist of three thousand years emerges today's beautiful Black queen," a male voiceover actor narrated. "Naturally beautiful. Radiant. She is Black essence, and her beautiful natural hair is her crowning glory. Today's beautiful woman uses Afro Sheen."

The musical jingle at the end of the ad sang, "Beautiful people use Afro Sheen!"

Such positive media representations of Black people on television never existed until Tom Burrell created them.

JPC's print ads were a far cry from the images of Black servants many of us had grown up with. They resonated with African Americans more than the "Black/White people" still being portrayed in the advertising of many mainstream products. They also stood out from the gangster Blaxploitation images also common during the era.

Soul Train broke ground in promoting Black culture and Black pride. Our positive imagery took the show to the next level. Add Don's far-out outfits, poetic hosting, and the scramble board. The world had never seen anything like it! People were awestruck by the show. Turns out, large numbers of White young people tuned in, too. In many locations, *Soul Train*'s White audience was larger than the Black audience.

Eventually, *Soul Train* was airing in two hundred markets, making Johnson Products the first Black financial sponsor of a nationally syndicated television show. In 1973 Dick Clark created a knockoff called *Soul Unlimited*. It didn't last long. Rumor has it that Black music's "godfather," Clarence Avant, along with Reverend Jackson and several other Black political leaders, threatened to boycott ABC because of Clark's imitation. In 1974 the songwriters Kenny Gamble and Leon Huff wrote and produced *Soul Train's* theme song "TSOP (The Sound of Philadelphia)," which topped the Billboard Hot 100 charts, sung by their house band, MFSB.

JPC's sales soared. By the end of 1972, we employed almost 260 people and had sales of over $18 million. The company was growing quickly, and we built a hundred-thousand-square foot warehouse, shipping facility, offices, and a research center. Johnson Products had reached a point where we didn't have to borrow a penny.

Almost a decade later, the three minutes of ads on every episode of *Soul Train* that skyrocketed Johnson Products to the top of the industry no longer produced the same sales growth. I had succeeded in my goal of making television work for JPC. But the time had come to make a difficult decision. We needed to let *Soul Train* go.

In 1980 I gave Don Cornelius JPC's half of the show. I didn't want Don to pay me a dime in exchange for my share. All I asked was that he set one minute of every show aside for JPC ads for the next ten years, without receiving any compensation. Plus, Don had a real vested interest in the show. He was the MC and the show's creator. I thought he should have an opportunity to own *Soul Train* outright and make it his own.

From then on, *Soul Train* was Don's show alone.

What *Soul Train* had done for JPC made my generosity well worth it. By coming together, we had grown both our businesses.

11

Going Public and Making
   History

IN THE LATE 1960s JPC showed up on the radar of some investment bankers. It was generating an exceptional amount of revenue. Profits were piling up in the company's bank account. JPC had about $2.5 million cash in the bank, about $21 million today.

"You've built quite a nice company," they told me. "You could be making a lot more money and raising money for Johnson Products to grow. You should think about taking it public."

By going public, they meant taking the company that was privately owned by me and the Johnson family and selling shares to investors. No Black-owned business had ever been traded publicly. I knew that going public meant JPC needed to answer to others about how we were running our company.

199

I wasn't exactly aware of how everything worked, but I was open to the idea.

One of these bankers, John Schriver, was a vice president at Hornblower & Weeks, a prestigious investment banking and brokerage firm. He started schooling us about what would need to happen to go public.

I hadn't paid myself a salary since I founded JPC. I'd been taking out whatever money I needed to pay my mortgage, get groceries, buy clothes for the kids, a new car, a house, or whatever. One reason I wasn't taking a salary was because my personal tax rate was extremely high. The federal personal income tax rate was somewhere between 62 and 70 percent, much more than today, primarily because the government was still paying down the debt from World War II. Paying that much in taxes didn't make sense to me.

The investment bankers told me that by going public I could reduce my taxes to 28 percent, a rate I could deal with. The more I learned, the more I was willing to take the risk. Going public offered a good way to monetize myself. It would give me financial security for the first time in my life.

We had to meet a number of qualifications, which would take about a year. For one, JPC needed to create a board of directors to set policies, oversee our operations, and represent shareholders. The Securities and Exchange Commission (SEC) required us to upgrade our accounting systems and publicly certify our tax statements.

Joan's basic accounting and bookkeeping skills were integral to getting JPC up and running. But the requirements had become a lot more complex over time. She didn't have the financial background to handle a $10.2 million company. We had been using the outside accountants Horowitz & Horowitz for help. Hornblower preferred that we switch from

Horowitz to a larger firm. We chose Arthur Andersen, which was both number one in Chicago and among the most pre-eminent accounting firms in the nation.

Ernest Lafontant recommended Norman Lebowski, a CPA and attorney, to assume the chief financial officer role. The accounting department would report to him.

"George, we have to close the books on time, but Joan is in there talking," Norm complained. Joan was notorious for closing the books late.

"Yeah, I know . . ." Joan was a talker.

"You've got to say something to her."

Little did he know how many times I already had. I needed to find a way to get my wife out of there with both our relationship and her dignity intact.

It was one of my most difficult decisions, but I had to speak to Joan.

"We have new requirements as a public company, and Arthur Andersen is watching us," I told her. "I am being required to replace you with a CPA."

I felt terribly because I knew how much Joan loved JPC, but I had to insist. I could not compromise the company. Eric and John were college age, but Petey and Joanie were just eight and six. Joan finally agreed to go home, but we kept her office, and from time to time she would come in.

Arthur Andersen advised me that once we were public, I would need a reason that I allowed $2.5 million to pile up in JPC's bank account. The Internal Revenue Service could require JPC to answer for what we planned to do with the money. It could include things like buying new machinery or building an extension onto our building. Either that or they could force us to pay dividends to me. I definitely didn't want any of JPC's hard-won profit taxed at 62 percent. And I didn't want to be paid those dividends, because I didn't need the money.

We talked about how a publicly owned version of JPC might be structured. We also discussed how much of the company to offer the public. Fifteen percent felt right to me. Because they saw the opportunity to make more money, the investment bankers wanted me to go beyond that percentage.

Hornblower also advised me to end JPC's profit-sharing plan.

"Investors won't tolerate giving away fifteen percent of the profits before taxes," the adviser told me. In this forthcoming reality of being a publicly traded company, our profit-sharing program would be viewed as taking away from investors' profits. I wanted to share JPC's profits with our employees, the people who were building the company. My philosophy hadn't changed. My employees—not investors—deserved the money.

I reflected upon how several years ago, I'd chosen business over the ministry. If ever there was a time to lean into my calling and the vision Dr. Faulkner described, it was now.

A good man with money can do a lot of good.

"If I can't give my employees fifteen percent as profit sharing, I will not go public," I told the Hornblower folks. The investors would be overwhelmingly White. Discontinuing the profit share would basically be taking away money from my majority Black workforce.

"You must be kidding—"

"No, I'm not."

"Come on, George, that isn't reasonable."

"I'm not worried about what's reasonable, I'm worried about what's right," I insisted. "If I were standing in my employees' shoes, that's what I'd want the president of my company to do."

"Well, if investors agree to a profit-sharing plan, they certainly won't tolerate one with benefits almost as strong as Sears's."

"They're going to have to," I replied.

"George, you don't understand. Sears has way more employees than you do."

"If Johnson Products Company is to go public, investors are going to have to swallow that," I insisted. "I'm not going to stop our profit sharing. That's a deal-breaker for me. It's a nonstarter."

They looked at me incredulously.

I valued my employees' loyalty and had provided them with an above-average livelihood. There was no way I would back down on my commitment to them.

Though Black people and White people lived in the same country, we inhabited entirely different worlds. While I was engaged in this debate with them, Dr. King and other activists were marching in the streets, leading protests to end segregation in jobs, housing, and education. One-fifth of the Windy City's Black residents were living in poverty. The Black unemployment rate was twice that of White people. In Chicago, Black males earned less than two-thirds of what White males did. Only 5 percent of Black folks were able to obtain either a white-collar job or a skilled position as a craftsman or machine operator. By contrast, more than half of White people held these types of high-paying jobs. A quarter of Black Chicagoans didn't have a decent home to raise their children and lay their head. Six percent of White Chicagoans had this problem. (Down south, many Black folks' plight was significantly worse.) I wanted to make a difference.

Before coming to work at JPC, many of our people may have worked in dirty or unsanitary places, as domestics, laborers, and factory workers, sometimes in dangerous factories, and for inconsistent or unreliable pay. The only skilled labor category where Black men were well represented was brutally hot and backbreaking factory foundry work. Some lived in tenements with broken windows, leaky ceilings, missing floorboards, and mice or rats. There were people in Black Chicago who didn't have food, or shoes, but aspired to have a good job and to further their education.

JPC's generous salary and benefits offered financial stability many never had before. Many of our employees were obtaining their first decent apartment, or a car that spared them standing in the wind, rain, and snow waiting for the bus. Others were buying their first home, giving their children a quiet place to lay their head, as Joan and I had. Some who hadn't completed or even gone to high school, or had dropped out like I had, were sending their children to college.

The folks at Hornblower didn't understand the way JPC transformed our employees' lives.

"You're not making any sense," they told me.

"What don't you understand?"

"You can make a lot of money here."

"I don't know how many ways I can say this. I don't mind making money, I just don't want all of it to come to me."

"What do you mean, you don't want the money?!"

"If I own 85 percent of the company, that means I'll make the lion's share of the money."

"Yes, that's the point."

"No, it's not the point," I insisted. "I have enough money. I don't need it!"

I did not believe in hoarding money and stacking it up

just for myself. My aspiration was to share money, to circulate it throughout Black Chicago and the nation, beauty salon by beauty salon, barbershop by barbershop. I wanted the entire community to benefit. My goal was to uplift the race as much as one man could. JPC wasn't only about me living well, it was about as many as possible living well.

Another thing that made me stand my ground was Dr. King being assassinated. People's grief manifested in different forms. On the South Side and in other communities around the nation, some Black people expressed their anguish, hopelessness, and rage by rioting. From Chicago, to Los Angeles, to Detroit, to Newark, to Baltimore and Washington, to Kansas City, and many places in between, some people burned businesses, ransacked communities, and caused a lot of destruction. On the West Side of Chicago, including in the Lawndale area where Dr. King and his family lived, both Black and White businesses got hit hard. People smashed windows, blocked streets, destroyed property, and there were too many fires to count.

I shared the heartbreak of our despondent community, but some folks set fire to complete neighborhoods. Yet I didn't fear that we'd be burned out.

The National Guard was called in to help create order and tear-gassed many protesters. For several days Mayor Daley set curfews, prohibited the sale of alcohol, and gave police the authority to shoot to kill. By April 7 in Chicago, eleven people were dead, more than five hundred were injured, and three thousand had been arrested.

Over in Detroit, my distributor Melvin Jefferson got caught up in the uprising. Melvin had become one of my best friends. His company, Superior Beauty Supply, carried all types of products, but he always promoted JPC and took pride in it. Melvin was light-skinned and his hair was straight. He'd been a captain in the army, and though his rank gave him the privilege of attending the segregated officer's club, and his White friends wanted him to pass, Melvin declined. In Detroit, somebody mistook him for White and burned down his store, and Melvin was out of business quickly. To help him get back on his feet, we shipped him everything he needed from JPC and didn't send him an invoice.

I imagine certain Hornblower employees cared about some of the same causes I did. But I didn't expect wealthy White investment bankers to understand what Dr. King or the civil rights movement meant to an oppressed community, or to me, a Black man who'd escaped the Cotton South.

After far too much debate about how I should run my own company, the investment brokers at Hornblower changed their minds. When a company goes public, the SEC requires a document called a prospectus to describe the investment to potential investors. We decided that we'd include in JPC's prospectus that management would contribute 15 percent of profits before taxes to the profit-sharing plan. That way investors would know what they were getting into. People could buy our stock if they liked that idea, or not buy our stock if they didn't like it.

Under normal conditions, because I was only offering 15 percent of our stock, the remaining 85 percent of the dividends would be paid to me. I added on the stipulation that one-third of my shares be non-dividend-bearing. On those shares I would not receive any profits. If for instance, the dividend we paid investors was five cents per share, I would receive dividends on only two-thirds of my shares. I could convert the non-dividend-bearing shares back to normal shares anytime I wanted. But I didn't need all the money, and I didn't want it.

Hornblower established my salary at a flat $200,000, about $1.5 million today. They could have set a much higher number, or a compensation plan that included stock options, bonuses, or other financial incentives. It was typical of what company presidents were offered, but it wasn't right for me.

In the weeks before we went public, John, Jim Middlebrooks, Norman Lebowski, and I went to New York. Hornblower arranged several dog-and-pony shows where I presented Johnson Products Company to Wall Street at Hornblower's New York offices. I gave a speech followed by a question-and-answer session about the company, our products, and our markets. I repeated my presentation in front of various investment bankers. We also presented in Detroit, Philadelphia, and Chicago. JPC was positively received almost everywhere, and once we went public, many bankers put their clients in our stock.

On December 10, 1969, Johnson Products Company became the first Black-owned company to be publicly traded in the United States. Right away, news of our accomplishment hit the media. We were the talk of the town, especially in the *Chicago Defender*, on Black radio, and in other Black media. We also hit the pages of the mainstream papers like the *Chicago Tribune*.

The day we went public, we opened at $19, and if my memory is correct, we closed at $22. In a single day, we had raised more than $7 million, about $55 million today.

We used some of the revenue to extended the plant by an additional fifty thousand square feet, for a total of eighty thousand. This expansion allowed us to hire more people. We ended 1969 with sales of $10.2 million; that's $86 million today. JPC was fifteen years old.

Nobody knew how much financial progress the company had made over the years. Once we went public, everything was exposed. Essentially, it meant taking our clothes off in public, in our personal life as well as professionally.

In January 1971, John, Ernest Lafontant, Dorothy McConnor, Norm Lebowski, Jimmy Middlebrooks, and several other JPC executives flew to New York when Johnson Products became the first Black-owned company to trade on a US stock exchange, the American Stock Exchange. Though all of us dressed up in suits on that historic day, Joan stood out in a collarless dress suit with a bold geometric print, lace-up boots, and a crocodile purse. Dressed to the nines, as always.

"Black Capitalist: Listing of His Concern on Amex Marks a 'First'" read a headline in the *New York Times* financial section. The writer, Marilyn Bender, went on to say, "Its president and majority stockholder, George E. Johnson, appeared to be a bona fide example of that rarest of species that only the Nixon Administration assures exists—a Black capitalist." I didn't appreciate Ms. Bender referring to me by the word "species," as though I'm an animal. Later in the article she quoted me as saying, "Black capitalism, that's a myth. It doesn't exist though it needs to be created." I had gone on to discuss how, early on, I'd been unable to get financing. Black capitalism may have existed for someone else, but it didn't exist for me. To be a capitalist you need access to capital. I didn't know any Black person with access to that resource. The *Times* always referred to me as a "Black businessman," never simply a businessman.

The Dow Jones news service reported on me as well. "Johnson Products Expects Higher Fiscal Year Sales and Earnings," the headline said.

The souvenir AmEx ticker tape from that day read:

AMEX.WELCOMES.JOHNSON.PRODUCTS.CO.INC.
331/2..2000s331/2..B 333/8.

At that moment, apparently someone was executing a buy order for two thousand shares at $33 ½ per share.

The dynamics change when investors own stock in your company. The investors get to ask questions, and you're there to answer them. They can't tell you what to do, but they help make sure that the business is moving in the right direction, performing financially, and that their investment is secure. JPC's board of directors now consisted of seven people: my brother John; John Schriver; our distributor, Melvin Jefferson; Dorothy McConnor; Alvin Boutte; Jesse Howell, whose wife owned Debbie's Beauty School; and me. After Johnson Products went public, I had to raise my game at work. We were no longer running a family-owned business, I was leading a company that was required to operate in the public's interest. This was a world I didn't completely understand.

"We need to move the company forward faster," our new board member John Schriver told me. Right away, Schriver made it clear he didn't have confidence in JPC's marketing team—meaning my brother John and me—because he believed we weren't professionally trained.

"Fifteen percent annual growth is not good enough," he told us. "We need to find a successful, experienced marketing man."

Though I'd created the company from scratch and had grown it to the point it had attracted attention from investors, apparently I was no longer good enough. I hadn't felt insecure before going public. But now, surrounded by Hornblower and some other "experts," I started to feel inadequate.

John Schriver was supposed to be on my board to help me, but doubt started to work on my spirit.

What if they're right, and I'm not good enough?

I sensed a subtle current of criticism creep in as I sat in meetings answering to people who believed in our company but lived outside the Black community. These people had no real understanding of our people or our market.

From time to time, I began to question myself. I didn't dwell on it much, but sometimes, in rooms like this, I felt insecure in not having finished high school.

I dropped out of high school in the eleventh grade. What do I know compared to what they know?

And at times, against my better judgment, I permitted others to make decisions.

Through Schriver, I allowed Hornblower to bully me into hiring a White marketing guy, John Moran, whom they recommended. John was experienced in the retail grocery store business. On day one, the New Yorker strode in with a confidence I'd never imagined anyone could possess. A part of me looked forward to the improvements my business partners promised he'd bring. Another part of me had serious doubts.

One of the first steps Moran made was to redirect our total sales volume. He took more than $10 million away from our sales force and put it into the hands of brokers in the grocery industry and other categories that did not represent our business closely.

"These guys have relationships with bigger distributors than we do," he told us. He promised the new brokers would sell our products to companies that had never participated in our category.

"Our sales guys have been building relationships for the past fifteen years," I argued, my body temperature rising. "We can't get rid of them just like that!"

"We need to become more efficient," he responded. "If

it's important to you, we can keep a couple of the salesmen to monitor the brokers."

I didn't think this guy knew what the hell he was doing. I demanded we keep as many of my salespeople as possible. But Moran impulsively fired twenty-one salesmen and women. Not only had these professionals been the backbone of JPC's sales force, they also depended upon JPC for their livings.

I received calls and letters from former members of my staff, confused as to why they'd been laid off. Now here I was, the believer in the Golden Rule, having to conform to the requirements of being a public company.

"We have to operate differently," I told them. "Our financial adviser insisted we make changes, and we're trying to comply."

Some felt betrayed and as though they'd received a dirty deal. This was especially true because the White retail grocery-chain brokers who Moran replaced them with knew nothing about our beauty market, distributors, and retailers. Because these brokers were powerful in the general market, Moran assumed he could translate that to the benefit of JPC.

Adding insult to injury, he awarded the brokers both the business and the commission that came with it without requiring them to increase our volume. They experienced a financial windfall for products that had been selling on their own. What did JPC get for this? Nothing. The brokers were as incompetent as I'd suspected.

Moran's hires did not increase our sales or distribution sufficiently.

For the first time in fifteen years, Johnson Products Company did not grow.

After several months, I fired John Moran. My brother and

I returned to collaborating. John rehired the sales force. I worked with our ad agencies, trusting in ourselves, and went back to operating JPC the way that made us successful.

Those seven months had a serious impact on our growth, and I had to work to repair long-standing relationships with people that this "trained New York marketing man" had broken.

Our first public offering was very successful, and the investment bankers made money. They started advising me that we didn't have enough stock in the market. They said we should make a second public offering of another 15 percent of the company. To hear them tell it, the lack of available shares made the stock price more likely to fluctuate. The securities business is about making money, and the investment bankers had made a lot and wanted to make more. I understood the benefits, but I wasn't willing to release more than an additional 15 percent.

At this point, the average CEO would have taken this opportunity to increase their compensation significantly. I had more than enough to live on quite comfortably. It was not about the money, I was working with my heart. I kept my salary at $200,000. Our department heads earned between $150,000 and $175,000 per year.

In January 1972, Johnson Products made our second public offering of that additional 15 percent of the company. We opened at $35 per share and at the end of the day closed higher. The price doubled to $70 per share within the next six months. A total of 30 percent of JPC could be owned by shareholders. Joan, my children, and I owned the other 70 percent. The Johnson family maintained absolute control.

12

A Company with a Conscience

WHEN I WAS fundraising for Chicago's Urban League, I ran into my old nemesis, Orville Nelson. Since Orville and the Lord had, in effect, put me into business, I had forgiven him long ago. Unforgiveness is self-destructive. Now Orville's business was struggling, and he tried to get in my good graces by volunteering to help me organize the Urban League's first Golden Fellowship dinner dance fundraiser. JPC's employees sold 60 percent of the tables.

Many people would not have welcomed Orville, but I believe when you truly forgive someone, you also clear your spirit of whatever they did to you. I'd resolved to run Johnson Products by the Golden Rule, so I didn't turn Orville away. I would want to be given a second chance. And forgiving others leaves space in your heart for other gifts.

I had been involved with the Urban League since 1957, when Edward C. Berry, the Chicago Urban League's new executive director, made an appointment to meet me. From a distance, I already admired this elegant man, who went by the nickname Bill. He had been making waves denouncing segregation in housing, which Chicago's mayor, Richard J. Daley, supported. Given the Urban League's mission of furthering economic empowerment, educational opportunities, and civil rights for Black Americans, I didn't think twice about joining the organization. In 1968, I became the president of the board.

After having been in the role for some time, Bill retired. I hired him as my special assistant. As the demands on me grew, Bill became JPC's face in the community. He also became my speechwriter as I was increasingly invited to speak at public engagements.

I knew of the Scripture in Luke 12:48: "To whom much is given, much will be required."

I thought one of the best possible uses of my newfound wealth was to help talented young people obtain a college education. I invested $1.5 million (roughly $10 million today) to start the George E. Johnson Educational Fund, which would provide scholarships to capable and deserving Black children from low-income families. Many Black teens were being admitted to college but couldn't attend because they couldn't afford the tuition. Some were A or B students going to a subpar public school. More than you might imagine, these young students were determined to pursue their education despite their disadvantages. I was just as determined to help them.

Bill Berry was in charge of the educational fund. A great woman named Clotee Betts ran the daily operations. Clotee went by the nickname Mike. Mike had gone to an HBCU (historically Black college or university) and been a longtime counselor and leader in Chicago's public schools. She, Loisteen Walker, and another community leader, Silas Parnell, collaborated to help Black kids get to college. Mike helped the students and families to prepare their applications and follow the process of applying. Our scholarship closed the gap between the financial aid and the total tuition, which was about $1,200 per year for a public four-year college. Recipients received roughly a $1,000 annual grant (that would be $6,500 today). We also provided two round-trip plane tickets so students could get back and forth to school and come home for the Christmas holiday break.

The students attended a wide variety of institutions. Some went to Howard, Xavier, and other HBCUs. A few went to Babson College, where my son Eric had gone. Over its life, the George E. Johnson Educational Fund helped pay for the schooling of almost one thousand deserving low-income Black and Brown young people. We focused on getting them advanced training in science, business administration, math, engineering, and technology.

In addition to that, I established the George E. Johnson Foundation to support local and national charitable organizations, like the Chicago Urban League, the Community Fund, the NAACP, the United Negro College Fund (now UNCF), Operation PUSH, and many others. For more than fifteen years, this foundation made financial contributions to Chicago's civic and cultural organizations. We rarely turned down any worthy nonprofit.

I also wanted to encourage more Black people to become

entrepreneurs. Even with some mainstream employers beginning to offer more opportunities, the vast majority of our
people were still stuck in the lowest-grade and lowest-paying
jobs. After centuries of financial exploitation of Black laborers, getting better wages alone wouldn't help our people
catch up economically. We also needed the profits that running a business generates, the type of profits God was blessing me with, giving me the opportunity to reinvest in the
community.

We joined Junior Achievement, which became a hit
among our employees. They worked with Junior Achievement staff and were generous mentors to aspiring young
entrepreneurs. For more than ten years, JPC sponsored
twenty-eight Junior Achievement companies in one of our
facilities.

I was the first Black person invited to join the board of the
Lyric Opera Company of Chicago Ravinia, a prestigious nonprofit and indoor/outdoor performing arts center in Highland Park, Illinois. Even today, Ravinia hosts America's oldest
music festival, summer concerts in a bandshell on the verdant
grounds, and performers in genres from opera to classical to
jazz to pop. JPC funded many cultural institutions.

JPC became known as "the company with a conscience."
Our employees were elated about and proud of our company's philanthropy. I was clearly living the concept that
when you cast your bread upon the water, it comes back
manyfold. When you help other people, you help yourself
more; you don't need to be stingy. When you receive a blessing, you pass the blessing.

Around this time, Dr. Faulkner retired from Park Manor
United Church of Christ with a meager retirement income. I
felt indebted to this great man and wanted to help him. JPC's

people could benefit from his counsel as much as I had. I put Reverend Faulkner on our payroll as the company chaplain. Once a month, he wrote a mini sermon we distributed to each employee to inspire them to demonstrate excellence at work and to encourage them in their personal life.

In 1972, I was on my way from Glencoe to the office, listening to the radio show aired by Reverend Jackson's People United to Save Humanity (PUSH) organization every Saturday morning, when I heard a booming baritone voice singing a song I'd never heard. The melody and lyrics were so compelling that I redirected my trip to PUSH's headquarters.

"I have to meet whoever sang that song," I told Reverend Jackson.

"That means you have to meet the wonderful Wintley Phipps," he told me, introducing me to a handsome chestnut-colored young man.

"That song was so wonderful I turned my car around and came over here," I said, shaking the man's hand. "I had to know who you were."

"Thank you, sir," the young, polite man replied in a slight accent, smiling and looking shy.

"Where are you from, son?"

"Well, I grew up in Montreal, Canada, but I was born in Trinidad and Tobago."

During our conversation, I learned that Wintley was twenty-two years old, newly married, and a graduate of Oakwood University, a historically Black Seventh-Day Adventist school in Huntsville, Alabama.

"Well, I've gotta tell you, your voice is just fantastic," I said. "I'd like to help you get it out into the world."

The young man looked both pleased and puzzled.

"I want to take you under my wing," I said to him.

He looked to Reverend Jackson for guidance.

"Do you know who you're talking to?" Reverend Jackson asked him.

"No sir," Wintley answered.

"Mr. Johnson owns the Johnson Products Company, the largest Black-owned haircare company in the world," Reverend Jackson bragged. "There's no better person to look after you."

"Praise the Lord," the young man said, his face lit up like the sun.

I put Wintley on JPC's payroll, rented him a car, and helped him get started for many years.

A few years later, I was contacted by the Robert Schuller Ministries and was surprised to learn that the same Dr. Schuller I was watching Sunday mornings on the *Hour of Power* wanted to have dinner with me. By this point, the *Hour of Power* was probably the number-one television ministry. Dr. Schuller was highly regarded. In addition to his large California congregation, he had a large television ministry in the United States and internationally.

Over a long dinner in Chicago, Dr. Schuller told me about the vision for his ministry and invited me to be on the board of directors. I knew he was extending the invitation because I was prominent and Black, but I agreed. On his board I met a number of heavy hitters, including people like Richard M. DeVos, one of Amway's founders, and Shirley Hufstedler, the nation's second woman secretary of education. I realized that my involvement created an opportunity to support Wintley Phipps. I told Dr. Schuller about him, exposed him to Wintley's amazing vocal gifts, and asked if he was willing to feature the young man on the *Hour of Power*. Dr. Schuller agreed, and Wintley performed "I Give You My

Life," the song that stopped me in my tracks, as part of the show. Dr. Schuller loved Wintley and invited him back three or four times.

Vocalist Minnie Riperton died of breast cancer at the shockingly young age of thirty-two. This wonderful young singer had grown up on the South Side of Chicago. She was known for her beautiful voice and her ability to sing unusually high-pitched notes, up in the whistle register. In 1975 Minnie's hit song "Lovin' You" topped the Billboard pop and R&B charts. Since the Black community was mourning her death and she had appeared on *Soul Train*, Don and I thought it would be good for an episode to be a memorial for her. Though Don had resisted featuring Wintley when I suggested him in the past, this time he agreed that Wintley Phipps should be a soloist. By this point, *Soul Train* was hot enough to make an artist's career. All the dancers sat at tables in front of the stage as Wintley sang to honor Minnie, and other groups performed meaningful songs.

These two appearances, on *Hour of Power* and *Soul Train*, played a significant role in getting Wintley on the map. In 1979, when Wintley cut his first album, JPC purchased thirty thousand copies, and gave them away in the Ultra Sheen Model Beauty Salon for a promotion. That's how great I thought Wintley was. Since then, he's gone on to found the U.S. Dream Academy. This nonprofit organization provides remedial educational support for the children of people who've been incarcerated. Over the years, Wintley's performed all over the world, in front of people like Mother Teresa and Nelson Mandela, and for six US presidents.

The year 1979 was also meaningful because it was the twenty-fifth anniversary of JPC. To mark that important milestone, I commissioned Black photo-realist Paul Collins to paint portraits of twelve remarkable Black women. A blue-ribbon panel of experts and scholars selected Madam C. J. Walker, Rosa Parks, Wilma Rudolph, Coretta Scott King, the Queen of Sheba, Mary Church Terrell, Harriet Tubman, Sojourner Truth, Marian Anderson, Josephine Baker, Fannie Lou Hamer, and Phillis Wheatley for this honor. We called it the Great Beautiful Black Women collection and it paid homage to our customers. The exhibit premiered to more than two thousand guests at the Chicago Cultural Center. It then toured for a year, visiting Lincoln Center in New York, the Frederick Douglass House in Washington, DC, the Piccadilly Museum in Memphis, and Spelman College in Atlanta, as well as other institutions and churches. At the end of the year, I donated the paintings to Spelman College.

The Bible tells us that when you help others, you also help yourself. As we helped others, JPC benefited immeasurably. The community supported us. People I didn't know spoke positively about us and began to perceive us favorably and respect us, personally and in business. I discovered that a positive reputation builds, and your name travels around with a lot of enthusiastic vibes associated with it.

13

The Rich Man

I GREW UP during an explosion of arts, culture, and politics in Black Chicago. With all the arts taking place around me, I envisioned myself going to plays, seeing musicals, attending the opera, and participating in all sorts of activities that weren't typical for Black male teenagers. I started going to venues by myself. Anytime Black entertainers were in the city and I had some money, I would go to the Regal Theater, or the Met Theater, where they were performing. Earl Hines, Fats Waller, Billy Eckstine, Louis Armstrong—everybody out there, I saw them. I watched Ella Fitzgerald sing her breakthrough hit "A-Tisket, A-Tasket" with Chick Webb's orchestra in what may have been her first live Chicago appearance. Inspired by Ella, Billie Holiday,

Billy Eckstine, and other famous singers, I started paying for voice lessons.

I was a clotheshorse. John and I started having our clothing made on Forty-Seventh Street, west of South Parkway, where a lot of Jewish tailors and clothiers owned shops. We wanted to wear "bigs," or zoot suits, large-shouldered jackets with pants whose fabric bloomed out at the knees but tapered tightly to hug the ankles. Browns and beiges were my favorite shades. I also started wearing either a suit or a shirt and tie with tailored slacks and a sports jacket to school. Though I don't think I ever owned more than three suits, I had a number of ties, and wore something different almost every day. I became the best-dressed boy at Wendell Phillips High.

But John and I didn't worship our clothes. We were trying to conform to the code people observed in public. In those days many men walked around in a suit, shirt, and tie. Women wore skirts and dresses. People looked down on you if they didn't consider you properly dressed. We were trying not to repeat the same outfit. Folks took a lot of pride in their appearance.

On Saturdays, John and I used our earnings to go to the movies and took Robert with us. We went to the Regal or the Met at Forty-Seventh and South Parkway, or the Louis Theatre on Thirty-Fifth Street. We watched *Tarzan*, Westerns starring Roy Rogers and Tom Mix, James Cagney movies, and Clark Gable in *Gone with the Wind*. I saw all the big men, all the cowboys. One particular day at the movies I will never forget.

"We've been bombed at Pearl Harbor," a paperboy shouted as we walked out of the Louis Theater. "The nation is about to go to war!"

The fact that the nation had been bombed terrified me.

What made it worse was that it had happened without warning. Theater newsreels showed people being killed and ships being sunk, and all sorts of frightening news began pouring in. It was horrible. Just one year earlier, the government had instituted the selective service for males who were eighteen or older. I worried I might be drafted. Several years later, when I received the letter to come to be examined, I was terrified. The injury to my leg and foot when I was hit by the car exempted me. I was classified 4F, unfit for military service. I walked out of the exam the happiest man in the world.

Probably inspired by going to the movies and watching lots of Westerns, I started taking horseback riding lessons at the Black-owned stables over on Fifty-First Street, on the far end of Washington Park, near the University of Chicago campus. I bought a pair of beige riding pants that bloomed out a little bit at the thigh, some black leather boots that came to my knee, and a riding crop. That turned a few heads.

Mama struggled to make sense of my fashionable dress, theatergoing, and the fact I walked around town wearing riding pants and carrying a crop.

"Don't you know you're poor?" she asked me one day, looking baffled and concerned.

"No, I'm not poor," my sixteen-year-old self responded.

"George, what do you mean?" she asked, her face all scrunched up.

"I've got money to do whatever I want to do, and I give you money, so I don't consider myself poor," I told her. And with all of the money I was making, I didn't. Whether my thoughts were foolish or not can be debated, but that was honestly the way I felt.

Family members started calling me "the rich man."

Maybe their nickname traveled from their lips to God's

ears, or their words combined with Mr. Fuller's and entered my spirit.

Now it was several decades later, and our family began to truly enjoy life's fineries. It didn't take long for Joan to become active in various activities in Glencoe and neighboring Lake Forest and Highland Park. Among them, she became involved with the North Shore Links, a nonprofit service organization of professional Black women.

Joan had very expensive tastes. I could afford to buy her furs, designer clothes, jewelry, and cars. These kinds of gifts made her happy. I also deposited money into a checking account for her to use at her discretion. She began to buy a lot of clothes. Nice clothes. Very expensive clothes. Fabulous clothes. Clothes by Yves Saint Laurent, Chanel, Karl Lagerfeld, Gucci, Louis Vuitton. Chanel loafers, Manolo Blahnik heels, Prada shoes. My favorites were the coats and multicolored jackets designed by Galanos and Valentino. I was happy to be able to afford to fulfill her dreams.

I do admit I was shocked the time I stumbled across a bill from Bonwit Teller, a luxury department store.

"Joan! Did you really spend six thousand dollars on clothes last month?"

"What difference does it make? We have it, and I liked the dress."

It was the first of many times I'd see a credit card statement the equivalent of about $50,000 today.

Earlier in our lives, Joan walked into a shop and asked how much something cost. Now she picked out anything she liked, said "Here," and handed it to the salesperson to ring up without considering the price. A salesman at Neiman Marcus named Morris Gearring dressed a lot of older Jewish women on the North Shore. He began dressing Joan. My wife's closets ran deep and wide, and they filled up quickly. Joan would look unbelievably stunning in any room we entered, but she was an absolute showstopper in a breathtaking gold beaded dress by Norman Norell.

We invited extended family, friends, JPC employees, our distributors, and other associates to enjoy our wonderful new Glencoe home. Our pool was sixty-five feet long, thirty-five feet wide, twelve feet at the deep end, and electrically heated. It was one of the first free-form swimming pools on the North Shore of Chicago. If Jerry Wexler had told me how much it cost to heat it, I probably would have never purchased the house.

After spending my childhood watching the good livers play, now I had my own tennis court. I took tennis lessons, as did Joan. We played regularly. Our neighbors gossiped that Wexler had built the court with lights as bright as Wrigley Field. They said he regularly played until two in the morning on weekends. They seemed happy to have us as neighbors, if only because we didn't play tennis under those blazing lights all night.

Joan and I also commissioned the young Black artist Richard Hunt to create a nine-foot outdoor sculpture for our front yard. I'd seen Hunt's enormous outdoor sculptures around 2300 North Lincoln, in Chicago, near his studio. They fascinated me. He created an abstract sculpture of a Black woman carrying something heavy on her head, entitled *Caritid*. We situated the sculpture in front of the glass living room wall. Hunt was also a civil rights hero. In 1960 he desegregated the Woolworths lunch counter in Alamo, Texas, single-handedly.

In time, we developed relationships with people in our

neighborhood. We occasionally socialized with the Pritzker family, founders of Hyatt Hotels, who had children Joanie and Petey's ages. One year we ran into them in Vail, Colorado, while we were skiing. I hadn't been skiing before. I had my first lesson there and I took my time on the hill while my kids went zipping past me. Jay Pritzker invited us to fly back to Chicago on their private plane. It was a new experience for me.

It felt good to be able to acquire whatever I had a taste for.

In 1972, I placed an order for the seventy-two-foot Burger yacht I once dreamed of. I was eager to enjoy it with my family and friends. I chartered a bus and took our loved ones and some JPC employees up to Manitowoc, Wisconsin, where I was to pick the yacht up. Joan popped a bottle of champagne across the bow. We christened the boat the *African Queen*, in the spirit of the movie starring Humphrey Bogart and Katharine Hepburn. We docked it in Belmont Harbor, on Chicago's North Side.

I hired a Miami-based navigation expert, Joe Figurado, to captain our yacht. Over the next few years, some of our family members spent a lot of time enjoying the sunshine, fresh air, and the pleasure of being out on the water on the *African Queen*. We sailed to Canada in the summer, passing through customs in a place called Little Current. We also stopped at a lot of small and sometimes uninhabited islands we hadn't known about.

We boated to Bailey's Harbor in Door County, Wisconsin. It's where Joan and I met Ray Kroc, the founder of the McDonald's hamburger chain. Ray and I both owned Burger boats, and yacht owners often show their boats to each other. We became friends and spent quite a bit of time on each other's yacht.

But sailing consumes a large amount of time. I wasn't as able as Joan and the kids to fully appreciate the *African Queen*. Because the boating season is longer and the weather so much better than in Chicago, we kept the boat at the Pier 66 Marina in Fort Lauderdale, Florida. I loaned Joe and the boat to Independence Bank's board members to use, when they were in Florida. Around this time I also purchased a single-engine Beechcraft aircraft. It helped me keep up with the boat. I would fly wherever the family was. Joe was safety conscious. Joan could be demanding and wanted her way. Sometimes she wanted things Joe thought were unsafe. It became too much conflict and aggravation for me. I got rid of the *African Queen* after four years, and then I had to deal with the fact that everyone was pissed at me for selling it.

Although I enjoyed what money could buy, I'm not a capitalist. In capitalism I see a lot of selfishness. When people make millions and billions of dollars, you ask yourself, "How much money does a person need to live well?" When I think of a capitalist, I think of someone who makes a lot more money than any human being needs, and too many stack it up, instead of sharing the wealth and using it to help other people. If companies paid people better, they would be able to spend more money and help keep the economy growing. Jesus said you can't serve God and money. If you're serving money, you're not serving God.

Achieving new heights in business and being able to assist others inspired me to confront my fears. I'd been struggling with a fear of flying since 1959, when Rose Meta Morgan invited me to New York for her grand opening. Every time the plane hit turbulence, I grabbed the armrest as tight as I could. With every bump, I gasped. After the affair, returning to Chicago meant flying again. More than a decade after that event, I was flying back to Chicago with Joan, from a live taping of *Soul Train*. The plane hit terrible turbulence. I could see the plane's wings, which were designed to move up and down with the air. Unaware of this feat of engineering, I leaned over and kissed Joan goodbye. We laughed about that for years, but flying remained a misery.

I decided the best way to overcome my fear was to learn how to fly an airplane. Before I purchased the *African Queen*, I started taking private flying lessons at Waukegan Airport, about thirty minutes north of Glencoe. I worked with my flight instructor, Dan Dickinson. First I began reading about aerodynamics, the science of how an airplane flies. I learned that once the plane's thrust equals gravity, the air creates a vacuum as it flows over the wings. The vacuum lifts the plane and keeps it in the air. The thrust that equals and overcomes gravity's vacuum is what makes it fly.

When the plane is in the air, it does whatever the air is doing. If the air goes up, the plane goes up. If the air is smooth, the ride is smooth. If the air is unsettled, the ride is, too. If you hit an air pocket, the plane will drop.

Reading and understanding principles of aviation quickly alleviated most of my fear. I went to ground school, where I learned about weather, flight planning, navigation, and how to read the instrument panel. Flight training came next.

After I got comfortable flying in normal conditions, I learned how to land in a crosswind. When the wind is blowing at an angle across the runway, you land by performing a maneuver called "crabbing." The maximum my plane could handle while crabbing was a thirty-five-mile-an-hour crosswind.

Learning how to fly took a helluva lot of time. But it absolutely cured my fear. It was part of why I decided to purchase a plane. I bought a sleek, high-performance single-engine Beechcraft Sierra 200 demo model that reached two hundred miles per hour, retracted its wheels, and operated as high as eleven thousand feet.

I began flying to Burger's headquarters in Manitowoc, Wisconsin, to check on my yacht's progress. Once I took off from Waukegan in clear weather, but before too long, I saw rain cells ahead. There also was a thirty-five-mile-per-hour crosswind, the maximum my aircraft could handle. I was trained to crab when I landed, but I'd never done it. For some reason instead of crabbing, I performed a cross control, which moved the plane's aileron and rudders in opposite directions. Somehow the wheels touched down smoothly.

"Man, you are something," a guy who'd been watching said when I arrived at the terminal. "That was a hell of a landing."

I had no idea how I did it. I couldn't believe I was on the ground. The guy's compliment gave me a big head.

I checked on my yacht, and then I headed back home. Between the boat and my plane, I was on cloud nine. On the way back, as I approached Waukegan's airport, I was feeling high on myself. I totally neglected to watch my speed. My altitude was too low. I also didn't reduce the plane's power. When my wheels touched the runway, the plane bounced back into the air. It scared me almost to death. My mind went blank. The plane came back down and bounced again. I was experiencing a phenomenon that pilots call porpoising. Each time I touched down, the plane landed harder. Each time the plane hit the ground hard, it bounced higher into the air.

Terrified, I did whatever came into my mind. As the end of the runway drew nearer, I was panicking. I responded instinctively by standing up as tall as I could and shoving the plane's yoke under my chin. I used my entire bodyweight to pull it higher. Miraculously, this time the wheels hit the ground and stayed there. The plane careened off the runway, and I used the foot pedals to pull it back onto the blacktop. My plane was damaged and wobbled to the terminal. When I got out to inspect it, my legs were shaking.

Turns out two FAA inspectors had been across the road, watching the airport.

"We thought we were going to have a ball of aluminum at the end of the runway," one said in disbelief when I walked into the terminal.

"We thought we'd have to sweep you up," the other added, rubbing his head. "You have to hand over your license right now."

God had spared me disaster. Who was I to complain? I reached into my wallet and handed it to them. I'd almost made Joan a widow twice in one day.

The mechanics discovered the motor mounts were contorted, and both propellers were bent about six inches.

Escaping two disasters left me with a sense of awe. I enjoyed flying until that day. I had a high-performance plane, but I was a rookie pilot. It was time to hang up my wings. I hired a pilot and purchased a larger plane, a Beechcraft Duke. The Duke seated six people and flew 275 miles per hour and thirty thousand feet high. As often as my brother John and I were traveling short distances, I needed it for the business.

When it came to my fear, faith carried the day.

14

The Big Lye

THE SEC REQUIRED Johnson Products, as a public company, to publish an annual financial statement. In 1971 JPC
generated a little over $12 million in revenue. Normally,
more than 15 percent growth year-over-year spoke for itself,
and was praised. We went above and beyond the SEC's
requirements that we depict our business clearly in our company annual report. We wanted to overcome the racist
assumption that Black companies were inferior.

In addition to our written narrative, we included charts
and graphs in our statement. They clearly portrayed how
much each JPC product contributed to our profits, and the
percentage of our total sales each brand represented. We
also showed the percentage of every brand's sales by product.

For instance, you could see Ultra Sheen Relaxer versus Ultra Sheen Conditioner and Hair Dress.

By doing that, we unknowingly overexposed ourselves.

Charles Revson, the CEO of Revlon Products, was sitting at his headquarters in New York City with his eyes on JPC. Revlon primarily sold cosmetics, nail polish, fragrances, and the permanent wave treatment White women used to create long-lasting curls for straight hair. Revson was watching Johnson Products Company and the Black consumer market.

The national economic expansion that had begun at the end of World War II was over, and the nation was experiencing challenging times. A mild recession was followed by significant recessions between 1973 and 1975, caused by debt from the Vietnam War, the OPEC oil embargo, falling stock prices, Watergate, President Nixon's resignation, and inflation. The sales and growth of many companies stagnated or declined. But you wouldn't have known it at the Johnson Products Company. Our sales catapulted from $11.2 million in 1970 to $37 million in 1975, just short of $200 million in today's dollars.

We learned that nothing stood between Black people and their hair—that is, the Black hair market wasn't sensitive to fluctuations in the economy.

Around that same time, two registered Black pharmacists, Cornell McBride and Therman McKenzie, founded M&M Products down in Atlanta. They began marketing a product to style Afros, which they called Sta-Sof-Fro.

Johnson Products engaged in a lot of market research. Some twenty-four million Black people lived in the United States, about 11 percent of the nation's population. Their median age—where half were older and half were younger—was about twenty-three, six years younger than that of White Americans. The race was growing 50 percent more quickly than the overall country. This translated into a greater proportion of Black people moving into the prime consuming ages of eighteen to thirty-five over the next two decades. Our typical customer invested more money in her hair than the average woman. This was not just about style; to be seen as professional at work, she had to. Getting her hair washed, pressed and curled, relaxed, conditioned, roller set, and styled might cost $30. People with straighter hair spent less than $12.

In haircare, the general market was increasing by 7 to 10 percent annually. The ethnic health and beauty aids industry was already growing by over 20 percent a year. The conditions were ripe for JPC to keep growing.

Until JPC went public, most White manufacturers looked at the Black haircare market as a nickel-and-dime business. For years, John H. Johnson, the president of Johnson Publishing Company, begged Charles Revson to run an ad in *Ebony*. Naturally, the magazine would want the ads to feature Black women to reflect their readership. Rumor had it that Revson had vowed never to use a Black model in a Revlon ad, though. Today, the Revlon website claims to have made history in 1970, when it became "the first beauty company to feature an African American model, Naomi Sims, in its advertising." This is not accurate. JPC had been hiring Black models for more than a decade.

Charles Revson could read our financial statements and see both that we were making strong revenues and exactly where we were making them. JPC had a hefty markup. It didn't take a lot of sales to build our bottom line. The Black haircare market was green, financially.

In 1973 Revson purchased Deluxol, maker of the relaxer Creme of Nature. It was the same product whose formula Leon Cooper had ripped off from me in the 1950s, and Jack the Barber had launched. Creme of Nature's name was changed to Revlon Realistic, and it was marketed as comparable to Ultra Sheen Relaxer. Suddenly, this company that had demonstrated no interest in Black people, Black hairdressers, Black customers, or the Black community began to turn its attention toward the Black haircare category.

After Revlon entered the market, other White-owned beauty product companies looked to increase their sales and profits by entering ethnic segments of the industry.

The largest ethnic market was Black.

During the 1970s and '80s, practically every major White-owned cosmetics manufacturer made a concerted effort to introduce an imitation of Ultra Sheen Relaxer, without improving upon the science of our original formulation. They felt they deserved the field that generations of Black entrepreneurs had labored in, cared for, and cultivated with their blood, sweat, and tears.

Revlon and the other mainstream companies entered the market without offering others a commensurate opportunity to participate. They didn't attempt to partner with Black entrepreneurs. They did hire the occasional management figurehead and Black salesperson. But they didn't hire members of our community in numbers reflecting the magnitude of the opportunity they were exploiting and benefiting from.

Many of the jobs they did offer Black people were in sales or marketing. In fact, they made attempts to poach JPC's salespeople. They didn't succeed often, but we did lose a few. The Black sales representatives these White companies hired became their public face in Black communities. The Black marketers they hired often created the campaigns that spoke to Black people. Together, these few Black sales and marketing people were the key to opening the lock Black companies had on the Black haircare market.

As the largest company, and with the most market share in the relaxer category, JPC took on the brunt of Revlon's blows.

We were in a fight for our lives. I prayed for God to give me the strength, the wisdom, and the courage I needed, and to lead me in the paths of righteousness and truth. That was part of my everyday meditation.

With a product close in quality, and all of their corporate glamour and money, Revlon should have easily wiped us out. It wasn't lost on me that they and like-minded mainstream firms might be planning to eliminate Black-owned companies from the industry altogether.

These enterprises had dollar signs in their eyes, unlimited resources, and a willingness to use every bit of their superior economic power. It goes without saying that the firms didn't give Black people a chance to participate in the mainstream beauty market. At this point, Black-owned companies had to compete with these big firms to keep Black people's business. We did not and could not take our customer base for granted.

I will never forget the day, in 1974, when Dorothy McConnor walked into my office, looking distressed.

"I think you should look at this right now," she said, handing me an envelope from the Federal Trade Commission addressed to the "President of Johnson Products Company." They wanted to investigate Ultra Sheen relaxers.

I was extremely concerned.

The first person I called to my office was my brother

John. Next, I invited our lawyer, Ernest Lafontant. John, Ernest, our new VP of marketing, Ivan Levinger, our sales manager, Jimmy Middlebrooks, and other members of our leadership team put our heads together.

Geographically, there were FTC offices located in most regions of the country, including Chicago and Cleveland in the Midwest. It seemed odd this letter was from the Seattle office. A few weeks later, the group of us flew to Seattle to meet with the FTC.

"We came across your ads running prominently in *Ebony* magazine," one of the FTC representatives told us.

"We wanted to do something for the Black community," another explained. Judging from their demeanors, I was sure they intended to unnerve us.

The first man went on to state that they were concerned about dangerous ingredients that might harm consumers, particularly sodium hydroxide, which they kept referring to as "lye." Lye had a bad connotation. People used it to unclog stopped-up drains. By then, Ultra Sheen had been on the market for more than a decade. Its safety profile was clean. Plus, every brand of hair relaxer contained sodium hydroxide.

"What other companies participate in this category with you?" the first man asked, before explaining that JPC needed to take measures to protect our relaxer customers, like putting a warning on our label.

"Well, there are several small competitors," I responded. "I'm most concerned about Revlon, though."

"What's your concern?" the man asked with a stone face.

"Revlon is coming after our category of business," I told him. "I'll do whatever I need to do if all our competitors have to do it. Anything you do to me, you've got to do to Revlon."

"We are not going to do something to a small company

like Johnson Products Company and steer clear of Revlon," they promised.

"Well, as long as you do to Revlon whatever you do to us," I replied, making my expectations clear.

The meeting was uncomfortable and, in a sense, frightening for all of us. We felt threatened.

When we got out of there, the JPC team headed straight to the airport.

"Am I the only person who thinks that meeting was bullshit?" I asked. Everyone felt the same way.

"Why was some White guy in Seattle reading *Ebony* magazine?" John asked.

"It definitely doesn't make sense," another member of our team replied. "Seattle, not Chicago, not Detroit, not Memphis or Atlanta. But Seattle, where not many Black people live."

It was obvious the entire thing was a setup, which unnerved me most.

"Whether it's bullshit or not, we are in one helluva damn fix," I said.

We had no way to know whether they were investigating Revlon, which was gaining on us but hadn't caught up in the relaxer category. We negotiated in good faith for months with the FTC. Because we made such an issue about Revlon being after us, the FTC assured us that if we signed their agreement, they weren't going to do anything to us they didn't do to Revlon.

In the meantime, Revlon kept on coming. They had deeper pockets than we had, and they were capable of spending it to wage a stunning advertising campaign.

I needed every bit of the strength, wisdom, and courage I prayed for each day.

On June 15, 1975, I was in Glencoe, sitting in the living room, watching the *NBC Nightly News*. The anchorman, John Chancellor, said, "Johnson Products Company has been ordered by the Federal Trade Commission to put a disclaimer, 'This product contains lye,' on the packaging for Ultra Sheen Relaxer." He also mentioned two small competitors.

I was stunned to hear JPC's name on television, and enraged that this was the first we'd heard that the FTC had reached a decision. Adding insult to injury, Chancellor didn't mention Revlon.

I called Ernest Lafontant right away. I was absolutely livid! We'd been duped — either the FTC wasn't investigating Revlon, was protecting them, or both.

The next morning, we called the FTC.

"Why are we learning about this on the *Nightly News* instead of from you?" we demanded.

We received no answer to that question. Instead, the FTC told us we had to label all Ultra Sheen relaxers with a disclaimer.

"I'm willing to list lye as an ingredient on our product if every manufacturer has to list lye as an ingredient," I responded, angrily.

"We're not talking about every manufacturer, we're talking about Johnson Products."

"Well, if you require that of me, then require it of Revlon, too," I replied. "They're almost as big in the category as we are, and they're a lot bigger than us in terms of company assets."

All day my telephone rang off the hook, as my distributors from around the country called me. "Hey, I just saw this notice in the newspaper that the FTC is making JPC put a warning about lye on the label," one told me.

"In the *newspaper*?"

How could this be happening?

"Hey, do you know about this article?" someone from another part of the country called to tell me.

I got some version of that call from Texas, from Nevada, from New York, from California. I heard about it from people working in large markets and small.

Within days, JPC customers and distributors were sending me newspaper clippings in the mail. Coincidentally, the family of Independence Bank's board member, Bob Bacon, ran a news-clipping service. He cut out some of the articles and sat down and showed me. Somehow Revlon had known what the FTC had not told me. And they knew it long enough in advance to simultaneously send press releases and place articles about the consent decree in newspapers all around the country, in big cities and small towns.

From television to newspapers, Revlon immediately involved all the communications systems possible.

Our employees, our distributors, our customers, everyone who knew, was extremely upset. Thankfully our distributors were loyal to us. Revlon was so new to our community perhaps they were not aware that JPC had put some of them in business.

The FTC consent decree required JPC to place the warning, "This product contains lye," on our relaxer products without requiring Revlon to do the same.

Suddenly, a cloud was hanging over Ultra Sheen Relaxers. The public, distributors, and hairdressers unexpectedly had to deal with the perception that a familiar and popular brand they had used for years seemed to have made a big formula change that caused it to receive a lot of negative press.

Revlon Realistic seemed not to have lye's downside. Their label read that it, too, contained sodium hydroxide. But their sales reps lied to beauticians, "We don't have lye in Revlon Realistic. This is a better and safer product."

It was a pretty convincing story, especially since Revlon's label didn't carry the warning. This created an unfair climate for competition. The disparity discredited us.

Not long afterward, Charles Revson invited all my major distributors to New York City. He wined and dined them. I even heard that he passed out cash for our Black distributors to put into their business.

With all that money, he didn't have a problem persuading some distributors to be interested in what Revlon could do for them. A small Black-owned distributor isn't often invited to get to know and engage in something glamorous with big-time folks. But many people had been using Ultra Sheen Relaxer and having no problem with it. They stuck with us. We had a lot of loyal customers and had generated a good measure of trust and goodwill over the years. And not everyone had seen the John Chancellor story.

Immediately after the FTC issued their ruling, I fought back, suing them in the Ninth Circuit Court in Detroit. Our lawsuit was pretty clear cut: if we had to apply a warning label, everybody else should, too. The goal was to force the FTC to order Revlon to put "This product contains lye" on their label.

On August 24, 1975, Charles H. Revson died. He passed away right before JPC signed the consent decree. I've been told that Simon H. Rifkind, the head of the FTC, offered a tribute at his funeral. Revson's successor, Michel Christian Bergerac, ran the company after Revson's death.

With their money, their image, a high-quality product, and an inside connection with the FTC, Revlon should have just wiped JPC out. But though they injured us, they hadn't killed us.

JPC fought against this big bear of a company.

We focused on being excellent and versatile.

JPC deepened our relationships with retailers, distributors, and "rack jobbers." Rack jobbers often determined what products were placed in stores' ethnic sections, stocked the shelves, and decided how much space to allocate each product. We also created modular displays featuring JPC products, making it easier for people to find our section and select our brands. John was key to making this happen.

As we engaged in market research, customers let us know that not enough beauty products were being made with Black people in mind. Our focus group participants identified many unmet needs in the haircare market, as well as in the cosmetics category. For example, our customers' hair and scalp tended to be dry. People wanted help addressing that. Doc Martini began working on an Extra Dry line extension to add to our Ultra Sheen Conditioner and Hair Dress brand. In facial cosmetics, almost all products were made with White people in mind, except the Fashion Fair beauty line sold by John H. Johnson. We knew there was a lot of room for expansion, and we launched Ultra Sheen Cosmetics.

In 1975, Johnson Products Company reached $37 million in sales, almost $225 million today, and employed more than four hundred people; most were Black Chicagoans. It was absolutely amazing we were doing as well as we were. Something greater than me was clearly working in our favor.

In early 1977, the Ninth Circuit Court of Appeals in Detroit finally decided in JPC's favor and against the FTC. It took far too long, but the court ultimately required Revlon to put the same warning on their Revlon Realistic relaxer as the FTC had forced JPC to display for almost two years.

By the time the court ruled, Revlon had eaten up approximately 45 percent of Ultra Sheen Relaxer's volume. JPC had gone from commanding 85 percent to about 40 percent of the relaxer market. Forty percent was still plenty—almost any businessperson would want their company to own that much of a category—but JPC had lost a lot.

Our company was David to Revlon's Goliath, when you compared the size and resources the multinational had at its disposal. Coming at JPC with everything they had, you'd think Revlon would have just wiped our company out.

Yet we were still standing.

JPC was hurt, for sure, but I was amazed Revlon hadn't done even better.

Though my formal education was limited, clearly God's arms were around my shoulders.

But if Revlon felt entitled to and could viciously come after the largest Black-owned cosmetic manufacturing company in the world, any White-owned company could come after any Black manufacturer, whether in the haircare industry or beyond. It meant not only was JPC's future at stake, the historic legacy of the entire Black haircare industry was also. And if Black haircare was in danger, Black entrepreneurship in general was, too. And if Black entrepreneurship was at risk, so was the well-being of the Black community.

15

Gold Rules

IN THE AFTERMATH of the FTC situation, I started thinking about more than my company. I spent time contemplating the well-being of the Black haircare industry, Black entrepreneurship, and the Black community, generally.

Black entrepreneurs created the Black beauty industry, back in the 1860s. During the early 1900s, the industry had provided Madam C. J. Walker the opportunity to become the first American woman of any race to earn $1 million in a business enterprise. There were legions of hairstylists and barbers who made independent livings. I reflected where the industry now stood during the 1970s, when revenues reached about $600 million, around $3.5 billion today.

Since its inception, the haircare industry had given untold numbers of Black men and women a way to earn a dignified living. The industry had been people's economic salvation, giving us control over our own destiny. Though it was hard to know the exact numbers, JPC's market research told us there were tens of thousands of Black-owned beauty salons. They created a way for many men and women with a modest education to provide for their family in a better-than-average fashion. Many doctors, lawyers, and other high-achieving professionals were children of haircare industry professionals. In fact, more wealthy Blacks had been created by the beauty industry than any other industry except entertainment. Our field of hair salons, beauty-supply stores, and manufacturers had grown even larger than other industries that produced many successful Black entrepreneurs, such as restaurants, music, insurance, and funeral homes.

During the 1970s, many White businesses were for the first time opening their doors to do business with Black people. That was partially because the civil rights movement had succeeded in making racial discrimination illegal—at least theoretically. It was also because civic and business leaders had been jolted into reality by Dr. King's assassination and the subsequent riots. But what would happen now that integration was more possible?

As both White multinational companies and new Black competitors entered the haircare market, I could see storm clouds gathering on JPC's horizon. I felt capable of navigating the competition from entrepreneurs, but multinational corporations, like Revlon, had bottomless pockets. They were a serious threat to me and my direct competitors. These large companies also posed a threat to Black salon owners, hairdressers, and all the people working in the industry. More than a century of Black economic progress was at stake.

This knowledge unsettled me. My role in the industry

and place of prominence in the community led me to believe it was my responsibility to warn my people about these threats. I also wanted to help organize the Black haircare industry to protect itself. In order to do that, I had to do a lot of public speaking, which I had a fear of and did not enjoy.

I began speaking publicly and sharing my thoughts about the future of Black haircare at various industry award dinners and trade shows. I shared about Black entrepreneurship, the Black community, and the economy as well. I also stood in front of the SCLC, the National Urban League, the NAACP, Operation Breadbasket/PUSH, Black fraternities and sororities like Alpha Phi Alpha and Delta Sigma Theta, and other social, civic, and civil rights organizations concerned with Black progress and economic development. I also spoke at high schools and colleges.

In 1973 I gave the commencement address at Xavier University of Louisiana. I'd never imagined myself speaking at a college. I toured Xavier's campus, spent time with faculty and students, and received my first honorary doctorate degree. I felt moved emotionally as I zipped up my black robe with velvet stripes, a gold-colored hood was draped over my shoulders, and I donned my mortarboard and tassel just like the students wore. Earning an honorary doctorate degree though I hadn't finished high school put me on cloud nine.

I delivered a commencement address titled "An Agenda for the Pursuit of Excellence."

"Our job ahead is to produce more and more and more Black Americans who are ready, willing, and able to do their jobs in an excellent way," I told the students, who sat before me in relaxers, naturals, and blowouts. "Our objective must be to produce more who have planned and prepared to go into the world and conquer it, while realizing full well that the real world is not the world we wish. It just happens to be the only world we have. In order to beat the odds presented by the terrible twosome of segregation and discrimination, our graduates must wear the mark of excellence at all times. They must become so good that no employer, no matter how culture-bound or biased, will be able to overlook them."

Afterward, Xavier's president, Norman Francis, reprinted and distributed the speech to the students.

In subsequent years I delivered the convocation speech at Tuskegee University, spoke at Fisk University, and gave the 1976 commencement address at Babson College.

As I spoke at HBCUs, I encouraged the business students to come work for us. I also suggested that some members of their generation should become entrepreneurs. Still others I encouraged to enter mainstream companies and try to work their way to the executive suite. I believed they should learn the skills a professional could only obtain in these environments, and then bring them back to the community. They had to be determined, and not give up and quit. This was particularly important for aspiring entrepreneurs. Finding a need they were passionate about would fuel their determination.

As more White-owned companies entered the Black hair and cosmetics business, our company wielded every strategy we knew how to use. The competition was fierce, but consistent with my values around excellence, we focused on the goal of superiority. We called our approach "the Johnson Way."

JPC opened a manufacturing plant in Nigeria, the largest Black nation in the world. We also explored new categories, including a cosmetic line called Ultra Sheen Facial Fashions. We continued to run superior advertising and promotional programs. The company was already known for offering high-quality products at reasonable prices. There wasn't much room to create an advantage there. We did seek more markets. We also hired the best people and trained them at the highest level. Our company worked to consistently improve our managerial and technical skills.

By 1974, JPC's rapid growth and the demands of the business were pushing John and me to the edge of our capabilities. We needed stronger marketing leadership than I could provide. When you don't know how to do something, it's important to ask for help and to surround yourself with strong people. A headhunter presented the résumé of Ivan Levinger, a White man who had worked for the mainstream haircare firm Alberto Culver. We hired him as our VP of marketing.

We also decided to venture into the general market, creating a new product everyone could enjoy no matter their race or ethnicity. Ivan Levinger proposed we launch a cologne. We created Black Tie, based on the bestselling men's fragrance Aramis. Black Tie smelled fantastic, and its reflective silver Mylar packaging was classy. We required our employees to handle the bottles with white gloves to avoid leaving fingerprints. JPC also pulled out all the stops by hiring an upscale new advertising agency.

In August 1975, we invited buyers to Las Vegas on JPC's dime to roll out Black Tie. We wanted to obtain distribution in the men's fragrance section of department stores, retail stores, and other outlets. Consistent with our elegant brand, the JPC team wore tuxedos to greet our guests. Geoffrey Holder was an actor, dancer, singer, and choreographer for the Dance Theatre of Harlem, the movie *The Wiz*, and many other productions. We hired him to create the entertainment.

Although our presentation was extraordinary, we ran

headlong into racism. Almost all of the buyers were White men. Most struggled to imagine how consumers of all races could be interested in our product, though cologne is unrelated to race or ethnicity.

"We're going to buy Black Tie for the Black consumer market, and that's it," some of them told our salesmen. Others refused to buy it at all.

We were terribly disappointed, but we worked with the buyers who wanted to work with us, then pressed on. After leaving Las Vegas, JPC launched Black Tie in Los Angeles, Chicago, Detroit, Cleveland, Memphis, St. Louis, and several other cities, encountering similar resistance time and time again. Many retailers that purchased Black Tie placed it alongside JPC's haircare products instead of with the cologne. Our experiences underscored the racism JPC always dealt with, everywhere and all the time, even after the gains of the civil rights era.

We also discovered that August is too late to present products, especially new items, to buyers for the Christmas season. Turns out we should have pitched Black Tie back in January. I wondered whether Ivan Levinger knew what he was doing.

Black Tie's rollout disappointed us, but our product won the industry's highest packaging award. The advertising agency was innovative, and other general-market fragrances copied their work.

Fortunately, the rest of our business was strong. In 1975, JPC experienced 15 percent growth, year over year, for the fifth straight year. So did Revlon.

The *Wall Street Journal* named me Outstanding Manager of the Year.

Me and Revlon's Michel Christian Bergerac.

*   *   *

Haircare wasn't the first to experience an assault from White-owned companies. By now, these businesses had invaded Black insurance, Black music, and Black restaurants. Entrepreneurs did their best to fight them off but had limited resources and ran into the brick wall of structural racism. By entering markets that Black entrepreneurs had built, mainstream companies were undermining the economic base of the community it had taken decades of struggle to build.

Black entrepreneurs did not merely hire Black people; they also reinvested and recycled their profits into their communities. The wages and profits from Black-owned companies filled church coffers, funded college tuitions, provided operating funds to HBCUs, helped subsidize voter-registration campaigns, and supported civic and civil rights groups.

Black banks loaned money to Black businesses when mainstream banks refused to. Black executives served as leaders and role models in Black communities.

Every single day, our businesses helped improve other Black people's lives.

But it takes only one generation to have your history wiped out. Only two industries remained in which Black entrepreneurs had a significant degree of economic power and control — Black beauty and Black funeral homes.

From my vantage point of running the largest Black haircare company, I knew our entire industry was undercapitalized and disorganized. That made us more vulnerable. From salons that couldn't afford the latest equipment to hairdressers who worked their own hours, the same opportunities to professionalize the industry existed in the mid-1970s as they had during the '60s.

I tried, once again, to help organize that change. I wanted to improve Black salons by eliminating the poor management, the hairdressers who came and went, the lack of high-quality standardized products, and the lost sales opportunities. I revived my idea to teach stylists how to run a profitable and well-organized business.

In 1975 we took a second stab at launching the Ultra Sheen Model Beauty Salon. This time around, we figured we'd offer beauticians the opportunity to franchise salons under the power of the Ultra Sheen brand. We envisioned JPC selecting the locations, securing the lease, and designing an attractive and comfortable interior. We would also provide franchisees with high-quality hair dryers and styling implements, JPC products, and training, so that hairdressers offered a high standard of service.

Not long after we opened, I also discovered that a White-owned Chicago beauty school, Pivot Point, had begun moving into the industry, and was teaching Black folks how to do Black hair. That concerned me, and I bought Debbie's Beauty School, in Chicago, to train students to work in the Ultra Sheen Model Beauty Salon. It gave me the opportunity to have newly trained hairdressers. JPC paid the stylists a 45 percent commission on sales to work at the Ultra Sheen boutique full-time, the same rate offered by White salons. We also provided the same vacation, health insurance, and benefits they would have gotten if they worked at our manufacturing plant. The White salons didn't offer that.

As wonderful and necessary as I thought the concept was, it didn't work out. We would help the hairdressers grow their "book," but they would quit and take the clients with them, often to run a business out of their home—the exact same dynamic that happened ten years earlier. What became clear to us was that beauticians cherished their independence more than they valued earning a commission.

During the early 1970s, Orville Nelson came to me and asked me to buy his company. I knew he had health problems and not a good income. Orville's brief presence in my life was key to developing the product I could take to make what I wanted—a company of my own. The fact that he made a mess on the road that JPC had the chance to clean up was critical to my coming out of poverty. Though he hadn't intended to help me, in the grand scheme of things I valued the pivotal role he had played in my life. I immediately bought Orville's company for $35,000, about $160,000 today. I also gave him a job, a good salary, an office, a title, and all the JPC benefits. The health insurance we provided Orville helped save his life. His office sat next to that of Walter Lepart, an executive we had hired from Clairol. Orville and Walter seemed to click, and Walter was assigned to train Orville.

Orville's time at JPC was short-lived. Our executive vice president, Mike Simms, caught him trying to steal our formulas. There had been rumors that Revlon, Clairol, and some of the other big companies had planted a "spy" at JPC to communicate confidential information back to them. I was aware of this scuttlebutt but wasn't sure it was true. I don't know whether Orville played that role or not. Some people just are who they are. Though I had forgiven him, he hadn't changed.

You don't always get every hire right. At one point, I signed on a young man who graduated with the first group of Black students admitted to Harvard Business School. I employed him because every entrepreneur needs a team of hardworking, smart people. I wanted the best. On paper, that's who he was. When he came onboard, I didn't know what to do with him, and called him the assistant to the president.

On his first assignment, I sent him to meet with the sales force in St. Louis. He told them I was preparing him to become JPC's president. It may have been wishful thinking on his part, but we never had any conversation like that. Not only was I not contemplating retiring, I had children, and hoped one of them would be my heir. I let this young man go quickly. Book smarts are important, but so are common sense and integrity.

From 1977 to 1978, when JPC was at its peak, the market was becoming a lot more complex. A number of new competitors entered the industry. The most popular product lines began to shift.

A Black inventor, William Morrow, tinkered with the Jheri curl and formulated a new product that made kinky hair curly. Morrow created a new Black haircare category. He called it the curly perm. He traveled the country selling his product, California Curl, to stylists. People loved it.

Around that same time, the founder of Pro-Line Corporation, Comer Cottrell, began marketing a relaxer for children. He called his product Kiddie Kit. It, too, became popular. In 1978 Pro-Line also launched Curly Kit, the first curly perm consumers could buy from retail outlets and apply themselves rather than going to the salon. Out the gate, Curly Kit was popular, lifting Pro-Line's sales from $1 million to more than $10 million almost overnight. Some years later, *Forbes* magazine called Pro-Line's Curly Kit "the biggest single product ever to hit the Black cosmetics market." Pro-Line became the second-largest Black haircare company, behind JPC. Our sales increased to $39 million. As

Black consumers flocked to this new curly style, M&M Products' Afro styling product Sta-Sof-Fro also began to gather momentum.

Soft Sheen Products' relaxer business, run by Chicago's Edward and Bettiann Gardner, hadn't been growing quickly because JPC—and now Revlon—commanded the category. But then the Gardners introduced their own curly perm, Care Free Curl. Between the product itself and all the sprays and oils they sold to maintain the look, Care Free Curl rode the wave. Suddenly, Soft Sheen's sales revenue passed JPC's. Hair weaves became more popular, as well.

JPC saw the curly perm coming and monitored the market to see where the hairstyle was going and how long it would remain popular. We needed to exercise caution in this marketplace. To get a curly perm, you first had to stop using a relaxer. You either had to grow it or cut it out of your hair. Since we were heavily invested in relaxers and led the category, we didn't want to launch a product that would both hurt our core relaxer business and promote this new category.

We also looked at the style, which required a lot of oils, creams, and sprays to maintain it. Curly perms also dripped, oozed, and stained shirt collars and pillowcases. Maybe we saw what we wanted to see, but I certainly believed the curly perm would run its course. I thought hairstyles would settle back down to where they had been, with women relaxing their hair and wearing it natural.

There were a few things that we hadn't prepared for. Music videos were one of them. Music Television (MTV) went on the air in June 1981. The network didn't showcase many Black artists. But in June 1982, the life of Bob Johnson crossed paths with mine. Bob, who is unrelated to me, launched Black Entertainment Television (BET) to fill the cultural gap.

And nothing could have prepared us for the King of Pop. In 1983 Michael Jackson released *Thriller*. The videos for "Billie Jean," "Beat It," "Thriller," and other songs from that album featured him wearing a curly perm.

Sales of the Jheri curl shot through the stratosphere.

BET helped elevate the careers of a variety of Black hip-hop artists, actors, and celebrities who carried the curly perm deeper into Black popular culture: Ice Cube, Eazy-E, Deion Sanders, Samuel L. Jackson, and others. Almost overnight, the number of Black people getting relaxers or wearing their hair natural plummeted.

Around this time Los Angeles–based hair and skin-care company Alberto Culver's president and CEO, Leonard Lavin, began to reach out to me almost every week.

"Mr. Johnson, if you ever decide you're successful enough and would rather retire and enjoy the fruits of your labors, I'd love to talk to you about buying your company," he said.

"I'm not interested in selling my company," I told him. "But if I do ever sell JPC, I'll only sell it to a Black person or company."

In reality, what Black person had the kind of money required to purchase our company?

"Well, you've achieved a lot," he continued. "If I can get you to reconsider, I'll compensate you fairly."

"Thank you, but I'm not interested."

"If you change your mind, you know where to find me."

I was invited to participate on corporate boards and sit at tables in rooms few Black people had ever entered. President Nixon appointed me a founding member of the governing board of the US Postal Service. I was also invited to join the board of directors of Commonwealth Edison, the area's largest electric utility company. As I participated in these conversations, I learned more about how America's economy works. I also had access to some of society's movers and shakers. I became familiar with how some powerful people think. The exposure caused me to consider Black America's future and economic well-being and the responsibility I had to help protect it.

Few other Americans shared my unique vantage point.

My life experiences had showed me that if Black Americans only participate in the economy as employees and consumers of goods, individual Black people may "make it," but our community overall will remain relatively powerless and poor. For our people to thrive, more of us need to become producers of goods and manufacturers.

I began to speak publicly about both my concerns and possible solutions at colleges, industry trade shows, gatherings of civic groups, and other organizations.

Our community was in quite a predicament. Across industries, Black entrepreneurs were in the fight of our lives. In the few fields where Black businesspeople exercised a bit of economic clout, "Johnny-come-lately" firms had begun moving in.

Now, adding insult to injury, the encroaching companies' enormous size made it extremely difficult for our firms to compete with them. Increasing numbers of Black entrepreneurs were being put out of business by competitors now feigning interest in Black people.

I was fighting for Johnson Products, of course, but I realized the situation was bigger than us. The overall well-being of Black families and communities was at stake.

In the beginning of the 1980s, I invited the heads of all the Black-owned haircare firms to a summit at my home in Glencoe. I hoped we might overcome our competitiveness and professional distrust. I hoped that we, as Black business owners, could develop a collective response to the assault upon our industry. I imagined us closing ranks to support our Black-owned businesses. I wanted us to join forces to protect one of the last remaining industries where Black enterprises could still compete with White-owned firms.

From Chicago, Dallas, Atlanta, and beyond, practically every leader of a Black haircare manufacturing business found their way to Glencoe. Some in attendance were Soft Sheen Products's Edward and Bettiann Gardner; Fred and Blondell Luster, the founders of Luster Products; Comer Cottrell, the owner of Pro-Line; Cornell McBride, one of the two founders of M&M Products; and one of the Bonner Brothers's sons.

Once everyone was seated in my living room, I stood before my peers, knees knocking, mentally asking God for strength.

"For more than seventy-five years, our Black beauty industry has liberated men and women from the clutches of abject poverty," I began. "Our industry has given our people the ability to earn a good living, in our own community, among our own people. It has provided freedom and independence from having to look to the White man for our livelihood, and of having to endure racial oppression at work."

"That's right," one responded.

"As a result, many Black people with even a modest educational background, like me, have raised our families in decent homes and provided for them in a better-than-average fashion," I continued. I realized I may well have been the least educated member of the group. Edward Gardner had a master's degree and Betty at least a bachelor's. Cornell and Comer had also graduated college. "Except for the entertainment industry, the Black beauty industry has produced more affluence among Blacks than any other industry I know."

As everyone nodded, I found my stride.

"As we face this threat from these massive corporations with bottomless pockets, I believe we have to seize the initiative to protect our businesses. And when we protect our companies, we protect ourselves and our financial viability as a community. The only way we can continue providing Black people with jobs, income, and opportunities that our White competitors do not willingly offer is if all of our businesses prosper. I am proposing an overall strategy for action that won't just benefit one of us but can benefit all of us."

"Yes," one of these great businesspeople replied.

I heard an "Amen." I almost felt like I was in church.

"What do you have in mind?"

"I believe we have to embrace ethnicity in all our business endeavors. This means patronizing Black businesses every chance we get," I proposed. "Loyalty is the essence of ethnicity. We have to build the economy in Black communities by going out of our way to support each other's businesses. We need to buy the goods and services our brothers and sisters sell, even if it means traveling a little farther, searching a little harder, and at times even paying a little more. We have to stop dollars from flowing out of the Black community into the economy of other communities, and we must teach this to all Black people. Without loyalty to our own people, we will not survive."

As owners of large businesses that generated profits, we all knew wages alone do not create an economic base sufficient to sustain a people. A person's salary may pay their bills and allow for some savings. But profits are far more sizable than wages. Profits can be reinvested in ways that create a viable economic base. As the folks in Tulsa's Greenwood community experienced, profits circulating among Black people over and over helped support each other's businesses and created the wealthiest Black community in the United States. Profits allow a company to pay people more and offer benefits its workers need. They allow it to upgrade its products, manufacturing processes, technology, training, and services. Profits can fund community scholarships, plant trees, and provide playing fields in local parks. They fund uniforms for the local community football team or bowling league. They contribute to veterans' funds and support jobs training and unemployment benefits. They help fund infrastructure and programs we often take for granted.

It was critical to fight Revlon and other companies like it because our community needed the profits that running a successful company produces. But as Black consumers patronized more White-owned companies, profits that once circulated in our communities were now being removed. Some of their benefits were being redirected into other communities. As owners, we knew that Black people would suffer unless free enterprise became a two-way street. That is, until White consumers bought from Black businesses to the same extent we purchased from them, Black people would come up short. We needed to protect and conserve not just our businesses but also the profits our own community produced to benefit our people in a significant way.

"If we lose this battle, we are destined to remain second-class citizens," I said. "From there, I believe we are likely to descend into third- or fourth-class consumers, and poorly paid workers."

All these great entrepreneurs shared their thoughts and ideas. Though we were competitors in the economic market, as Black people we shared a common history and experience. Overwhelmingly, we agreed with one another.

That afternoon, we joined together to fight for our collective survival.

Black entrepreneurs had a long historical legacy to protect, and we wanted each other's firms and our industry to make it. We bonded together, as previous generations of Black businesses had. We discussed our respective business situations and the challenges we faced, and strategized about how to endure the corporate onslaught.

Cornell McBride and I made a verbal commitment that if he ever wanted to sell his company, he would sell to JPC. We sealed our agreement with a handshake.

Collectively, our companies created a trade organization, the American Health and Beauty Aids Institute (AHBAI). I became the founding chairman. We envisioned AHBAI as a resource and advocate for Black-owned businesses in the hair and beauty industry. We didn't use the word "Black" in our title because we didn't want to open ourselves up to attack. The artist Richmond Jones designed our logo, the Proud Lady, a profile of a Black woman with long braids flowing down her back. This image made our message and identity clear.

AHBAI then launched an advertising campaign to help the Black public differentiate products made by Black manufacturers from products made by White-owned firms. We encouraged consumers to support our "buy Black" campaign.

As all this was going on, Ronald Reagan became president. In Chicago, US congressman from Illinois Harold Washington was running to become the city's first Black mayor. White Chicago was likely to split its vote between Jane Byrne, Chicago's first woman mayor, and Richard M. Daley, the son of the man who had governed Chicago for twenty-one years. Black people helped put Mayor Byrne in office, but some of her actions and policies had lost the community's support. The older Mayor Daley started many of the policies that further segregated Black people, led to overcrowded schools, and made jobs hard to come by. He also knocked down a lot of tenements and implemented urban renewal, forcing my mother and thousands of other Black Chicagoans to move out of their homes.

After clearing Black people out of large areas, Daley then packed many into twenty-story high-rise slums, like the Cabrini Green projects. By doing that, he concentrated poor Black folks even more densely into certain neighborhoods. These housing projects became like vote banks for him. Ninety percent of Black folks living in them voted Democrat because they had no better option. It helped keep him in office. The unfortunate people living in these projects were poor, just as I had been. But in these high-rise slums, the residents couldn't see anyone who was doing better socio-economically the way I had when I was coming up. There was no lady next door who had a Rolls-Royce, or neighbors two blocks down with a tennis court. There were no lawyers, teachers, or postal workers living on the same block, only the very poor who had no other option. Many aspiring people lived in those projects as a stopgap until they could afford to move out. Sadly, there were others who did not.

By 1983, the city was almost 40 percent Black, but

Chicago had never had a Black mayor. Once I realized Harold Washington had a chance, I put money and JPC people behind him. I never personally got involved, but I loaned my right-hand man, Bill Berry, to run Harold's campaign. As the race heated up, more than twenty-five people from Johnson Products volunteered full-time for the campaign. Some came from the factory, others from the front office. They included three lawyers and my director of communications, Grayson Mitchell. I kept them on JPC's payroll. When Harold won and became Chicago's first Black mayor, he asked me if Grayson could come work for him. With Mayor Washington in place, there was finally hope that the needs of Black Chicago would both be heard and treated more equitably. Sadly, he died suddenly at work in November 1987.

While all this was going on, Bryant Gumbel, the son of Judge Gumbel, became the first Black anchor for a major television network at NBC's *Today* show. Martin Luther King's birthday became a federal holiday. Jesse Jackson ran for president of the United States twice. In his first primary campaign, he won one-fourth of the votes. I donated money to his efforts. For about a week, I also sent the Beechcraft Duke pilot and airplane to help him get from place to place.

In 1984 the Johnson Products Company experienced our first annual loss. For the first time in its thirty years of existence, JPC was unable to contribute to the profit-sharing program. You can't share what you don't make, and it was heartbreaking.

The following year, the head of Revlon's Professional Products division, Irving Bautner, boasted that Black companies would soon be sold to White companies and disappear. According to him, Black products were inferior. This came from the man who was selling a product that was mighty close to the Ultra Wave Hair Culture formula stolen from me twenty years earlier. A huge uproar followed, and it didn't take him long to apologize. But according to some sources, by 1988, White manufacturers dominated more than half of the Black haircare market.

16

I Give Joan the Business

IN THE FALL of 1944, the prettiest girl I'd ever seen floated down the stairway of Wendell Phillips High School.

Ooh, wowww! I thought, immediately enchanted by this brown-skinned young lady. Without thinking, I spun on my heels and followed two steps behind her. I felt like I had to get her attention. My right hand reached out and pulled her long, shiny pigtails.

"Who the hell do you think you are?" she turned and blasted at me, her neck rolling, eyebrows scowling, and lips curled. Then she turned right back around and strode into a classroom.

I wasn't the least bit concerned that the girl cussed me out. I had gotten her attention, and now I could figure out my next move.

Who is this girl, and how can I find out more about her?

The next day, I was undeterred. Lacking a better strategy to get her to notice me, my hand reached out and pulled her pigtails again.

This time, the girl whipped around, put her hand on her hip, and wagged her finger at me.

"Dammit! Didn't I tell you to leave me alone? Don't you dare touch me!" She disappeared into the classroom.

My heart plummeted.

After being sworn at twice, it was clear she couldn't stand me. I didn't have a chance of getting to know her. But I learned her name was Joan Warden. She was a sophomore and quite popular. She was involved in the school's dance group and already quite good, my spies told me. Though only fifteen, Joan had a reputation for being a smart-ass. I learned she had a boyfriend. Red was one of the stars of Wendell Phillips's football team, which had won the state championship the previous year.

I didn't stand a chance.

Later that semester, I dropped out and left Wendell Phillips and Joan behind. I went to work for Mr. Fuller and concentrated on my work.

During the spring of 1945, I saw a young lady with a beautiful, rounded booty bent over trying to fix her bicycle. I knew how to fix a bike, and I crossed the street, eager to assist.

"Can I help you?" I asked.

The woman stood and turned around. Suddenly Joan and I were face-to-face.

"*Oh, my goodness!*" I exclaimed, excited to see her again. "Let me fix that for you."

I proceeded to fix the tire.

"Do you want to go to my apartment and wash your hands?" she offered, after I finished and as I tried to brush off the dirt. I discovered we both lived on Vernon Avenue, half a block apart.

Joan led me into the small living room of a two-bedroom unit. She introduced me to her mother, whose appearance she favored, except that her mom was plump. Her mother took an immediate liking to me. Before long we were all talking and laughing. Joan had a strong personality like my mother, and I liked that. After I left, my mind overflowed with thoughts about her. From time to time, I would see Red sitting with Joan on the front steps.

As I passed by her place one day, I saw Red straddling his bicycle and speaking with her at the curb. Something I can't explain came over me. I walked up to them.

"Man, do you know you're talking to my wife?" I asked.

"You better get out of here," he yelled, as I turned and hightailed it down the street.

At five-foot-seven and weighing all of 130 pounds, I wouldn't have stood a chance against the taller, well-built Red. But the next time Red came by, I was sitting with Joan on the stoop. It was the beginning of the end of Red.

The more time I spent with Joan, the more interesting I found her. She was talkative, loved to learn, and her nose was always in a novel. She also read a lot of magazines, especially the ones that came with the Sunday paper. Before long, I invited Joan on a date.

We shared interests in cultural activities. She was studying modern dance at the Abraham Lincoln Center, where I was taking voice lessons. The dance and choreography of

Martha Graham and Katherine Dunham inspired her. Ms. Dunham started one of the first Negro ballet groups in America, Ballets Nègres, in Chicago.

I was listening to the radio, reading the entertainment section of the newspaper, and learning about musicals and operas in town. I went to the theater by myself, because I was the only person I could afford to take. Now I had a girlfriend to court who loved the arts. Falling in love with Joan took me to a different level of life.

I also became friendly with Joan's stepfather, Al Henderson, a Pullman porter. After running on the railroad for many years, he reached a point where he worked only on the private train cars that wealthy people chartered. Sometimes they took these private cars to South Dakota so rich White men could hunt pheasant for several days. The Pullman porter took care of all their needs—made the beds, served drinks, cooked meals, and so on. Mr. Henderson made good money and often returned with the uneaten steaks and other food the customers encouraged him to take home.

Hanging out with Joan and her family gave me the sense of a nuclear family.

Mrs. Henderson liked drinking beer. Drinking seemed to activate her. She talked and laughed her butt off. I found her delightful and a lot of fun. I often drank beer with her and caught a buzz. When I went home, my mother smelled the beer on my breath.

"You'd better know what you're doing," she warned.

Joan had already been drinking before age eighteen.

It didn't take long until I discovered that Joan had a temper. If I said something she didn't like, she lost control and became volatile. Occasionally Joan turned violent, cussing me out, scratching, or smacking me.

"Hey-hey-hey, what's going on?" I asked when she started swinging. "Stop it, you have to calm down!"

To keep her from hurting me when she lashed out, I might wrap my arms around her so she couldn't move, or try to restrain her until she cooled down.

"Shh . . . ," I told her, holding on tight as she tried to pull her arms loose. "It's okay, it's okay . . ." I tried to comfort her. I never knew exactly what to do.

Sometimes Joan calmed right down, and we had a nice makeup. Other times, she broke up with me.

When I returned home after Joan's outbursts, Mom would give me the side-eye.

"Why are there scratches on your face, George?" she asked, inspecting me closely. "Why are you having all this trouble? This isn't how a woman who cares for you treats you, son."

Sometimes my relationship with Joan felt like a battle royale. Our relationship was up and down, on and off.

My girlfriend had been born out of wedlock when her mother was sixteen, the same age my mother was when she had me. She didn't have a relationship with her biological father. When Mrs. Henderson drank, there were times she picked on Joan. It seemed like Joan was always fighting for her mother's love.

One of the things I found increasingly attractive about Joan was how she seemed always to be caring for somebody's child. A few of her girlfriends had babies. Practically every weekend I saw Joan, she had a different infant on her hip. She really loved children, and she spoke to them sweetly. I was fascinated.

In June 1947, Joan graduated from high school and turned eighteen. She attended Northwestern University, working her way through school by doing clerical work for the Montgomery Ward catalog. After about six months, Northwestern became too expensive, and she dropped out.

Early the following year, when I was twenty, I bought Joan a diamond engagement ring. I asked Joan's mother, godmother, and adoptive father for her hand. They agreed.

"She doesn't know the value of a dollar," her stepfather warned me.

Right away, I started saving money, anticipating our marriage and starting a family. For me, having a family was always a foregone conclusion. Because my parents didn't live together, I deeply longed to have what I considered a "proper family." I wanted to have enough money to make a good start of it.

I left my mother's apartment and rented a room in a three-bedroom apartment on the second floor of a two-flat building at 6136 South Evans Avenue. What was supposed to be three bedrooms had been subdivided into four. The living room was converted into a large bedroom. The dining room became the living space we six occupants shared. We also split the kitchen and the apartment's one bathroom.

Between the Black folks migrating from the South, soldiers returning from the war, and the inflexibility of the color line, the Black community was becoming more and more crowded.

Even though Joan and I planned to tie the knot, Joan remained volatile. She'd return the ring to me, then want it back immediately.

After we'd been engaged for a year, and I had saved $500 to marry her, about $6,000 today, Joan and I got into a fight and broke up. One day, as I was walking, I saw Joan float down the front steps of her building and get into a car. Some man was driving.

Now she is with him? Is it because he has a car and makes a lot more money than I do? The hell with you!

I went to a bar around the corner, drinking and crying into my beer. Billy Eckstine sang Duke Ellington's "Sophisticated Lady" in the background. I blew all my "wedding" money on new clothes and a Browning Automatic shotgun I could use to go hunting with Joan's stepfather.

For some reason, on Christmas Eve I went by the Hendersons' apartment. By now my on-and-off courtship had lasted more than four years. "Let's stop this," I said. "Let's get back together."

We realized we loved each other, and we reunited.

Joan's mother had begun drinking more heavily. It seemed the more Joan blossomed into a young woman, the worse her mom treated her. I will never forget the day when Joan's mother told her, "Girl, as beautiful as you think you are today, you couldn't hold a candle to my ass when I was your age."

Joan was crushed, absolutely devastated, by how her mother demeaned her. I was furious.

"Look, I don't have any money because I spent it," I told her. "But we can go down to City Hall, and get a marriage license, and get you out of this house. We will figure out the money part as we go."

On Saturday, March 4, 1950, Joan and I dressed up, went downtown, and got our marriage license. Saturday, March 18, we walked into the pastor's study at Metropolitan Church and the Reverend Joseph Evans married us in front of her mother, her sister, her two best friends, and my mother. Afterward I took everyone to lunch on Sixty-First Street.

After paying my bills and the check for lunch, I had $5 left. It had to last until the following Friday.

I moved Joan into my place. She and I stayed in my room and shared the living room area, kitchen, and bathroom. My paycheck from Mr. Fuller wasn't adequate to support two people. Suddenly I had to get on the ball and start doing a lot of things as a married man that I hadn't had to consider while I was single.

"I'm late," Joan told me three months into our marriage.

"I'm sorry?" I asked, not certain I'd heard her correctly.

"I think I'm pregnant," she replied seriously. "I was due last week."

"What?!"

What am I going to do? I gotta get us out of this apartment.

The first thing I did was get a second job in a bowling alley, manually setting up bowling pins. I didn't get off until about ten at night, but bowling alleys paid you the same day. I remember feeling financial pressure because Joan needed a coat before the weather got cold. There was no money left for anything extra. Mama bought me lunch and paid my carfare quite often.

As Joan started thinking about baby names, I began looking for an apartment. I needed to rise to the occasion to find a place where we could raise a family. I also needed to give Joan confidence in me as a husband and provider. Being a good provider was one of the most important things a man could do. During World War II, no one had been building homes. There was still a shortage of affordable housing. When you could find a flat, it cost a premium.

One day I walked into the office of William Knighten Real Estate, a Black-owned business. "I want to fill out an

270

application for an apartment," I said to Mr. Knighten, who was sitting at the desk.

"Well, everybody wants an apartment," he said, and laughed. "What makes you think that *you're* going to get one?"

"My wife is expecting a baby," I proudly told him.

"*Maaan,* nobody wants children!" Mr. Knighten responded, incredulously.

"Whatever it costs, I'll try to pay it," I persisted.

The man humored me, and I filled out the application. When I got to the section for references, I put down my friend Walter Knighten's name, in the event they were related.

While at Fuller Products, I had befriended Walter Knighten and his business partner, a Fullerite whose last name was Bimms. They were starting a direct-sales business, essentially trying to become another Mr. Fuller. The two had opened a little store called the Bimms and Knighten Company. They needed someone to help produce their items, basically hand lotions and face creams. Because I compounded Mr. Fuller's products, Knighten asked if I would help them follow our mentor's advice to get their own company started. I knew they were struggling, but I wasn't willing to be disloyal. I made it clear I would not duplicate or make anything similar to Mr. Fuller's products, give them Mr. Fuller's formulations, or help them improve upon their own formulas. I compounded their products and formulas after work. Joan bottled and labeled them. Though the guys promised to pay us, they never did. But she and I didn't quit.

Several months later, I received an unexpected call.

"Mr. Johnson, if you go out to 209 East Sixty-Ninth

Place and Indiana Avenue, my wife will be there, and you can take a look at a place," Mr. Knighten said. "But you have to go now."

Mrs. Knighten walked me up to the second floor, unlocked the door to an apartment, and ushered me in. This was a real apartment. It hadn't been subdivided. There was a front door, a living room, one bedroom, a bathroom, a small kitchen, and a back door.

"I love it!" I told her.

"You have to put down $105 to secure it."

I called our current landlord, Agnes Lewis. I told her I needed to borrow $105, one month's rent (about $1850 today). Mrs. Lewis, who had three children, was very fond of us. Joan often tutored and helped them with their homework. Mrs. Lewis loaned us the money.

Joan and I finally had our own apartment!

The building had recently been purchased by a Black woman. Walter Knighten was related to William Knighten, after all. Walter had told his brother about the goodwill Joan and I had shown him six months earlier. It was nice how our generosity unexpectedly came back to benefit us when the odds were stacked high against us.

Joan and I now lived in the Park Manor neighborhood, named after the all-White Park Manor United Church of Christ at Seventieth and South Parkway. When we moved into the building, White flight had begun. Another apartment opened quickly, and we helped my mother move in on the first floor. Soon Park Manor became an all-Black congregation. When the area's White Democratic precinct captain moved out, I replaced him.

Our baby was due sometime in April. Joan was scheduled

to deliver at Cook County Hospital, which had a bad reputation for how they treated Black people. Joan wanted to deliver at Provident Hospital, a private facility staffed mostly by Black doctors, including her own physician, Dr. P. C. Williams.

One Saturday I only had $5 left after paying that week's bills. With Joan's due date drawing near, I knew I had to get some money so Joan could have our baby at Provident. I decided to go to a racetrack bookie. I read that day's form and picked out five long shots. Miraculously, three of the horses won. I left with $85. I gave Joan my winnings, and she put them down as a deposit at Provident on Monday morning.

On Monday, Joan caught a cold and developed a temperature. About 1:30 a.m., my wife began experiencing labor pains. We went to the hospital. While I paced back and forth in the waiting room, Joan delivered our son, Eric George.

This was March 29, 1951.

I was *amazed* that this baby had come out of Joan's body. I felt overwhelmed.

How am I going to pay for our child?

I worked six, seven days a week. I'd rather be tired than worried.

When Eric was close to a year old, I started bussing tables at Harrison's, a restaurant downtown on Madison near the financial district. I got off from Fuller Products at 4:30 p.m. and worked at Harrison's until 10:30 or 11:00, and headed home after that.

I'd walk in the door to find Joan physically and emotionally worn out from caring for Eric all day. Joan loved Eric and expressed such kindness toward him. I adored that about her. Our little baby also had nine-month colic and cried for much of the day. I took Eric from Joan and let her go to sleep.

Then I rocked him. I didn't go to sleep until after our baby fell asleep. Many nights he didn't fall asleep until 1:00 a.m. In addition to working at Fuller Products and Harrison's Restaurant, I washed cars on Saturdays and Sundays. New parenthood was hard on both of us. We were young, under a lot of pressure, and had no time to figure things out.

All of my long hours at work and Joan's parenting at home without adequate support began taking a toll on our marriage. Sometimes I wished she'd be as sweet to me as she was to Eric. It seemed like some of the loving and hugging I used to receive had shifted over to him. Sometimes I felt a little bit jealous.

On January 29, 1953, our second son, John Edward, came into the world. Once he became a toddler, he loved to follow his big brother around the apartment.

In 1962 Petey was born, followed by Joanie two years after that. By then I had met my goal of becoming a good financial provider. JPC was doing very well as a business, employer, and member of the community.

I tried to keep myself grounded in my spiritual life and not be seduced by the glamour that began to surround me. But all sorts of new challenges began to pop up.

When you start experiencing good fortune, it's easy to think that you did it yourself.

Look at what I've done!

People were willing to become yes men to me, buttering me up and telling me only what I wanted to hear. It all began to go to my head.

People in the community liked and admired me. Of all the praise I was receiving, I most wanted it to come from my wife. But I consistently felt that Joan didn't express her appreciation for what I was doing, and it led me to become increasingly unhappy with our relationship. JPC was receiving accolades for our business achievements and good work in the community. Our employees felt good about how we treated them, and twice voted against unions attempting to organize in our plant.

Why didn't Joan encourage me, reassure me, and compliment me from time to time? I needed her to be proud of me. I wanted to feel her appreciation. A term of endearment. A random embrace. A kiss when I accomplished something. I did everything I knew to let Joan know I loved her and wanted to please her. But no material or physical expression of my love seemed to be enough.

Periodically, I'd fish for a compliment or hug after I received some public recognition. It was to no avail. Joan was always reticent to communicate loving feelings. Nor did she affirm or attempt to inspire me.

Why does everybody else see good things in me that she can't see?

Her lack of admiration and affection began to bother me.

Given all that my efforts had provided for her, our children, and extended family, I didn't think I should have to ask for a pat on the back. I thought she should have felt enough love for me to offer one herself. Everything I'd done was obvious. I wasn't going to beg her.

On the other hand, Joan consistently complained that she didn't get the recognition she believed she deserved for the company's accomplishments. She did deserve recognition for being involved in the company, especially during the early days. She was right by my side doing anything and everything necessary.

Our marriage also took a hit when I was forced to eliminate Joan's job. Overnight, the joy and satisfaction she got from being Mrs. Johnson, chatting with our employees, and working at JPC was gone. Joan and I had different parenting styles as well. I worried about her permissiveness and I didn't want the hired help raising our kids.

I also discovered that when people get wealthy, their attitudes can change. Joan always had the tendency to speak her mind, especially after we moved to Glencoe.

As her stylist Morris Gearring put it, "If Joan liked you, you knew it. If Joan didn't like you, you knew it."

It was bad enough that she could sometimes be cold and unfeeling toward me, which I found confusing because I loved her very much and sensed she still loved me. What bothered me most, though, was when she was sharp-tongued with others. Whatever Joan thought at that moment, that's what you got. Much of this happened when she was drinking. Both of us were drinking. Having a martini before dinner and a couple of nightcaps afterward was a mark of living the good life, back then. But when Joan drank a lot, she changed.

My spiritual devotion and development had been growing in leaps and bounds. But I fell short in my desire to bring my wife along. Joan wasn't interested in joining me on my spiritual journey.

Though I understood that my devotion to the Spirit had gotten me to success, I entered a period of spiritual struggle. A part of me fell under the allure of the affluent life, which wielded a double-edged sword. I didn't realize how strongly I needed to stay disciplined, especially as it related to resisting temptation.

I invited some distributors who were doing well to our plant. We walked around the facility together and had a nice conversation. I said encouraging things about their businesses. I also tried to share some constructive feedback in an affirming way, as one Black businessowner helping others.

Experiencing JPC's beautiful offices and witnessing several hundred people working in the plant made them feel proud. I recall a few saying what a great guy I was. What a wonderful place. What a wonderful company. They kept using all these superlatives and stroking my ego.

"George, you're a helluva guy!" one man said. Somehow that got stuck in my head.

Well, maybe I am a helluva guy!

I started wondering why, if I was such a great guy, my wife couldn't see it. I began to feel sorry for myself, and my attention began to wander.

At first, I was unfaithful with my eyes. Increasingly, in the company of other successful men, I witnessed how worldly success makes it easier to make a move on a woman. I saw how some women become less likely to resist accomplished men's romantic advances.

A part of me knew it was just a matter of time before I crossed the line.

In the late 1970s, after Joan left JPC, I started having an affair. I'm ashamed about this weakness. I deeply regret my infidelity.

In my affair, I sought the affection, appreciation, and fulfillment I wasn't receiving from my wife. Because I was discreet, I deluded myself into believing I was being unfaithful in a more positive way than I witnessed among some other men. I tried to keep the relationship from affecting my family routines. I also made up a lot of lies, excuses, and alibis to be in the lady's presence.

One part of me knew that what I was doing wasn't right;

another part of me rationalized it. I tried to ignore the small voice that reminded me I was wrong, but I couldn't fool my conscience. Guilt plagued me throughout the affair. I thought that when I ended the relationship, my shame would go away. But temptations grow, and I engaged in another discreet extramarital relationship.

I didn't divorce because I wanted it all. The truth was, I was still in love with Joan, and I yearned for her to love me. I continued to be physically attracted to her. Even as she matured, I thought she looked fantastic! I also adored my children. My sons needed love and a man's guidance. My daughter needed my love and protection. I knew firsthand what it was like to see other kids with their dad but not have yours there. I couldn't fathom living apart from my wife and children.

I contacted a marriage counselor at Lutheran General Hospital, a Protestant hospital with a spiritual mission, and tried to get Joan to go to marital counseling with me. By now, we were both drinking too much. I could stop and did stop for years at a time; Joan could not. She wasn't interested in counseling. That, to me, was a bad sign.

I became extremely disappointed and stopped trying to make our marriage work.

As I started walking apart from the Spirit, I also began to slack off in some of my spiritual discipline. After I stepped away from the righteous path, I lost a lot of power and strength. God does not reward unfaithful behavior.

Joan loved Europe, and we decided to get an apartment abroad. We found a seventeen-hundred-square-foot pied-à-terre exceptionally well located along the river Seine.

Though living on the first floor wasn't our first choice, from our windows we could see the Eiffel Tower, at the northwest end of the large public park the Champ de Mars. The Bateaux Mouches cruise boats that ran up and down the river turned around outside our window. We could see all the lights the city is known for. The ambience was wonderful.

Shopping became one of our favorite pastimes. Paris is clothing paradise, and Joan loaded up when we went there. She frequented at least four couture boutiques, buying Yves Saint Laurent, Givenchy, Karl Lagerfeld, and Christian Dior. She liked Chanel, and they *loved* her. I bought her Cartier watches.

But though we found lots of entertainment in the City of Light, no amount of clothes, or escargots, or champagne seemed to help us rekindle our romance. We would have a wonderful time and an awful time within the same day.

One day, I left the apartment to go for a walk.

"Monsieur, you should take your wife to Deauville—there's a Black film festival there."

I turned around and saw an attractive, well-dressed French woman coming down the stairs behind me.

"You might like it," she continued. "Maybe you'll see people you know."

Curious, I listened while this woman, who introduced herself as Renée, told me about the festival taking place a couple of hours away along the English Channel.

Joan and I never went to the film festival, but I started running into this friendly, pleasant-looking brunette, who lived on the third floor. I learned she had a law degree and played classical piano. She hit on me at some point when

Joan was back stateside, and Renée and I began an affair. I had completely drifted away from my spiritual discipline.

After working a year for Procter & Gamble after graduating from Babson, Eric came to work for JPC. In 1975, he also began at the University of Chicago Booth School of Business. A rung at a time, my oldest son started climbing JPC's managerial ladder, rising from district manager to sales manager to the head of professional sales. Eric had a brief assignment, in 1986, as VP of sales. We never spoke about a succession plan, but with his business school education he was my obvious heir.

In 1987, I made Eric president of JPC, and I continued as chairman of the board. By then, JPC needed to borrow money, and through his knowledge and networks, Eric secured a source of financing. Borrowing was expensive, but at least our bills were paid. Early on, Eric hired two Arthur Andersen staff members who had been working on our account: Tom Polk became the VP of finance, and a man named Corey became manager of operations. As Eric began restructuring the company to survive the competitive onslaught, he laid people off to save money and cut prices to increase sales.

He also dissolved the profit-sharing plan.

When Continental Bank distributed the money, my employees were ecstatic. Dorothy McConnor received $250,000, about $1 million today. Vera Williams received more than $200,000. My brother Robert took about $220,000 to the bank. Supervisors pocketed more than $100,000. Line employees were paid between $50,000 and $100,000.

In December 1987, Reginald F. Lewis purchased Beatrice

International Foods for $985 million. This company, which he renamed TLC Beatrice International, was the largest African American–owned and –operated business in the United States. Lewis became the first Black man to own and run a billion-dollar corporation. Reginald had an apartment on Paris's Left Bank. Our apartment was on the Right Bank. He and I talked on the phone from time to time. I admired the way he was charting new heights as a Black entrepreneur.

In the summer of 1988, Joan went to Paris without me. While she was gone, I had the absolutely rotten idea of bringing Renée to Chicago. I thought I'd show her where I lived.

I drove up the driveway and pulled around to the back—only to find my daughter standing there washing her car.

I backed the hell up, beat a hasty retreat, and got out of there as fast as possible. But Joanie had seen Renée and me. I knew the consequences of being caught with another woman were going to be severe. Joanie called her mother in Paris and told her, "You'd better come back home and get a lawyer!"

I didn't want to get divorced, but I knew I was wrong. After I was served with divorce papers, I bought an apartment downtown and moved out of the house. I had backed myself into a corner and had to face the consequences of my infidelity.

Joan obtained legal representation from Rinella & Rinella, one of the most prominent divorce law firms in town. Phillip Rinella, Joan's lawyer, wanted me to sell JPC and give her half of the money. To keep from selling the company, I would have had to take out a loan to buy her out. But in 1989

JPC was losing money, and the stock was way down. Under these circumstances, I could not borrow enough money on my share of the company. Two choices remained, and both were painful—I could sell the company and leave, or give Joan half my shares and take other assets equal to the value of my shares.

My greater priority was to keep the company in the family. I gave Joan my stock. In other words, I just gave her the whole company. I negotiated a combination of cash and assets for myself, including the Paris apartment and the house in Jamaica. There was also my investment in McClurg Court, a thousand-apartment complex in downtown Chicago; a cattle farm we owned in McHenry, Illinois; and some other real estate we owned, equal to the value that she received.

On October 10, 1989, I sat in Rinella's office, emotionally drained and in a fog. I signed all the settlement papers and resigned my role at JPC. When I stood up and walked away from the table, Joan looked back at me with a strange look on her face.

Though I had plenty of regrets, I wasn't bitter. My behavior had been rotten. I certainly wouldn't have wanted her to treat me the way I'd treated her. My priority had been to keep the company in the family, and I'd accomplished that. I took a position at Independence Bank and expanded my role as chairman of the executive committee.

I had lost JPC, ruined my marriage, ruptured my relationships with my children, and lost my purpose. Joan and I had been married for thirty-nine years and courted for five years before that. I was reeling and grieving my losses and mistakes.

My mother was one of the few people I confided in, but she was not all that sympathetic.

After several weeks, I returned to Paris. I clung to Renée closely for a while and did crazy things such as spending too much money at auctions.

About six months later, Renée asked me to marry her. On June 9, 1991, I married her. We honeymooned in Saint-Tropez, France, stopping in Cannes on the way. To my surprise, she brought her grown daughter on our honeymoon.

I knew I needed help healing and finding myself again. I sought out Dr. Harold Visotsky, the chairman of the department of psychiatry at Northwestern Memorial Hospital. I spent the next couple of years in therapy, trying to straighten myself out.

During Joan's reign, Eric became both president and CEO of JPC, and Joan became chairman, at a salary of $400,000, almost $1 million today. By then JPC's sales had dropped to $29 million, about $72 million today. The stock price had fallen to about $2.50 per share.

In 1989 M&M Products was having similar problems. I heard through the grapevine that my friend Cornell McBride had accepted a letter of intent from a financial dealmaker, Bertram Lee. Bertram wanted to buy the entire company. By the time I discovered this, M&M was already on the market. Even though I was no longer involved in JPC's business, I reached out to Cornell to remind him of our handshake agreement in Glencoe, when he promised me first refusal if he decided to sell. I knew buying M&M would improve JPC's bottom line by adding $12 million to JPC's $29 million in sales. It would immediately move Johnson Products out of the red and into the black.

Bertram was unable to raise the money. Cornell told me he would sell M&M to JPC. I immediately called Eric and implored him to jump on Cornell's offer. In February 1990, JPC paid $5 million for M&M's domestic business.

M&M Products was JPC's savior. It raised Johnson Products' sales to $41 million and put the profit back into the business. JPC's stock rose from about $2.50 to around $26 a share.

In 1991 Johnson Products was the seventh best performing stock on the American Stock Exchange. After the company recovered and became profitable again, Eric reassessed the situation and decided that running Johnson Products wasn't his calling. He soon left JPC to start his own company.

Losing Eric didn't bode well, as Joan didn't know how to run JPC. She had not worked in the company since 1970. Tom was a CPA, not a CEO. He had only been with JPC as VP for about three years, and he didn't know the company's history. Still, Joan made him president.

The person that I'd become wasn't the person I'd been for most of my life. In therapy, I came to the realization that though I was married to Renée, I was still reeling from my divorce from Joan. I was miserable not having my family. Counseling helped me become more clearheaded. I could see where I was and where I wanted to be.

Early in 1992, the telephone in the Chicago apartment I shared with Renée started ringing regularly during the evening. From the caller ID, I knew it was Joan. I didn't answer. Once Renée picked up the phone, heard Joan's voice, and hung up.

A couple of weeks later, Renée went to Paris to check on some family matters. While she was away, the phone started ringing at 6:00 p.m. and kept on ringing until about 11:00. I don't know why I didn't take the phone off the hook. Finally I picked up.

"What do you want, Joan?" I asked.

"Hello, sweetheart," she purred. I could tell she'd been drinking.

"Joan, you can't be calling me that."

"But I am," she insisted. "Why don't you come over to see my apartment?"

Joan had sold our Glencoe home, and she had moved into a condo in Chicago, two blocks from Renée and me.

I got up, got dressed, and went to her apartment. I intended to humor her and check out her apartment then go back home and get some sleep. When she opened the door, she smiled. Then she kissed and hugged me tightly. I was stunned by her warmth. It was the first time in decades I had felt real affection from her. I realized Joan remained the love of my life.

Turns out Joan wanted to get back together. It was the answer to my prayers. Several days later, I called Renée in Paris to tell her I was returning to Joan.

I'd made many mistakes in my personal life, but it doesn't make sense to keep making mistake after mistake. Joan and I began courting and trying to renew our relationship. I went back to her apartment each night, and we talked. We were affectionate. I felt like I was living in a fantasy.

We left our mistakes in the past.

A few weeks later, I moved in with Joan. The first thing I did was pour her J&B Scotch down the damn drain. She went off hard liquor. We started drinking wine with dinner, and I was the one who poured it. Joan and I wanted each other. We wanted our family together again.

I was one happy man.

After I got back with Joan, my life returned to normal. I resumed all my spiritual practices. I returned to God, and I have worked hard to be with the Lord ever since. Thankfully, ours is a forgiving God, and Jesus's gospel is one of forgiveness.

My family was mending, and things were going well as chairman of the executive committee at Independence Bank. Joan and I had been living happily together for more than a year.

At noon on June 15, 1993, the telephone rang.

"George, I need to talk to you about something."

It was my friend Jim Lowry, who had worked for McKinsey consulting and was the firm's first Black consultant. Joan had invited Jim to be on JPC's board after she took over as chair. He was a good adviser.

"Listen, George, there will be an announcement today that JPC is being sold to Ivax Corporation," he told me.

My body slumped forward onto my desk.

I had been living with Joan for more than a year and sleeping in the same bed with her every night. This was the first I'd heard about Johnson Products being sold.

The news gave me a horrible feeling. There's no way I could comprehend what I was hearing. I had to think about her situation, but I had no answer for why Joan had never said anything to me. I was angry. I was hurt.

After I calmed down and thought rationally about it, I realized that monetizing the company was Joan's best bet. She did not know how to build or protect the Johnson Products Company. I wished she had sold JPC to a Black company, but the more I thought about the situation, the more I realized how fortunate Joan was that Phillip Frost, the chair of Ivax, had made her an offer.

The only way I could survive the situation was to forgive Joan for not informing me. If I wanted to stay with her, I had to forgive Joan from my heart. The fact was, I wanted to stay with her. I knew I would never be able to sleep in the same bed with her if I held a grudge against her. I had to forgive her instantly.

The next day, I turned sixty-six. I'd been given a helluva birthday present.

I learned later that Phillip Frost's offer had come out of the blue and Joan could not afford to refuse it. Joan received $67 million for the entire transaction, of which $32 million was hers. She and Joanie appeared on the cover of the November 1993 issue of *Black Enterprise* magazine beneath the headline "The $67 Million Question: Should We Sell Our Firms to Whites?"

Of course, hindsight is always twenty-twenty, but knowing what I know today, I would never have taken the Johnson Products Company public. Though we were blessed to be Black "firsts" in many areas, nothing could have prepared Joan, our children, or me for some of the challenges and situations we encountered.

A year after Ivax purchased JPC, Joan and Joanie left the company. Our son John, who worked in sales, was laid off. Within a couple of years, my brother Robert was let go after almost forty years. Many people stayed on until the company was sold to L'Oréal.

A few of our women employees, including Gwen Butler and Maryann Fitzgerald, started an annual JPC reunion. It was such a big compliment that they wanted to keep the love and relationships going. For about fifteen years, they kept our JPC family together. Each reunion, they printed a program listing the JPC employees who had passed away. Over time, it filled up with names.

There was a lot of love at JPC, and that love hasn't died.

On April 22, 1995, Joan and I remarried and embarked

upon another twenty-seven years of love, devotion, and fidelity. All told, our marriage spanned sixty-nine years; including our courtship, we were together for seventy-four. Joan and I spent most of our lives together, from the time I fixed her bike as a teenager until she died on September 6, 2019.

Epilogue

IN 1997 IVAX sold to L'Oréal. But to get the FTC to approve the merger, L'Oréal had to divest itself of some of its brands, including Ultra Sheen Conditioner and Hair Dress. The Wella Company bought several brands Ivax divested. In 1999 L'Oréal moved production from Chicago to a plant in New Jersey. Only a few of our former employees relocated East. The move left the JPC building empty, and it stayed that way for many years. At one point Procter & Gamble bought some of our brands, including Ultra Sheen Conditioner and Hair Dress.

The companies milked our products, kicked them around, and exploited their historic Black haircare legacy. Rather than investing in the brands and making them even better, they used them as a cash cow.

As much as it pained me to witness, that's capitalism.

In 2009 a multiracial group of investors bought Johnson

289

Products Company from Procter & Gamble, reestablishing it as a Black-owned company. But like many Black businesses, they eventually ran out of money.

Racism trailed my mother, Priscilla Johnson, but she and the six million Black Americans who participated in the Great Migration helped reshape our nation. John, Robert, and I all lived successful lives. Thinking about those who both stayed in the South and departed, if Black America were its own country, our spending power of over $1.6 trillion would make us one of the fifteen largest economies in the world. America remains awash with racial inequality, but Black people now participate in all aspects of American society, from the farm life my mother left behind to service workers, middle managers, the C-suite, and the vice presidency and presidency of the United States. Black people are central to all aspects of American life and culture, including the nation's economy. I am heartened that stories like those of Annie Turnbo Malone, Madam C. J. Walker, Berry Gordy, Clarence Avant, and other Black businesspeople who succeeded in the face of overwhelming odds are being told on the stage, the big screen, and streaming services. It's thrilling that their lives are inspiring new generations of Black entrepreneurs.

It satisfies me to know that my story now contributes to the growing body of knowledge about Black enterprise and Black-owned businesses in the United States. I wish life here were fair and equitable, but that continues not to be the case. Even though in some ways things are much better, in other ways things seem as bad as, if not worse than, they've been in my lifetime. Everyone will have to struggle in some or maybe many areas. Life is harder for Black people, women, and other folks with marginalized identities. Still, it's important not to fear or steer clear of difficult things. Life's journey includes some uphill travel. As Dr. Faulkner taught me, the struggle of climbing brings the growth. And I believe Mr. Fuller's maxims. *God did not intend for you to be poor. Latch on to those gifts and use them to create the life you want.*

One lesson I learned stands above all others: living according to the Golden Rule is the most rewarding approach to life. It's one whose infinite outcomes can't be predicted or forecast by any man-made tool or instrument. I find the Golden Rule far more powerful than any business plan. It more than compensated for my eleventh-grade education, as well as a multitude of blind spots, shortcomings, and errors.

The financial things I accomplished, I did not seek. They were just one type of reward for treating other people the way I wanted them to treat me.

One of my greatest joys was being able to retire my mother at a reasonable age and take good care of her. In 1995, after she was diagnosed with lung cancer, the doctors told us she had about three months to live. Many nights, I'd sit next to her in the hospice bed for hours. We'd reminisce about our lives together, laughing, talking, and crying.

"You have given me a wonderful life," she told me.

I could only imagine what mine would have been like if she hadn't been courageous enough to leave Mississippi as a teenager, with her sister and three young children.

Looking back with the perspective of an almost one-hundred-year-old man, I realize that by giving of myself to other people, I helped myself even more than I helped them. I put all my heart into my family, my business, and my community. Above all, I devoted myself to my relationship with God. My good intentions returned manyfold, beyond what I ever imagined.

For forty years, the Johnson Products Company helped countless Black Americans engage in a biased society with dignity. We helped people relax their hair to make haircare easier, to express fashion and style, to meet society's definition of professionalism in the workplace, and to be seen as fully human. JPC also helped Black people wear their hair as naturally as it springs from their head, and to express pride and authenticity in their natural appearance.

JPC provided hundreds of Chicagoans with meaningful jobs, generous benefits, and a loving environment during a time when many Black people experienced a lack of fairness and opportunity at work. There's no way to know the impact of the company's Golden Rule philosophy—how many people were able to get a job, buy their groceries, pay the rent, purchase a new car, put a down payment on a house, or send their children to college because JPC's compensation was well above average. Our company also served as a training ground that prepared many people who moved on to work in nonprofits, government, corporate America, and entrepreneurship.

Millions of dollars of JPC profits have been cycled into the City of Chicago, and particularly Black communities on the South and West Sides. Civic organizations around the Windy City benefited from thousands more dollars of company contributions, making Chicagoland a better place for everyone. And who can calculate the value of college? One thousand deserving Black and Brown youth obtained a college education they may not have been able to access without the help of the George E. Johnson Educational Fund.

The Golden Rule's ripple effect over generations remains incalculable.

Acknowledgments

I had no intention of ever writing a book. In fact, for thirty years, people asked me to tell my story, and for thirty years, I always gave them the same answer: "I don't like to talk about myself." Why didn't I like to talk about myself? Once I started taking inventory of all the blessings I received from the Lord, the next thing I knew, I'd be crying. On Sunday, November 21, 2021, at about 10:30 in the morning, I had an epiphany. In that experience I clearly heard five words: "You must tell your story." Had I ever intended to write a book, I certainly would not have waited until I was ninety-four to start.

I want to thank so many people for making this book possible.

I want to especially thank my mother, Priscilla Dean Johnson Howard, whose courage when she was just eighteen years old opened a world of possibility to me that would not have existed if she'd stayed in Jim Crow Mississippi. Though my mother left my father behind, I'm grateful to my dad, Charles David Johnson, who showed me his love, warmth, and nurturance through his letters and in person.

I will always be indebted to Mr. S. B. Fuller, who poured priceless lessons about spirituality and entrepreneurship into my young heart and mind. I'm also grateful to Dr. Herbert A. Martini, who gave me invaluable advice about creativity and perseverance, and Dr. William J. Faulkner, for his spiritual guidance as my pastor.

I can't express enough gratitude to Joan Johnson, who was my partner in love and life for sixty-nine years and the mother of our four wonderful children. Joan worked alongside me after I founded the company, in the production room with her sleeves rolled up, as well as in our offices as a bookkeeper dressed to the nines. Not only that, Joan covered the home front. She was a doting and generous mother and grandmother who raised our children, tended to our house, and nurtured our family as I traveled and worked strenuous hours.

Joan worked on several boards, including at Spelman College, the Chicago Museum of Contemporary Art, the Women's Board of the University of Chicago, and the Women's Board of Northwestern University. She was a terrific fundraiser. During the 1980s she put on three charity fashion shows for the Congressional Black Caucus and was the first chairperson of the Black Creativity Gala at the Museum of Science and Industry in Chicago, which is still going strong today.

My brothers, John and Robert, supported me, lifting a big load from my shoulders and making great and noteworthy contributions to JPC. When he joined me in 1965, John was a Godsend for JPC. He gave me a lot of confidence and built the legendary salesforce that became the foundation of JPC's success. Robert researched shipping and warehousing best practices and implemented them, running both departments masterfully. I am grateful to have had brothers as supportive and loving as they were.

When I was a young man, my children Eric, John, George Jr., and Joan Marie opened my heart to a love and the family I'd always longed for. I experienced tremendous joy and inspiration watching my children grow. Being responsible for my young children's lives made me hustle as I'd never hustled before, working two and three jobs in an attempt to make their childhoods better than mine. I am incredibly proud of them.

My grandchildren Lucretia, Erin, Cara, John, Eric, Katja, David, George III, Olivia, and Taddeo light up my life and bless me. I love them dearly and am proud of how they're carrying on the Johnson family legacy. Today, Eric and his two daughters, Erin Tolefree and Cara Hughes, are continuing the family tradition as entrepreneurs. In 1997 Eric purchased a company doing $42 million in annual revenue; today the sales of Baldwin-Richardson Foods exceed $500 million. Erin and Cara are running the company and Eric continues to coach them effectively. Though Erin, President and CEO, and Cara, Executive Vice President of Sales and Marketing, are tremendously capable, from time to time their grandfather checks in and shares a bit of his wisdom, encouraging them always to follow the Golden Rule.

I'm grateful to Veronica Farfan for her years of loyalty and support.

God uses all people to share his blessings, and God used Orville Nelson to light the spark and open the door for me to step into my destiny.

What would I have done without Bill Berry, my right-hand man for nearly two decades? I cannot forget the dignified and professional way he represented me throughout Chicago when I couldn't be present because I was running the company. A confidant who also wrote speeches for me, Bill helped me find my voice and present myself professionally at various events. JPC would not have made the mark it did upon Chicago if he hadn't been by my side.

From the moment I heard the Reverend Jesse Jackson speak when he was just a twenty-four-year-old student at the University of Chicago Theological Seminary, I knew I was in the presence of a brilliant mind, a young man with tremendous potential. Little did I know the impact this courageous leader would have upon the city and the country when I put my arms around him and supported him. I feel blessed to have had a long relationship with him, and I am honored that he once said, "George Johnson was the foundation of my career."

If it weren't for Tom Kuehn, my account executive at our advertising agency, I wouldn't have met Don Cornelius in 1970, and *Soul Train* wouldn't have been sponsored by JPC. Don was one of the most creative people I've ever met. His chutzpah and instincts for music, fashion, and popular culture helped JPC ride the current of many of the latest trends. Between JPC's vision and Don's creativity, we were a great team. I'm thankful to have known and worked with him.

My executive vice president and administrative assistant, Dorothy Middlebrooks McConnor, was like my alter ego. Loyal and protective, Dorothy knew me so well that she understood how I thought. I could trust her to make decisions that were almost the same as mine. Dorothy ran the whole office, and her administrative abilities were remarkable. I don't know how I would have managed without her.

I am incredibly grateful for Ernest Lafontant, one of my closest friends and among the smartest people I've ever known. He transformed JPC's purchasing department into an efficient operation and was our lawyer for many years.

I am deeply indebted to the hundreds of proud, loyal, and hardworking Johnson Products Company employees, including Hilton Tregg, Jim Middlebrooks, Pat Johnson, Andrew Bright, Francine Hurst, Gwen and Edris Ford, Clotee Betts, Norman Lebowski, Grayson Mitchell, Tom Polk, Vera Williams, and so many more.

I am particularly grateful to Gwen Butler, Dave Corner, Mary Rollison, Loisteen Walker, and Pam Young, who generously allowed us to interview them about their experiences working at JPC.

I am also thankful for Mike Simms, who came to JPC at a critical time, professionalized our operations department, and worked his way up to executive vice president. Mike performed his duties like a hawk. He caught Orville trying to steal our formulas and fired him.

The Lord blessed me to be one of the first customers of two trailblazers in Black advertising. Vince Cullers was a visionary and ahead of his time. Tom Burrell was legendary, and produced many of the groundbreaking, innovative, high-quality, and iconic television and print ads JPC became known for over the years.

I'm grateful to Leon Cooper for taking a risk on me by letting me rent the production area in the rear of his store.

Thanks to Millard Frazier, who left his business, sometimes two days a week, to travel with or without me to teach barbers how to use Ultra Wave Hair Culture safely and finger-wave hair properly. For four years, he was indispensable to me.

And where would I have been without JPC's distributors, especially Don Robey, Melvin Jefferson, Joe Bailey, and Chico Foote?

The writings of Thomas R. Kelly, Harry Emerson Fosdick, and Professor Rufus Jones inspired me and helped broaden my spiritual foundation.

I'm grateful to Max Holzman, a dependable supplier and friend.

I believe the Spirit directed me to meet the incredibly talented Wintley Phipps when he was just twenty-two years old. I feel blessed that Wintley has inspired me with his baritone voice and uplifting music for more than forty-seven years. I'm also thankful to the Reverend Robert Schuller for being a great television minister to me and for helping to launch Wintley's amazing career.

Thank you to Dan Dickinson for helping me overcome one of my greatest fears and teaching me how to fly an airplane.

My relationships with John H. Johnson, founder of the Johnson Publishing Company; Edward Lewis, Clarence O. Smith, Cecil Hollingsworth, and Jonathan Blount, the founders of *Essence*; Earl Graves at *Black Enterprise;* and Bernice Calvin at *Beauty Trade* created a supportive ecosystem that helped all our businesses thrive.

I'm grateful to Dr. Harold Visotsky, who played a pivotal role during a very difficult time in my life.

Thank you, Julieanna Richardson and the priceless *Historymakers* online resource, for bringing countless stories of Black excellence to the Library of Congress and the world. We relied on several *Historymakers* interviews to help ensure the accuracy of this book.

ACKNOWLEDGMENTS

Thanks to the City of Chicago and particularly the South Side, where I learned some of my most valuable lessons in love, life, and business. Chicago embraced the Johnson Products Company for more than forty-four years, offering the most wonderful workforce any entrepreneur could imagine and providing fertile ground within which we could sow the seeds of JPC's financial prosperity in the South Side and West Side communities.

I'd also like to acknowledge one of our city's favorite sons, John W. Rogers, the founder and co-chairman of Ariel Investments, the first Black-owned capital management firm in the world. I've known John since he was six years old, and we've been friends throughout his adulthood. In fact, JPC was among Ariel's earliest supporters. But what stands out most to me among John's many impressive attributes is how he has diligently followed the Golden Rule in his business life, earning my admiration.

I'm grateful to Hilary Beard, who I believe God sent me. The very next day, after the Lord instructed me to write this book, I told Christopher Rabb, the son of my soon-to-be wife, Madeline Murphy Rabb, that I was looking for a very smart writer who was both Black and spiritual. This Pennsylvania state representative from Philadelphia introduced me to Hilary, who was one of his constituents. When we spoke, I immediately sensed her warmth and spirituality. Compassionate, patient, and excellent at drawing my stories out of me and shaping them, Hilary and I enjoyed a wonderful rapport working in person and via Zoom, getting to know each other for over two years as we created this book together.

We couldn't have gotten a publishing deal without our amazing literary agent, Jennifer Lyons. She was so enthusiastic about my story and the Golden Rule that she fought to represent us. I will always remember her tenacious efforts on our behalf as we shopped and later completed the book.

What a blessing to have the opportunity to work with our editor, Tracy Sherrod, who immediately understood the importance of preserving and sharing this untold Black history and the power of the Golden Rule. Thanks to Peyton Young and all the editorial, marketing, publicity, and production people at Little, Brown and Company who helped make this book possible.

I've overcome a lot of fears in my life, but stage fright is one I have yet to conquer. I am indebted to Harriette Cole for her expert coaching to help me find my voice, so I can share my story through the media and live in public.

Of course, none of this would have been possible without the indescribable blessings of the Lord, who has wrapped His arms around my shoulders from the earliest days of my youth all the way to the present, helping me make the impossible possible and share the abundance I experienced with others.

Indeed, the Lord's blessings never cease. I experienced one of the greatest surprises of my life when a longtime acquaintance, Madeline Murphy Rabb, unexpectedly became a part of my life. Madeline's presence in my life raised me out of a depression and brought me new love and happiness, which led to our marriage, a joy I never expected to experience at ninety-four years of age. And who knew that this art connoisseur and master's level swimming champion was also a writer in her own right? Madeline was a tremendous help, supporting me as I reflected upon all the amazing occurrences of my life and standing at my side as a writing helpmate as Hilary and I honed and revised my story.

Hilary Beard's Acknowledgments

If the good Lord blesses you and the stars align, you may experience days like November 26, 2021, when I received a text out of the blue from my friend Christopher Rabb, asking if I knew who George Johnson was. Through Chris's thoughtful and gracious introduction, I found myself at Mr. Johnson's kitchen table two weeks later about to embark upon an amazing journey. Chris, thank you for opening the door for me.

Words cannot express my gratitude to Mr. Johnson for offering me the opportunity to document his essential but untold life story, so central to American and African American history. Mr. J., our countless hours of exploration blessed me with your amazing narratives, deepened my understanding of God, African American history, life, and culture, and helped me understand my deceased parents' and ancestors' lives more completely. What a joy it has been to explore Black history, entrepreneurism, spiritual development, and life with an almost centenarian.

I am deeply indebted to Madeline Murphy Rabb Johnson, who brought her warm heart, joyful spirit, and sharp intellect to bear, transforming what normally would have been a team of two into a trio. Madeline, thank you for sharing time that under normal circumstances you would have devoted to your new husband alone to help us complete this book more easily. From sharing your inside-Chicago insights, to patiently reading chapters and helping us sharpen revisions, to the constant behind-the-scenes support that kept us working so smoothly, your many contributions were pivotal to this book. Not to mention your homemade granola.

Jennifer Lyons, thank you for recognizing the priceless-ness of Mr. Johnson's story and for being such an enthusiastic champion as we scrambled to document Mr. Johnson's life quickly, and outside the typical industry sequence. Where would we be without your dogged perseverance and industry insights? I deeply appreciate you.

Tracy Sherrod, I'm thankful you took the risk of publishing an almost-centenarian, squeezing us onto your already overflowing plate, lending your brilliance and shepherding us through the editorial process so quickly and masterfully. Thank you, as well, to Peyton Young, for being a life-saver; the entire art department, production team, and marketing and public relations departments for all their amazing support.

I am indescribably grateful to my ancestors and angels, especially Charles and Peggy Beard, who encouraged me to read, write, and be free, and my grandparents, from whom I learned to love and value elders. Thank you, as well, to Noel Gordon, who bore witness to this project unfolding and loved and supported me every step of the way; Jonathan and Alison Beard, who I can always count on to be in my corner; Alex Montilla, Kailey Essa, and Jadon Beard, my inspirations; Uncle Ray Morgan and my Beard family elders, who both root me and root for me. To my Beard and Lanton extended families, I cannot tell you how proud I am to be one of you. I deeply appreciate the support I've received from Natalie Bell, Sekou Campbell, Phyllis Goltra, Valerie Harrison, Bill Harvey, Rockelle Henderson, Erin Johnson, Alex Leonard, Dr. Susan McElroy, Jeffrey Morgan, Gilda Smith, Dr. Robin

L. Smith, the Reverend Adriene Thorne, Linda Villarosa, the Reverend Dr. Alyn E. and Dr. Ellyn J. Waller, and my family at Enon Tabernacle Baptist Church, as well as my fabulous Cleveland, Shaker Heights, Princeton, and Philadelphia communities.

Mr. Johnson and I are eternally indebted to the authors, researchers, and editors of these books that helped us frame his story historically, double-check memories, contextualize accomplishments, and ensure we captured events accurately: *Black Bourgeoisie: The Book That Brought the Shock of Self-Revelation to Middle-Class Blacks in America* by E. Franklin Frazier; *Black Families in White America* by Andrew Billingsley; *Black Folk: The Roots of the Black Working Class* by Blair L. M. Keeley; *Black Fortunes: The Story of the First Six African Americans Who Survived Slavery and Became Millionaires* by Shomari Wills; *Sundown Towns* by James W. Loewen; *Black Metropolis: A Study of Negro Life in a Northern City* by St. Clair Drake and Horace R. Clayton; *Building the Black Metropolis: African American Entrepreneurship in Chicago*, edited by Robert E. Weems Jr. and Jason P. Chambers, especially the essays "King of Selling: The Rise and Fall of S. B. Fuller" by Clovis E. Semmes and "Positive Realism: Tom Burrell and the Development of Chicago as a Center for Black-Owned Advertising Agencies" by Jason P. Chambers; *The Color of Law: A Forgotten History of How Our Government Segregated America* by Richard Rothstein; *The Hippest Trip in America: Soul Train and the Evolution of Culture and Style* by Nelson George; *Hair Story: Untangling the Roots of Black Hair in America* by Ayana D. Byrd and Lori L. Tharps; *Labor of Love, Labor of Sorrow: Black Women, Work and the Family, from Slavery to the Present* by Jacqueline Jones; and, of course, *The*

ACKNOWLEDGMENTS

Warmth of Other Suns: The Epic Story of America's Great Migration by Isabel Wilkerson.

Finally, though I grew up in Cleveland, I tried my best to do right by the city of Chicago, especially Black Chicago, both by capturing its pulse and by elevating great legacies for the world to celebrate. I pray we succeeded.

About the Author

GEORGE ELLIS JOHNSON SR. is the founder of the Johnson Products Company, a business made famous for creating products such as Ultra Sheen and Afro Sheen. It was the first Black-owned company to trade on a major stock exchange, the financial sponsor of *Soul Train*, and once likely the largest Black-owned manufacturing company in the world. Known for his generosity around Chicago and nationally, Johnson has received numerous honors for the philanthropic contributions of the George E. Johnson Foundation and the George E. Johnson Educational Fund, which awarded more than one thousand college scholarships.

In 1964 Johnson cofounded Independence Bank—the first Black-owned financial institution to operate in Chicago after the Great Depression—and became its chairman. He served on the boards of the Chicago Urban League, Commonwealth Edison, Lyric Opera of Chicago, MetLife,

Northwestern Memorial Hospital, Northwestern University, and Operation PUSH.

Johnson is the recipient of nine honorary doctorate degrees, including several from historically black colleges and universities. He has also received the Harvard Medal, Stanford Graduate School of Business's Marketing Man of the Year recognition, and Chicago mayor Harold Washington's Lifetime Achievement Award. In 1999 the *Wall Street Journal* included him in its special report "Ten Who Changed the World: During the Past Century, Through Action or Thought, These Lives Have Had a Major Impact on Business."